An Alternative Labour History

About the editor

Dario Azzellini is assistant professor of sociology at the Johannes Kepler University. His research and writing focuses on social transformation, self-administration, workers' control, democracy and social movements. Azzellini has published several books, including *They Can't Represent Us* (co-authored with Marina Sitrin, 2014), *Ours to Master and to Own* (co-edited with Immanuel Ness, 2011) and *The Business of War* (2002). He serves as associate editor for *Cuadernos de Marte* and is co-founder of workerscontrol.net. He served as associate editor for *The International Encyclopedia of Revolution and Protest: 1500 to the Present* (2009) and was primary editor for Latin America, the Spanish Caribbean and the new left in Italy. Azzellini is also a documentary filmmaker, co-directing, among other films, *Comuna under Construction* (2010) and *5 Factories – Workers Control in Venezuela* (2007).

www.azzellini.net

An Alternative Labour History

Worker Control and Workplace Democracy

**Edited by
Dario Azzellini**

Zed Books

LONDON

*To my partner, comrade, friend and wife Marina Sitrin and
to our wonderful son Camilo Turi Azzellini Sitrin.*

*An Alternative Labour History: Worker Control and Workplace
Democracy* was first published in 2015 by Zed Books Ltd,
7 Cynthia Street, London N1 9JF, UK

www.zedbooks.co.uk

Editorial copyright © Dario Azzellini 2015
Copyright in this collection © Zed Books 2015

The right of Dario Azzellini to be identified as the editor of
this work has been asserted by him in accordance with the
Copyright, Designs and Patents Act, 1988

Typeset in Bembo by Swales Willis
Index: Kerry Taylor

Cover designed by www.stevenmarsden.com

A catalogue record for this book is available from the British Library

ISBN 978-1-78360-155-4 hb
ISBN 978-1-78360-154-7 pb
ISBN 978-1-78360-156-1 pdf
ISBN 978-1-78360-157-8 epub
ISBN 978-1-78360-158-5 mobi

Contents

Foreword

When workers organize themselves, occupy their workplace, and begin working under their own control, their action is often met with astonishment that such a thing could happen. People around the world were electrified, for example, when in 2001 Argentine workers took over two hundred factories, a hotel, and many other enterprises and began running them themselves. Yet "such things" have happened over and over again in different times and places. Now *An Alternative Labour History: Worker Control and Workplace Democracy* rescues this important aspect of worker history and action from the memory hole and makes available a wealth of historical understanding about it.

If the world of work under capitalism is largely a realm of unfreedom, workers taking over the companies that employ them and running them under self-management is emblematic of the emancipation of labor. Yet the relation between such workplace "recuperation" as it is now known and broader social change raises a host of issues. What, for example, is the relation between the control of a single workplace by its particular employees and control by society over the economy as a whole? How can a recuperated enterprise acquire the supplies it needs to produce and pay its workers without becoming captive to the dictates of lenders and the market? What are the similarities and differences between recuperated workplaces and more traditional worker cooperatives? Between recuperated workplaces and the worker councils and assemblies that have repeatedly sprung up in many countries in times of crisis? There is a long but little-known tradition of reflection on such questions, and this book recounts those reflections as well as the actions themselves.

Since the wave of recuperations in Argentina in 2001, such experiments have been going on around the world, and this book brings the story right down to the present with accounts of recuperated workplaces from Italy to Brazil to Chicago. Many of these have been closely connected to the wave of "occupy," "indignados," and "anti-austerity" movements that spread around the world in response to the global Great Recession. The book brings out some of the important new characteristics that are emerging in these new recuperations. For example, they often use the facilities they acquire to produce useful goods and services, but to produce different products and for different end-users – in many cases for the local community or for the popular movement. They often modify products and production processes with an eye to ecological protection and the needs of the local economy. And they often use popular assemblies and network forms of organization in an effort to coordinate on a larger scale without establishing new markets or hierarchies.

These new approaches make clear that the possibilities opened by such worker takeovers, far from being just history, are a matter of living experiment and reflection. There is every reason to believe that workers will continue to turn to "such things" in the future as they have from time to time in the past. When they do, they will find in *An Alternative Labour History: Worker Control and Workplace Democracy* treasure trove that will be invaluable for making their action a truly effective contribution to the liberation of workers – and society.

Jeremy Brecher

Acknowledgments

I want to thank first and foremost all workers who fight and take over workplaces as well as those who support them in different ways. I thank also a long list of researchers and organizations who have inspired radical thinking about workers' struggles and social transformation, and who are supporting and conducting research on labor insurgency and workers' self-organization. Special thanks go to all who have contributed to this work through writing, translating, editing and contributing important information. The list is not complete. If I have forgotten to thank anyone, I apologize. Many thanks to Carolina Cositore, Patrick Cuninghame, Milenko Srećković, Benoît Borrits, Kika Sroka-Miller, Gigi Malabarba, workerscontrol.net, Alan Tuckman, Ralf Hoffrogge, Pina Toscano, Andrés Ruggeri, Laura Gottesdiener, Stiftung Menschenwürde und Arbeitswelt and the Rosa Luxemburg Foundation Berlin.

Notes on contributors

Patrick Cuninghame is a sociology lecturer and researcher and member of the Area of Labor Studies of the Department of Social Relations of the Autonomous Metropolitan University – Xochimilco, in Mexico City. His main area of research has been on autonomism as a social movement, from the Workers Autonomy movement in Italy in the 1970s to the neo-Zapatistas in Mexico since 1994. Currently, he is researching on the relation between cognitive capitalism and the university in a comparative study on Mexico and Italy.

Alex Demirović is professor at the Goethe University Frankfurt am Main, Germany, and senior fellow of the Rosa Luxemburg Foundation. His work focuses on critical theory of society, materialist and state theory, political theory and the theory of democracy.

Maurício Sardá de Faria is a professor of sociology at Federal University of Paraiba in Brazil and holds a PhD in political sociology from the Federal University of Santa Catarina, where he studied labor. He is the director of the National Secretariat of Solidarity Economy at the Ministry of Labor and Employment of Brazil.

Franck Gaudichaud is a lecturer in Latin America history in the Department of Latin American and Iberian Studies, Grenoble 3 University, France and a doctor in political science. He published:

Popular Power and Industrials Belts: An Oral History of Allende Government (1970–1973) (in Spanish, 2004) and *Condor Operation and International State Terrorism in South America* (in Spanish, 2005) and he edited *The Latin-American Volcano: Lefts, Social Movement and Neoliberalism in Latin America* (in French 2008; in Spanish 2012). In 2013 he published *Chile 1970–1973: A Thousand Days That Shook the World* (in France). He is on the editorial board of the academic journal *Dissidences*, the political magazine *ContreTemps* and the web site rebellion.org. He contributes to *Le Monde diplomatique* (Paris).

Peter Haumer learned organ building and worked as a metal worker in machine construction and the car industry. He worked as an instructor in apprenticeship workshops in Austria. He has been politically active since the age of 15 and started union activities when he was 19. He has been a shop steward and shop steward leader for 12 years.

Kimiyasu Irie is a lecturer in sociology, labor movement history and social thought at Toyo University, St Paul's University and Musashino Art University in Tokyo. He is the author of *Sleepless Workers* (Japan, 2008) about the destructive influences of neoliberalism and globalization on workers. The book also discusses the relationship between the labor movement and fascism in Japan and the history of Japanese revolutionary labor movements. Irie is also a member of the part-time lecturers' union and is active in various struggles over academic labor problems.

Theodoros Karyotis is a social activist based in Thessaloniki, Greece. He studied sociology in Bristol, UK, and did his postgraduate dissertation on the global justice movement at the University of Granada, Spain. He currently works as a translator and participates actively in social movements promoting self-management, solidarity economy and the defense of the commons. He also participates in the organization of the annual Direct Democracy Festival, an international event that brings together collectives, activists and academics around the issue of the construction of radical alternatives to capitalism from below.

Alexandros Kioupkiolis has studied Classics and political theory. He is now a lecturer in contemporary political theory at the Department of Political Science, Aristotle University of Thessaloniki, Greece. His teaching and research interests focus on contemporary democratic theory, post-Marxism, anarchism and theories of justice. His books include *Politics of Freedom. Radical Democracy, Post-Anarchist Utopias and the Emergence of the Multitude* (2011) and *Freedom after the Critique of Foundations* (2012).

Henrique T. Novaes graduated in economic science at São Paulo State University, Brazil. He earned his Master's degree at the State University of Campinas (Unicamp) in Brazil, where he conducted research on Latin American recuperated factories and the history of workers' self-management of factories and of agrarian class struggles. He completed his PhD at Unicamp. His dissertation examines the relationship between the university and Latin American social movements. Novaes is author of the book *The Fetish of Technology: The Experience of Recuperated Factories* (2007).

Anabel Rieiro has a MA in sociology and is finishing her PhD in sociology. She is adjunct and coordinator of the Extension Unit of the Faculty of Social Science and she is a lecturer and assistant researcher in the area of political sociology of the Department of Sociology, University of the Republic, Montevideo, Uruguay.

Elise Thorburn is an activist and organizer based in Canada. She is active in workers' and feminist movements, including the Greater Toronto Workers' Assembly and the Feminist Action Committee, and is an editor on the radical political action journal *Upping the Anti*. Her PhD is in media studies at the University of Western Ontario and she is currently raising one amazing child, Olive Josephine, while completing her dissertation.

Introduction

Dario Azzellini

Over the past 135 years, in all kinds of historical situations and during various political and economic crises and in different political systems, workers have taken control of their workplaces. Yet this story of workers self-administered production is rarely told. Capitalists, bourgeois governments and administrators of systems based on the exploitation of workers usually have little interest in disseminating the history of self-organized workers; those who have successfully run factories without bosses. In the early 20th century workers tried to gain control over production in social and socialist revolutions, like those in Austria, Germany, Hungary, Italy, Russia and Spain, and under state socialism, as in Yugoslavia, Poland or Hungary; they did so as well in anti-colonial struggles and democratic revolutions in Argentina, Algeria, Indonesia and Portugal, to just name a few examples. Factory take-overs by workers and the perspective of workers' control was also present in labor struggles against capitalist restructuring in the last third of the 20th century in France, the UK, Italy, Canada, Australia and elsewhere. Company occupations and workers' self-administration have again manifested themselves strongly since the 1990s in Argentina and in many parts of South America, as well as in India and some European countries. Workers and communities have recuperated hundreds of factories and companies contending against the consequences of global capitalist crises (Ness and Azzellini, 2011).What can be seen from all these examples is a common struggle of workers for the democratic control of production. They show how, even without knowledge of previous worker control initiatives or an explicit socialist consciousness, the collective administration of workplaces has frequently emerged as an inherent tendency among the rank and file. Workers' councils and assemblies discuss, decide and work in a horizontal and directly democratic way. In the long run workers' control has not been able to impose itself on a large scale. Media and expert discourses often suggest that the many problems worker-controlled companies faced internally were the reason for their failure. But despite all claims that workers' control is not viable or the supposed loss of enthusiasm of workers and the adverse conditions of the capitalist context surrounding them, workers' control almost always failed because of the threat or use of violent repression.

This illustrates that workers' control in production is only one necessary step for transforming society and moving towards overcoming capitalism and "the exploitation of men by men" (as Marx said: today we would say "men and women"). In order to create a perspective for overcoming capitalism it is indispensable to gain control of production. But revolutionary organization and self-administration must be extended to all areas of society to be able to consolidate the transformation process needed.

However, this tendency is inherent to workers' control. As Alex Demirović states in Chapter 1, council democracy is not limited to the economy but challenges "the social division of labor, and consequently the separation and configuration of economics and politics, everyday reproductive labor and social decision-making, as well as the public and private spheres" and by extension, also the state (p. 34). "From this perspective", Demirović argues:

> [D]emocracy is no longer a political regime but instead constitutes a way of life that determines every sphere and as such constitutes a different community, which Marx identifies as the association of free individuals. (p. 34)

This is what makes workers' control so interesting and crucial and it is also the reason why it has so many enemies.

During the last 15 years the question of workers' control was mainly connected to the developments in Latin America. The crisis of capitalism in the 1990s that hit Latin America in particular, and the crisis of the neoliberal model imposed upon it, provoked factory take-overs across the region. The best known case is Argentina, where economic and political implosion and the failure of employers and traditional union strategies to respond to unemployment and pauperization resulted in more and more workers across various sectors taking matters into their own hands through occupation and the self-management of their workplaces (Sitrin, 2013). Today 15,000 workers administer 350 recuperated companies, among them not only industrial production sites but also hotels, restaurants and print shops. But recuperations by workers also took place in Brazil and Uruguay. In Venezuela the "entrepreneurs' strike" in 2001–2002 and the intentional disinvestment by factory owners opposed to the leftist government led workers to take over dozens of factories. Responding to mobilizations of workers and communities, dozens of occupied factories were expropriated by the Venezuelan government. Since then, more companies abandoned by their owners have been recuperated by workers, bringing the total number of recuperated factories to approximately 100 (concrete numbers are difficult to obtain) (Azzellini, 2011, 2012, 2013, 2014).

The current global economic crisis has led to a new shop-floor militancy, radical forms of protest and new worker take-overs in France, Germany, Greece, Ireland, Italy, Spain, Scotland, Canada, the USA, South Korea, Russia, Turkey, Egypt, Tunisia, Venezuela, Brazil and, once again, in Argentina. In the context of the current crisis, workers started occupying and recuperating their companies even in the USA and Europe. In the USA the former Republic Windows and Doors in Chicago, now New Era Windows, started production under workers' control in May 2013. In Greece workers attempted to take over and run their own hotel, hospital, newspaper and radio station, as well as a factory. In mid-February 2013, Vio.Me., a factory producing industrial glue, started to produce organic cleaning products under workers' control (see Chapter 10). Moreover, workers recuperated at least two factories in Italy, two in France and one in Turkey (see Chapter 2). Beyond these recuperations in industrialized countries, since 2009 workers have also recuperated around 50 companies in Argentina and some more in other Latin American countries. Workers' control seems back on the agenda.

It is my intention in this collection to advance scholars' and workers' understanding of, and appreciation for, the historic significance and necessity of self-administration, workers' control, collective decision-making in assemblies and workers' councils. The contributors take the position that, as history repeatedly shows, workers always have the ability to run their enterprises on their own. This is especially important and opportune now that capitalism is undergoing a structural crisis. In this way the book contributes to the understanding of contemporary working-class struggles and to the current debates on how workers and communities can regain control of their working lives. The chapters of the collection recount real examples of how the precarious nature of many people's work (and lives) created conditions for worker takeovers. All the contributors take the point of view of rank and file workers, those struggling on the shop floor for workers' control. These accounts, it is hoped, will also inspire more take-overs. If capital is not going to be confronted by unions and political parties, why not take it on in the workplace?

Workers' control and self-administration as emancipatory and anti-capitalist praxis

An Alternative Labour History: Worker Control and Workplace Democracy contributes important historical and contemporary case studies of worker control and labor resistance to current debates among scholars and activists, and adds to the publications on popular struggles, social movements, the commons, alternative and solidarity economies and alternative organizations. The case studies span the globe and provide international, cultural, national and regional examinations of relevant experiences of worker control, from the Global South as well as the Global North. Some chapters contribute in-depth theoretical and philosophical reflections.

The examples given in this collection fall outside the region of traditional cooperatives and experiences of institutionalized forms of workers' participation:

> Workers' councils or committees can only become serious expression of working-class interests when they challenge authority relations in the enterprise, are based on some under-standing that the prevailing division of labor reinforces these relations, and when they possess the power and the desire to transform the workplace in accordance with a new conception of the relations between work and play and between freedom and authority. Workers' control demands that are instruments of trade union and bureaucratic institutions merely reinforce the powerlessness of workers because they sow the seeds of cynicism concerning the possibility of actually achieving the vision of a self-managed society. (Aronowitz 1991: 426–7)

The focus of the collection examines cases in which council and assembly forms, meaning forms of democratic self-administration through non-hierarchical, participatory means, have prevailed, even if for short periods. Hence, this is an examination of work-ers' actions of insurrection against the capitalist system, played out in the form of plant take-overs. It is about workers questioning and challenging capitalist relations, explicitly or implicitly, through what the workers of the recuperated factory Ri-Maflow in Milan, Italy, call "conflictive self-administration" (see chapter 2). "If there is no struggle there is no progress", stated Frederick Douglass:

> Those who profess to favor freedom and yet deprecate agita-tion are men who want crops without plowing up the ground;

they want rain without thunder and lightning. They want the ocean without the awful roar of its many waters. . . . Power concedes nothing without a demand. (Martin, 1986: 175)

Through their activities and forms of organization the workers in our examples in this collection question property rights, hierarchies and the capitalist division of labor. They do not aim only to solve their specific situation but see themselves as part of a bigger struggle for change. They support other struggles and try to build networks with other worker-controlled companies, communities and movements. Even so, the recuperated factories under workers' control have to be seen as part of a much broader context of initiatives pointing at a different kind of society, encompassing cooperatives, small producers, barter networks, alternative currencies, consumer–producer networks, efforts for building a solidarity economy, struggles revitalizing the commons and all kinds of movements struggling for emancipation and freedom and against any form of oppression. Nevertheless, workers' control or conflictive self-administration comprises several characteristics that other forms of workers' participation in production and its administration, whether as cooperatives, co-management models, union participation in management decisions or the central and northern European company councils (*Betriebsräte* in Germany and Austria) do not have.

Limits and contradictions of the cooperative model

It is important to distinguish clearly between workers' councils, models of directly democratic and collective self-administration and cooperatives. While the first, as shown before, directly challenge capitalist logic and hegemony almost automatically – if they are based on workers' autonomy and not on institutional or bureaucratic concessions – the latter tend to operate within the capitalist logic of productivity and profitability. This general tendency has also its exceptions, usually in small workers' cooperatives, but the pressure on them to adopt a capitalist business logic is immense: not to follow the logic often requires a huge exercise of will. On the other hand, recuperated companies, including various cases studied in this collection (especially contemporary examples) have taken the legal form of workers' cooperatives, due to the fact that it is often the only legal form of collective ownership and administrative structure possible in a capitalist society. Nevertheless, the traditional cooperative model encompasses basic orientations and general tendencies that limit the emancipatory potential of cooperatives in capitalist surrounding.

Cooperatives rarely question private ownership of the means of production. They tend to see this individualistic notion as the source of the right to participate in decision-making and benefits. This idea, and its logic, is also fundamental to capitalism. Hence, cooperatives may represent a positive step in democratizing the ownership of enterprises within the frame of the capitalist economy, but they are not automatically an alternative institutional form.

Imagine that all cooperatives founded during the last 100 years remained cooperatives with non-capitalist ideas: they would make up a huge part of the economy. But they do not. Most cooperatives see their ideals fading away as their members age. Having to act in a capitalist economy while not following its rules is extremely difficult. Capitalism is a vortex. Most cooperatives start with great ideals and with time sell out – both ideologically and materially. Often, cooperatives are sold to corporate business or investors once they reach a certain size. Their individual notion of property makes that possible. As Rosa Luxemburg noted:

> Co-operatives – especially co-operatives in the field of production – constitute a hybrid form in the midst of capitalism. They can be described as small units of socialized production within capitalist exchange. But in capitalist economy exchanges

dominate production. As a result of competition, the complete domination of the process of production by the interests of capital – that is, pitiless exploitation – becomes a condition for the survival of each enterprise. The domination of capital over the process of production expresses itself in the following ways. Labor is intensified. The workday is lengthened or shortened, according to the situation of the market. And, depending on the requirements of the market, labor is either employed or thrown back into the street. In other words, use is made of all methods that enable an enterprise to stand up against its competitors in the market. The workers forming a co-operative in the field of production are thus faced with the contradictory necessity of governing themselves with the utmost absolutism. They are obliged to take toward themselves the role of capitalist entrepreneur – a contradiction that accounts for the usual failure of production co-operatives which either become pure capitalist enterprises or, if the workers' interests continue to predominate, end by dissolving. (Luxemburg, 1900)

That most cooperatives are embedded in the framework of the capitalist economy and compete on the capitalist market following the logic of profit-making has serious consequences for the company model they develop. Many cooperatives have employees who are not part of the cooperative, and have wage differentials as that, although the differential is perhaps smaller than in common private enterprises, a manager's income nevertheless ends up being several times that of a worker. And while many cooperatives might be worker-owned, they are rarely worker-managed, especially larger cooperatives.

Because in most areas in the economy it is impossible to compete with capitalist businesses, the cooperative sector will always grow more slowly than the private business sector that strictly follows the rules of capitalism. This happens even under advantageous conditions, such as those in Venezuela during the last

15 years (Azzellini, 2012). Without a notion of common property, cooperative solidarity will suffer. Each cooperative tends to view itself as a separate business, disconnected from other coops – neither supporting them, nor being supported by them. What has been called "enterprise consciousness" will outweigh the commitment to build and maintain a truly worker and community controlled economy.

The famous and often praised example of the Mondragón cooperative's complex in the Basque country which started in 1956 and tuned into the Mondragón Cooperative Corporation (MCC) in 1990, one of the most advanced cooperative networks, is a good example of the tendencies and developments described. The constitution of the MCC was justified with the necessity to compete with transnational companies and went along with introducing more and more traditional capitalistic incentives and administrative practices (Huet, 1997). MCC is worker-owned but not worker-managed. In order to survive in highly competitive markets it has outsourced production to other countries in Europe, Africa, Asia and Latin America. In 2014 it had 105 production plants in different countries, including Brazil, Chile, Colombia, Mexico, Morocco, Turkey, Thailand, Taiwan, India, Romania, Slovakia, Poland, Czech Republic, China (18 plants!), Vietnam, several Western European countries, Australia and the USA (Mondragón, n.d.), none of which are worker-owned or worker-managed, and none of their employees are members of the MCC cooperative. Even in the Basque Country MCC has various non-coop businesses, mostly in the form of joint ventures with capitalist partners. Contrary to "the original Mondragón commitment to never employ more than 10% nonmembers", already in 1997 about one-third of Mondragón workers were nonmembers (Huet, 1997).

MCC's industry area reported record sales for 2012, surpassing sales figures from before the crisis and 11 new international production subsidiaries were opened (*TU lankide. Mondragón Corporation's News*, 2013). Nevertheless one of the major MCC businesses, the white goods manufacturer Fagor Electrodomésticos – which, ironically, was the first cooperative founded in Mondragón in 1956 – filed for bankruptcy in October 2013, after the Mondragón Group General Council decided not to save the heavily indebted company due to its heavy losses during the crisis and bad financial management. At the time of writing, in the Basque plant 5600 workers are about to lose their jobs. More jobs are in danger in the more than 50 Basque firms that supplied Fagor. In November 2013 several hundred workers occupied the plant. One of their demands was not to penalize individual investors, who are mostly workers who invested their savings in it. MCC has been heavily criticized for its decision, which seems to be no different from what any privately owned company would have decided (Bibby, 2013). Nevertheless the Mondragón Cooperative complex also has important positive lessons to teach. It could consolidate and expand because beyond concrete production facilities it also built an independent bank, a job education system and a social security system.

In Italy, once famous for its huge cooperative networks, "the coop model is the new paradigm of precarious labour organisation" (Curcio, 2015, in Azzellini, D. and Kraft, M.G. (eds) *The Class Strikes Back. Self-Organized Workers' Struggles in the 21st Century*. Amsterdam: Brill forthcoming). In the logistics sector, for example, the

> accumulated surplus value depends on the exploitation of a low-skilled labor force (or better, low-paid), whose working activity is managed by the unregulated co-op system operating in conditions of formal illegality.

About 98 percent of workers employed in the cooperatives subcontracted by transnational companies consist of a heavily exploited migrant work force:

> Workers employed in the cooperatives usually neither enjoy any sort of social security protection nor any labor rights as

cooperatives are not subject to the mandatory application of the National Collective Labor Contract (CCNL). According to Italian Public Law the CCNL is supposed to regulate employer/employee relations but workers of the cooperative are employed as associate-workers. This means they are dependent workers, but they are also members of the cooperative at the same time. Thus, as they are dependent workers, they have no access to profits. As they are members, they do not enjoy the labor rights they should and they have to take on the full job risk. Furthermore, they also have to pay – as a payroll deduction – up to five thousand Euros per year as a percentage of their capital share to the cooperative. (Curcio 2015)

Workers' autonomy versus unions

The supposed representatives of the workers, parties and unions, viewed the councils with suspicion. They saw their authority challenged by workers' self-organization beyond party and union structures. Furthermore, as Karl Korsch and other council communists noticed in the early 20th century, once workers begin to discuss their needs, aspirations and strategies in assemblies on the shop floor, party affiliation does no longer matters: workers develop autonomy. That obviously challenges the existing mechanisms of representation and with that, the core logic of parties and unions. Representational politics is no longer possible. A union can no longer sign an agreement rejected by the workers, just because the union leaders consider it to be the best option strategically. Autonomous workers, as historical experiences show, are able to question and to achieve much more than unions, which usually stick to the pre-established official set of rules in order to be a "reliable partner" mediating the interests of work and capital. Almost all the approximately 350 companies recuperated by workers in Argentina since 2000 were recuperated by autonomous workers' struggles, since unions rarely engage in conflicts outside a legal framework regulating the conflict and guaranteeing a successful outcome or a mediated settlement.

Moreover unions represent – by their own logic – employed workers. Once workers are unemployed the traditional instruments of representation, struggle and negotiation of unions are no longer effective – and even less so if the workers become, either formally or de facto, owners or entrepreneurs, as it is the case with the recuperated factories. There are obviously exceptions among unions. Some are real rank and file organizations with a political and social perspective extending beyond bargaining wages and working conditions and some do not stick to the official conflict and conflict resolution script. But they are in a small minority. Sometimes traditional unions respect and support rank and file decisions and support struggles beyond their pre-established role, as the communist General Confederation of Labor in France, in the case of the recently recuperated factory, Fralib. In such situations unions merely follow workers' initiatives, they are not the ones that come up with a proposal for occupation and workers' controlled production. Nevertheless, union support is an exception. In Greece the Communist Party and its union reject company recuperations and accused the workers of the occupied Vio.Me. of being petty bourgeois and capitalists when they started production under workers control (see Chapter 2).

But even in those rare cases when unions respect workers' decisions, workers' autonomy on the shop floor goes much further. Autonomous workers making decisions in assemblies on the shop floor are able to react much faster and more powerfully to changes or threats than unions and they are able to achieve much more, as workers' struggles and achievements in the 1960s and 1970s have proved. They are able to develop mechanisms of struggle and alliances that unions usually do not (because of their commitment to legality and pre-established conflict mechanisms). Moeover, autonomous workers can develop struggles around issues that unions accept on a broader level or do not touch because of their limitations on mediation:

> The purpose of labor unions is to help workers sell their labor power as advantageously as they can. Unions will always be needed for this purpose. But while unions are necessary, they are not sufficient. (Lynd and Lynd, 2000: 1)

Workers' control in revolution and state socialism

Among the best known examples of workers' control, one of the oldest and most far-reaching cases is the Paris Commune. The short revolutionary socialist administration of Paris (18 March to 28 May, 1871) was, in fact a workers' government with the principle of decision-making being the workers' council democracy. Karl Marx (1871a, 1871b) immediately recognized the significance of the Paris Commune and stated that it

> was essentially a working-class government, the product of the struggle of the producing against the appropriating class, the political form at last discovered under which to work out the economical emancipation of labor. (Marx 1871b)

Nevertheless, after Marx, socialist and communist parties rarely supported the notion of workers' control and often fought against its manifestation. Workers' control was usually welcomed by communist parties during revolutionary struggles in order to build "dual power", as Lenin called the situation when structures built by revolutionaries exist in parallel to official institutions and powers. During the struggle self-organization and self-administration would be accepted as necessary, but once "the party" seized the state it would claim that dual power was no longer necessary, since the real power, the state, was now under revolutionary guidance and the party represented the common interest of all proletarians. Spinning the argument further, workers fighting for workers' control were even often accused of being counter-revolutionary since they would contradict the revolutionary leadership and defend only individual or group interests.

In Russia the councils were repressed by the Bolsheviks once they had seized and consolidated state power (Mandel, cited in Ness and Azzellini, 2011). In Italy the Italian Socialist Party (the PSI, precursor of the Communist Party) and its leader Antonio Gramsci supported the great council movement in the factories of the industrialized north in 1919–1920, and Gramsci's accounts and analyses in the newspaper *L'Ordine Nuovo* (The New Order) are still among the most compelling descriptions of and inquiries into workers' control. But the refusal of the PSI to extend the strike in the northern Italian industrial region of Piedmont to the national level and the PSI's demand for a full mandate for negotiations decidedly contributed to the workers' defeat and was seen by many workers as a betrayal (Di Paola, 2011). In Germany the revolutionary shop stewards, being the backbone of the German revolution and at the forefront of organizing, nevertheless had to struggle hard against both the Social Democratic Party, which was trying to impose a reformist agenda, and against different communist parties trying to co-opt and impose their party line on the councils. Once they decided to join a party they had to struggle hard to maintain their autonomy as a workers' organization (Hoffrogge, 2014). Something very similar happened during the Austrian Revolution (see Chapter 4 in this book).

Attempts by workers to install workers' control under "state socialism", were repressed either by the ruling party or, if the ruling party gave in to the workers' demands, the *Union of Soviet Socialist Republics* (USSR) imposed the suppression of workers' control either politically or even militarily. In the Hungarian uprising of 1956 against Soviet-imposed policies workers established councils following the vision of "communalizing" state socialism and preventing the capitalist restoration and the ruling party opened up to the movement. The uprising which started on 23 October 1956, was definitely crushed after the USSR invaded Hungary militarily on 4 November. Fighting between Hungarian rebels and the Soviet Army continued until 10 November with hundreds of deaths on both sides. The workers councils maintained themselves in place until January 1957, when they were definitely defeated.

In the course of the Prague Spring in Czechoslovakia, the government under the leadership of Alexander Dubček agreed to the necessity of socialist reforms demanded from below in February 1968; in April it launched an Action Program of reforms. Workers built councils and took control of factories. But on August 20–21 1968 armies from five Warsaw Pact countries (the USSR, the German Democratic Republic, Bulgaria, Poland and Hungary) invaded the Czechoslovak Socialist Republic, repressing the reform movement. In socialist Poland (1944–1989) there were several workers' council movements. In 1956 a strong workers' movement was even able to achieve a law on workers' councils. But by December 1958, that law had been replaced by a new law that again reduced the councils' role and power. Councils arose again in workers' mass protests in 1970.

Then again, the Polish independent union movement, Solidarity, was so strong in 1980–1981 that the military and the ruling *Polish United Workers' Party* staged a coup on 13 December 1981:

> The military council decreed a "state of war" or martial law, confined nearly ten thousand Solidarity activists in internment camps, surrounded all the occupied enterprises with tanks, and crushed the working-class movement in Poland. (Kowalewski, 2011: 205)

The only exception among state socialist countries was Yugoslavia, where a new doctrine of "workers' self-management" became law and state policy in June 1950. But in reality the self-management councils could not serve as democratic organs in order to express dissent and discuss different opinions, since their primary purpose was to play a managerial function in the operation of firms, not to serve as political organs of the working class (Musić, 2011: 189). The so-called worker-managed companies were mostly controlled by the ruling bureaucracy through party delegates. And on

> a larger scale, the apparent contradiction between the self-interest of a single factory or a given region and the interests of society as a whole was not resolved through centralized democratic control of the overall economy by the working class. (Musić, 2011: 189)

However, many workers and minority currents on the left, ranging from council communism, Trotskyism and Italian *operaismo* to socialists influenced by the early Marx and the writings of Antonio Gramsci and Rosa Luxemburg, autonomist movements, social revolutionary currents (including several Latin American Marxists and revolutionaries), anarcho-syndicalism and other "heretical" left currents – have always viewed workers' control and councils as the base of a self-determined socialist society.

Workers' control and the emancipation of humanity

The experiences accumulated in over 135 years of workers' self-organizing and taking control of production sites are an immense treasure for emancipatory politics and prove again and again that workers do not need bosses to organize production and they usually even do better without them. Even if most people today assign universal and trans-historical validity to capitalist economic categories, these categories are only part of capitalism. Capitalist categories are simply the structure of rules in capitalist societies; social structures that human beings have historically entered into (Agnoli, 1999). That means they can, of course, also exit these societies.

Workers' control and collective democratic self-administration provide several elements for building a path towards overcoming capitalism. As Immanuel Wallerstein argues, "Capitalism has been a program for the commodification of everything. . . . Socialism ought to be a program for the decommodification of everything", specifying that decommodification, "does not mean demonetization, but the elimination of the category of profit" (Wallerstein, 2000: 157). A serious attempt at this will be possible only if the economy and society are controlled directly by workers and communities. If we look at the praxis described in the chapters of this collection we can see clear steps of decommodification. Democratic debate and decisions in the workplace become more important than profit, and the necessary time is dedicated to them. Workers' health, education, solidarity, ecological sustainability and so on stand over profit, as do social relations and free time. Especially in the contemporary cases of company recuperations, the quality of work and ecological aspects play a central role. In Argentina, Venezuela or Italy workers get time off to support other struggles, in Venezuela workers get time off to participate in educational programs, in Italy, Greece, France and Venezuela ecological aspects play an important role in production choices. Meaningless consumption and production is questioned in most contemporary cases and the accessibility of quality products to other workers and communities becomes an important issue (Azzellini, 2012; Azzellini and Ressler, 2014; Ness and Azzellini, 2011; Sitrin, 2013, see also Chapter 2 in this collection).

By regaining collective control over the product of their own work, the workers engage in a process of "progressive disalienation", as Ernest Mandel described a crucial element of social transformation, based on Marx' early writings on alienation (Mandel, 1971: 187–210).[1] In light of the long history of humanity, the fact that wage workers do not own the product of their own labor is quiet news. It is a product of bourgeois society. Craft workers and farmers up to the Middle Ages still controlled the production process and were owners of most of the fruit of their labor, even if they had to hand over a part of it to rulers. When workers are in control of the work they do, work is a means of self-expression. The creative capacity inherent in every human being is unleashed in the labor activity.

In wage labor (or even in modern wage labor such as most "independent" work relationships), the alienation, the control of the capitalist over workers, their time, their activities and the product of their work, this is no longer the case. Work is no longer a means of self-expression but just a way of obtaining money with the goal of satisfying material needs. The importance of the worker's subjectivity has meanwhile also been recognized by the capitalists and put to use. While it was a disturbing factor in the rigidly organized Fordist production process, the post-Fordist mode of production tries to absorb the workers' subjectivity to dynamize the production process. By doing this alienation is even deepened since capital does not appropriate only workers' labor power during work time, but also the workers' subjectivity.

Victor Wallis correctly states: "What workers' control points to is more than just a new way of organizing production; it is also the release of human creative energy on a vast scale" (Wallis, 2011: 11). The practical experiences and case studies in this collection proof that workers invent new products, new forms of organization, new ways of production and, most important of all, they build new social relations. The clear focus of the book is to bring these remarkable histories and cases to light. Most of the chapters go beyond the history of workplace take-overs to point to the impact they made on the consciousness of the participants and on the social relations between them, and how the take-overs influenced their surrounding communities. These are important contributions to the few existing works on workers' control.

Building a workers' economy

Recuperated factories are gaining more visibility and take-overs are becoming increasingly an option to be considered in workers struggles. Considering that the financial, economic, political and social crisis that generated the current recuperations still persists, it is likely that more occupations will follow. It is impossible to predict which of those occupations will endure and present a positive model for other occupations, and which will be evicted by the police, given up because of economic difficulties or fail due to internal disagreements among the workers.

One might object that in most of the alternative models presented here had little staying power and that, looking at the result, the rebellions were not worth the sacrifice. But as Michel Foucault stressed in 1979:

> I do not agree with those who would say, "It is useless to revolt, it will always be the same." One does not dictate to those who risk their lives in the face of power. Is it right to rebel, or not? Let us leave this question open. It is a fact that people rise up, and it is through this that a subjectivity (not that of great men, but that of anyone) introduces itself into history and gives it its life. (Foucault, in Afary and Anderson, 2005: 266)

Every single experience can help us to develop a new society and economy by the people and for the people. Therefore, the examples in this collection also have to be seen as an inspiration.

Gigi Malabarba, worker and participant in the recuperated Italian factory Ri-Maflow states:

> We can win if we are part of a larger struggle and increase tenfold and a hundredfold experiences such as these, to nurture the idea that another economy is possible. If the economy of the bosses is in crisis, we need to develop a different idea of economics. (Azzellini and Ressler 2014)

In this context it has also to be asked: which new forms of distribution could be realized? If recuperated, workers' controlled factories do not want to be subjugated by capitalism or repeat the failure of bureaucratic planning, alternatives to planning or markets have to be developed.

Michael Albert's (2003) book is among the better known theoretical works expanding the idea of democratic decision-making to the sphere of consumption and coordination between producers and consumers. A closer look to international experiences shows that practices and experiments are already on the way. The most far-reaching experiences are to be found in Latin America. There, the influence of István Mészáros, who traced his basic ideas for a transition to socialism in his book *Beyond Capital*, have become an important theoretical reference in Argentina, Brazil and Venezuela. Mészáros, whose central critique of first-epoch socialism is that it failed to establish "the socialist mode of control, through the self-management of the associated producers" (Mészáros 1995, xvii), proposes a communal system involving communal production and consumption cycles. In Venezuela this idea started to materialize through the creation of directly democratic administered communes with enterprises collectively and directly democratically administered by community assemblies (Azzellini, 2012, 2013; Azzellini and Ressler, 2011). In Argentina recuperated companies interrelate between each other and with communities (Sitrin, 2013).

In early 2014 the first European and Mediterranean meeting of The Economy of the Workers was held in the recuperated factory, Fralib, near Marseilles. Some 200 people attended the meeting, among whom were activists, workers from five recuperated factories in Europe and researchers from Europe, Mexico, Brazil and Argentina. The idea came from Argentina, where several meetings of this kind have been organized during the past 8 years. Starting at a national level, subsequently regional meetings for Latin America, and world meetings took place in Brazil and Mexico; with the next world meeting in the second half of 2015 being planned to take place in Venezuela.

The idea behind these meetings is to create a self-organized space to debate the common and different challenges the recuperated companies face, and how they can use the different experiences to build a network among themselves and with other alternative, self-organized and democratic forms of production and self-administration to create a new economy at the service of the workers and communities and not vice versa:

> Common challenges faced by occupied factories include state repression, huge bureaucratic hurdles, lack of an institutional framework, and the hostility of the ex-owners, political parties and bureaucratic trade unions. They often operate within economies that are already in great recession (such is the case of VioMe and most Argentinian factories in the early 21st century) and thus re-entering the market and ensuring an income are tough feats to accomplish.
>
> Dangers also lie ahead in the case of economic success. How can the workers safeguard the radical character of the experiment and avoid becoming an "alternative" multi-shareholder capitalist enterprise guided by the profit principle or using wage labor? In answer to that, many participants pointed toward the close relationship with the wider community. It is not sufficient for production to be worker-controlled, although it is a necessary first step to break the vicious circle of capitalist exploitation. Production should also be socially controlled, it should be environmentally and politically sound and grounded in the values of respect and solidarity. (Karyotis, 2014)

The meeting offered not only an extraordinary opportunity to exchange ideas and experiences among the recently recuperated factories, participating cooperatives, and researchers, but strengthened various concrete projects, from the promotion of recuperated factories and their products, the exchange of products among the factories, a self-organized research network, the use of workerscontrol.net in order to collect and promote contemporary and historical experiences, and many more. The network that arose from the meeting has since fostered an intensive exchange and numerous visits among workers of the different factories in order to continue debates and the exchange of experiences on the shop-floor.

The content of the collection

The first three contributions in the book address three central aspects of workers' control. In Chapter 1, "Council Democracy, or the End of the Political", Alex Demirović discusses the contemporary significance of council democracy as democracy originated by workers and the problems it has failed to solve. He starts by pointing out a series of conceptual problems and the limitations of representative democracy from the point of view of democracy theory and discusses how the council form has repeatedly arisen as an alternative in times of social unrest. As the author shows, council democracy is not only relevant to companies or factories, it also questions the foundations of bourgeois society and capitalism. Demirović connects Marx' early writings with his analysis of the Paris Commune and analyzes different approaches to council democracy, with a focus on the writings based on the experience of the German Revolution of 1918–1919. Finally, Demirović points out a series of unsolved questions on council democracy, which have not been addressed or satisfyingly answered by council theorists nor have they been solved in practice by the short-term council experiences up to now: where beyond workplaces should councils be formed? Who is entitled to vote and who to be elected? How can democratic participation be guaranteed and how can it avoid that a specialization and "efficiency" that leads once again to a separation of the political from the social?

In Chapter 2, "Contemporary Crisis and Workers' Control", I address factory recuperations and workers' control in the current crisis. The seven short case studies encompass the most recent conflictual factory recuperations in the USA, France, Greece, Italy, Turkey and Egypt. The examples differ from the traditional cooperative model in terms of their internal mechanisms as well as their approach and the contextualization of self-administration, having a lot in common with recuperated factories in Latin America. They all are inspired by and see themselves as part of broader movements. As the author shows, they share common characteristics, such as a conflictual relationship with bosses and authorities, workers' self-administration, and the change to eco-friendly and sustainable production.

In Chapter 3, "Workers' Assemblies: New Formations in the Organization of Labor and the Struggle against Capitalism", Elise Danielle Thorburn addresses the urgent question of how to organize workers' control under circumstances of modern and post-Fordist capitalism, when work is no longer an automatically unifying and homogenizing factor but instead plays the role of dividing and dispersing workers. She suggests that movements with the characteristics of the new global movements, such as Occupy and the neighborhood and students' assemblies in Canada in 2012, and the model of the Greater Toronto Workers' Assembly, contributed to "the embryonic stages of a recomposition of the working class in the Global North, after a long and decisive period of decomposition" (p. 102). Thorburn focuses on the example of the Greater Toronto Workers' Assembly and discusses the experiences of this extraordinary example of self-organization.

The seven case studies following these chapters illustrate a wide range of experiences over epochs, scope and socio-political context. In Chapter 4, "The Austrian Revolution of 1918–1919 and Working Class Autonomy", Peter Haumer shows the extraordinary potential of workers' councils in the organization of economic productivity and the emancipation of workers, as well as the repression and political errors – such as social democratic reformism and class collaboration – which led to their defeat. The Austrian Revolution is an important example of workers' councils and self-administration during times of revolution in the early 20th century. Along with the council movements in Russia, Germany, Hungary and Italy, the Austrian Revolution may be said to be the moment when the modern workers' councils' movement was born.

Chapter 5, "Chile: Worker Self-organization and *Cordones Industriales* under the Allende Government (1970–1973)", addresses struggles for workers' control in a democratic revolution. Franck Gaudichaud first describes the context of the Chilenean way to socialism in which "transition was seen as a gradual political-institutional path towards transforming the relations of production based on a mobilization of the majority of the people and the unity of the left, but without interrupting the current legal order" (p. 158). In this reformist scenario, labor struggles increased and workers took control of factories to guarantee production and distribution. Case studies show how the struggles for worker control took place on the shop floor. Workers' take-overs reached a peak after the large-scale lockout in October 1972 and were decisive in defeating the reactionary attack. Gaudichaud analyzes relationships and contradictions between unions, leftist parties, the state and the self-organized workers. He presents the subjective voice of the workers and discusses why the workers could not oppose the coup d'état on 11 September 1973.

In Chapter 6, " 'Production Control' or 'Factory Soviet'? Workers' Control in Japan", Kimiyasu Irie gives an insight into the post-World War II (1945–1947) Japanese "production control struggle", which encompassed different degrees of worker control of production. Production control emerged during the first year after the end of World War II and was massively endorsed by Japanese workers. In a situation of a totally collapsed war economy and paralyzed production, the Japanese bourgeoisie was systematically sabotaging production and provoking shortages in order to make bigger profits. Therefore, strikes were not an adequate means of struggle. Production control, in contrast, was an effective instrument of struggle while it also democratized the extremely hierarchical internal structure of companies. The workers gained influence "on production plans, wage levels, time administration and other matters" (p. 183). The Japanese Communist Party did not launch the production control struggles but adopted them as basic policy, accepting workers autonomy in the struggles. But their limited influence on management and state repression led to the workers' defeat.

In Chapter 7, "The Factory Commissions in Brazil and the 1964 Coup d'État", Henrique T. Novaes and Maurício S. de Faria describe the struggle of Brazilian workers against capitalist restructuring in the 1960s and 1970s. The chapter places the factory commissions and their struggle for workers' control in a broader sociocultural context going back to the social struggles of the 1950s and 1960s of workers, students and agrarian workers, and revolutionary cultural movements, especially film productions. The factory commissions faced resistance by bosses, government authorities and pragmatic trade union leaderships. Originally inspired by the different examples of factory councils in history, as a tendency of self-administered socialism, the factory commissions were finally assimilated and turned into integrated shop-floor representations as spaces of corporative conflict resolution.

The three final chapters deal with workers' control in the contemporary era, meaning from the 1990s to the present. In Chapter 8, "Self-management, Workers' Control and Resistance against Crisis and Neoliberal Counter-reforms in Mexico", Patrick Cuninghame addresses different examples of workers' control and self-administration in Mexico and situates them in the context of the struggle against neoliberalism and privatization. Cuninghame provides several examples. The case studies encompass tire producer Euzkadi in the state of Jalisco, formerly part of the transnational corporation Continental Tires. The Euzkadi workers led a 1100-day labor struggle between 2001 and 2005 and regained control of the factory; restarting production as a workers' controlled cooperative. They were also supported by the Pascual Boing soft drinks producer cooperative, which represents the second case study. This cooperative has been functioning since 1985 after a more than 3-year-long struggle. The third important example from Mexico is the Urban Passenger Motor Carrier Route 100, also known as R-100, a partially worker-controlled decentralized organism under the control of the Mexico City government. R-100 functioned from 1981 to 1995, when it was declared bankrupt and subsequently disappeared. The last and most far-reaching example regards the self-managed cooperativism in the Zapatista autonomous municipalities in Chiapas. Cuninghame concludes that, in contrast to most other workers, the Zapatista National Liberation Army cooperatives and other rural and indigenous initiatives are the most emblematic and far-reaching examples of self-management with an anti-capitalist perspective.

In Chapter 9, "Collective Self-management and Social Classes: The Case of Enterprises Recovered by Their Workers in Uruguay", Anabel Rieiro analyzes the recuperation of more than 20 different, mainly industrial companies with a total of approximately 1500 workers. The recuperations followed the crisis of 2002 that provoked the closure of 35 to 40 percent of all Uruguayan companies. But as Rierio shows, "the fact that these collective actions were inspired by defensive rather than offensive reasons did not stop them from becoming intense experiences that led to deep subjective transformations for the workers involved" (p. 275). The recuperations represent a collective resistance to processes of growing individualization. The workers chose collective and assembly-based forms of administration. The recuperations can therefore revitalize class struggles and deter exclusion processes.

In Chapter 10, "Self-managing the Commons in Contemporary Greece", Alexandros Kioupkiolis and Theodoros Karyotis describe the long history of rural cooperativism in Greece going back to the 18th century and give examples of workers' control at the beginning of the 20th century. In the 1980s the "socialist" Panhellenic Socialist Movement government claimed to support cooperatives and introduced forms of co-management and workers' control in industrial companies. The result was negative. Government interference destroyed many cooperatives and attempts at workers' control. But in some cases, as shown by the authors, workers developed struggles and concrete forms of workers' control and participation in administration. The contemporary economic crisis, with its devastating consequences for Greek workers, led to the emergence of a network of self-organized collectives engaged in commerce, exchange, production and social services. A significant feature of these new self-administered activities is that they relate to other movements and place themselves in the context of a broader resistance movement, relating to the recent social movement. They put an enhanced emphasis on autonomous self-organization, social solidarity, networking and opposition to neoliberal capitalism, as the authors show in three case studies ranging from a collectively managed café, and the recuperated factory Vio.Me. to the social center Micropolis.

An Alternative Labour History is organized as a collection drawing from a range of historic epochs, although it is by no means comprehensive. It stems from a larger body of work that includes the web site workerscontrol.net (a multilingual, virtual archive on workers' control founded by Alan Tuckman, Ralf Hoffrogge and myself, with the goal of promoting and sharing knowledge of different experiences of workers' control), as well as the book *Ours to Master and to Own*, edited by myself and Immanuel Ness (2011). workerscontrol.net is a self-organized network with autonomous nodes and has grown to have edited areas in English, French, German, Greek, Italian, Portuguese, Spanish and Serbo-Croatian. Even so, we are still far from having documented all the important experiences of workers' control. There are still several better and lesser known examples of workers' control that need to be made accessible, such as in Hungary (1919 and 1956), Bolivia (1950s), Czechoslovakia (1968), Australia, Switzerland and France (late 1960s and 1970s), as well as South Korea (1980), to name only a few, and it is to be hoped, also many more to come.

Note

1. Frantz Fanon (1952) used the term disalienation in *Black Skin, White Masks*, in which he analyzes he negative psychological consequences of colonial subjugation on Black people. The internalization of inferiority by the oppressed means that the process of emancipation is primarily a process of disalienation.

References

Afary, J. and Anderson, K.B. (2005) *Foucault and the Iranian Revolution: Gender and the Seductions of Islamism.* Chicago: University of Chicago Press.

Agnoli, J. (1999) *Subversive Theorie. Die Sache selbst und ihre Geschichte.* Gesammelte Werke. Vol. 3. 2nd edn. Freiburg: Cairá.

Albert, M. (2003) *Parecon. Life after Capitalism.* London: Verso.

Aronowitz, S. (1991) *False Promises.* New York: McGraw Hill.

Azzellini, D. (2011) Workers' control under Venezuela's Bolivarian revolution. In Ness, I. and Azzellini, D. (eds) *Ours to Master and to Own: Workers' Councils from the Commune to the Present.* Chicago: Haymarket.

Azzellini, D. (2012) From cooperatives to enterprises of direct social property in the Venezuelan process. In Harnecker, C.P. (ed.) *Cooperatives and Socialism. A View from Cuba.* Basingstoke: Palgrave Macmillan.

Azzellini, D. (2013) The communal system as Venezuela's transition to socialism. In Brincat, S.K. (ed.) *Communism in the 21st Century. Vol. II: Whither Communism? The Challenges Facing Communist States, Parties and Ideals.* Westport: Praeger.

Azzellini, D. (2014) Venezuela's social transformation and growing class struggle. In Spronk, S. and Webber, J.R. (eds) *Crisis and Contradiction: Marxist Perspectives on Latin America in the Global Economy.* Leiden: Brill Press.

Azzellini, D. and Ressler, O. (2011) *Comuna Under Construction.* Film. 96 minutes. Berlin, Caracas and Vienna: Azzellini and Ressler self-production.

Azzellini, D. and Ressler, O. (2014) *Occupy, Resist, Produce – Ri-Maflow.* Film. 34 minutes. Berlin and Vienna: Azzellini and Ressler self-production.

Bibby, A. (2013) Workers occupy plant as Spanish co-operative goes under. *The Guardian.* 25 November. Available at http://www.theguardian.com/social-enterprise-network/2013/nov/15/spanish-co-op-workers-occupy-plant (accessed 28 November 2014).

Di Paola, P. (2011) Factory councils in Turin, 1919–1920 "The sole and authentic social representatives of the proletarian class". In Ness, I. and Azzellini, D. (eds) *Ours to Master and to Own: Workers' Councils from the Commune to the Present.* Chicago: Haymarket.

Fanon, F. (1952) *Black Skin, White Masks.* Paris: Gallimard.

Hoffrogge, R. (2014) *Working-Class Politics in the German Revolution. Richard Müller, the Revolutionary Shop Stewards and the Origins of the Council Movement.* Amsterdam: Brill.

Huet, T. (1997) Can coops go global? Mondragón is trying. *Dollars and Sense* (November–December). Available at http://www.dollarsand-sense.org/archives/1997/1197huet.html (accessed 28 November 2014).

Karyotis, T. (2014) Report from the "Workers' Economy" international meeting, January 31 and February 1, occupied factory of Fralib, Marseille. Available at autonomias.net. http://www.auto nomias.net/2014/02/report-from-workers-economy.html (accessed 28 November 2014).

Kowalewski, Z.M. (2011) Give us back our factories! Between resisting exploitation and the struggle for workers' power in Poland, 1944–1981. In Ness, I. and Azzellini, D. (eds) *Ours to Master and to Own: Workers' Councils from the Commune to the Present.* Chicago: Haymarket

Luxemburg, R. (1900) Co-operatives, unions, democracy. In Luxemburg, R. *Reform or Revolution.* Available at www.marxists.org/archive/luxemburg/1900/reform-revolution/ch07.htm (accessed 28 November 2014).

Lynd, S. and Lynd, A. (2000) *The New Rank and File.* Ithaca and London: Cornell University Press.

Mandel, E. (1971) *The Formation of the Economic Thought of Karl Marx.* 1843 to Capital. New York and London: Monthly Review Press.

Martin, W. (1986) *The Mind of Frederick Douglass.* Chapel Hill, NC: University of North Carolina Press.

Marx, K. (1871a[1986]) First draft of 'The Civil War in France'. In *Karl Marx, Friedrich Engels: Collected Works.* Vol. 22. Moscow: Progress Publishers.

Marx, K. (1871b[1977]). The Civil War in France. In McLellan, D. (ed.) *Karl Marx: Selected Writings.* Oxford: Oxford University Press.

Mészáros, I. (1995) *Beyond Capital: Towards a Theory of Transition.* London: Merlin Press.

Mondragón, (n.d.) Home page Available at http://www.mondragon-corporation.com/eng/ (accessed 23 February 2014).

Musić, G. (2011) Yugoslavia. workers' Self-management as state paradigm. In Ness, I. and Azzellini, D. (eds) *Ours to Master and to Own: Workers' Councils from the Commune to the Present.* Chicago: Haymarket.

Ness, I. and Azzellini, D. (eds) (2011) *Ours to Master and to Own: Workers' Councils from the Commune to the Present*. Chicago: Haymarket.

Sitrin, M. (2013) *Everyday Revolutions*. London and New York: Zed Books.

TU lankide. Mondragón Corporation's News (2013) Internationalisation consolidates Mondragon's industrial business with sales abroad in excess of €4bn. 17 June. Available at http://www.mondragon-corporation. com/eng/internationalisation-consolidates-mondragons-industrial-business-with-sales-abroad-in-excess-of-e4bn (accessed 28 November 2014).

Wallerstein, I. (2000) A left politics for the 21st century? Or, theory and praxis once again. *New Political Science*, 22 (2) 143–59.

Wallis, V. (2011) Worker's control and revolution. In Ness, I. and Azzellini, D. (eds) *Ours to Master and to Own: Workers' Councils from the Commune to the Present*. Chicago: Haymarket.

ONE

Council Democracy, or the End of the Political

Alex Demirović, translated by Joe Keady

Democracy, as it is widely understood, is equated with parliaments, periodic elections, parties, and representation. This form of liberal democracy has repeatedly been in crisis since the 19th century, but it has consistently been able to revive itself and, if anything, expand further. Parliamentary democracy has once again been diagnosed as being gradually eroded and in crisis in recent years: the dominance of business interests in politics, the distance of parties and parliaments from the general public, the imperviousness of public opinion to the interests of the populace, the executive decisions made to benefit institutional investors, and the spread of corruption, as well as that of right-wing populism and nationalism, are all symptoms of this erosion. Critics often pin their hopes on forms of direct democracy, but contrary to what this term suggests, it offers little potential for participation or agency. Direct democracy operates within the framework of liberal democracy, which is based on finding majorities to pass bills and therefore ultimately on a dichotomous yes or no position. As a result, social relations themselves are not constituted in a directly democratic way. Rather, direct democracy adds yet another procedure arises which is supplementary to the parliament instead.

The council democracy tradition represents one alternative to this. This may appear at first blush to be a museum piece, but during periods when social movements no longer oriented themselves to the parameters enforced by the ruling classes and no longer demanded these standards to be reinforced, but instead have transitioned into constitutive action, they have repeatedly updated their demands for a radical democratic alternative (see Arendt 1963). That demand has assumed various forms, including control over production, changes in the distribution of property, self-government, the cooperative management of production and distribution, anti-authoritarianism and self-determination of all social relations from the workplace to the school to the family. It can be expressed as "Work differently, live differently". The forerunners of the council democracy tradition are the English and French revolutions; the fundamental impetus comes from the Paris Commune and the council communist movement in Russia as well as in Germany, Hungary, Austria and Italy following World War I (see Ness and Azzellini, 2011). It was revived by the uprising in Hungary in 1956, by the social protest movements since 1968 and finally, by new initiatives in Latin America in recent years. Often spurred on by the social movements of their time, intellectuals such as Marx, Trotsky, Gramsci, Max Adler, Karl Korsch, Hannah Arendt and Cornelius Castoriadis have addressed the matter of council democracy at various times.

In this article I address certain aspects of council democracy. My intention is neither to apply old debates to the present-day situation without comment nor to suggest that they are directly applicable to it. Instead, I call attention to a particular problem in the debate on council democracy and therefore read older texts from the perspective of democracy theory. If the impulse towards council democracy has repeatedly renewed itself in the prevailing historical conflict, then a critical reading of this kind will be useful in three ways. It will recall these older discussions; it will show that council democracy utilizes important ideas in pursuit of fundamental democratization that are useful for today's social movements, and finally, it brings to light the problems connected with the demand for council democracy. I would first like to show that liberal democracy innately produces the necessity of a radical alternative. In the second section, I introduce the reasons for this with support from observations by Marx and the significant perspectives he developed on council democracy based on the experiences of the Paris Commune. The third section examines the problems that developed in the council democracy movement after World War I that are instructive for any new considerations of democracy theory.

The failure of liberal democracy

Council democracy is an alternative to liberal representative democracy. From the perspective of council democracy, parliamentary democracy is a principle that does not challenge the bourgeois class. Rather, parliamentarianism must be seen as a form of bourgeois domination (see Adler, 1919: 134–5; Pannekoek, 1946: 67–8, 266–8). The shortcomings of parliamentary democracy are therefore not simply incidental to it: they systematically contribute to the dominance of the bourgeoisie and its specific structure of ownership. Liberal democracy operates in the context of a two thousand-year conception of democracy. In this understanding of political organization, democracy is a regime in which, as a form of compromise, common people to a certain extent participate in that domination, alongside the rich. From this perspective, therefore, democratic institutions are not controlled through the shared and equal participation in the shared production of shared living conditions and shared interests. If the mechanisms of liberal democracy are not explicitly aimed at preventing the will to develop from the bottom up will, together with the collaborative formation of social relations, then they are designed to break down, postpone, filter and then selectively accept this will and its enactment. This happens through the process of representation, the institution of parliament and political parties, the separation of the legislative and executive branches, and the particular form of the state's management of people.

Liberal democracy separates the economic from the political sphere, the public from the private sphere and the universal from the particular in the social sphere. Universal interests are represented in the political. The political sphere constitutes the terrain of a universal will that is separate from society, which is to say it acts according to its own specific logic in terms of its juridicial subject-position, autonomous free will, universality and representation. By contrast, life at work, at school, or in the family is regarded as a particular, private matter. To prevent the state from restricting freedom in these private spheres, it is permitted to set down binding universal conditions only when they protect the rights of the individual. No consideration is given to cooperation or the shared planning of the structures of everyday life. While decisions are made that have an impact on the whole of social life in the fields of production, technology or the family, the state often serves only the particular interests of certain powerful groups whose interests are generalized within society as a whole in the form of the state itself.

Council democracy, by contrast, extends collective self-determination to much more than the economic sphere alone. More importantly, it comprehends all social labor as well as the social division of labor, and consequently challenges the separation and configuration of economics and politics, everyday reproductive labor and social decision-making, as well as the separation of the public and private spheres. It makes that challenge in the interest of reorganizing and democratically structuring social life in its entirety rather than simply for the benefit of individual workplaces or regions. The state, as an ostensibly neutral authority enthroned above society, consequently becomes superfluous because the planned management of production and distribution in the society is organized from below (see Korsch, 1919a: 164). From this perspective, democracy is no longer merely a political regime but instead constitutes a way of life that determines every sphere and as such constitutes a different form of community, which Marx identifies as the association of free individuals.

Marx's understanding of the political and his assessment of the commune

With respect to his view of the state and politics, there is a great deal of overlap between Marx's analyses of the Paris Commune in 1871 and his early writings. He saw the measures taken by the commune as steps towards the goals that he had articulated in the 1840s. Marx drew on those developments in his critique of the political state at the level of its principles, which is to say the representative state or the democratic republic based on national sovereignty (see Marx, 1843: 352, 1875: 29). He used the method of critique to tease out this representative system. According to Marx, the political, representative state is a free state that emancipates itself from society by defining social differences such as birth, status, education or occupation as apolitical; proclaiming that, "every member of the nation is an equal participant in national sovereignty". In contrast to these particulars, which the state regards as private, it then asserts a claim to universality. Consequently, modern life is divided into two spheres: one ethereal and the other mundane: one a life in a political community in which people are citizens and the other a life in civil society in which they act as private individuals.

Marx noticed a chiasmus. Living individuals in their concrete reality are regarded as merely private and particular and therefore false. But this is where individuals are perceived as a species-being (*Gattungswesen*), as a member of the community, and as a citizen, while it is within the state, that they are "robbed of [their] real life and filled with an unreal universality" (Marx, 1843: 46). So the representative state operates on a higher historical plane in lieu of religion. The individual relates to all other individuals through the medium of the state. But that means that individuals relate to one another only on a limited, partial basis and many aspects of their lives, specifically everything that is considered private, are necessarily disregarded. Given that the political state becomes the intermediary between people and that they demand their freedom solely through the state's laws, Marx identifies that state as religious and Christian:

> What makes political democracy Christian is the fact that in it man, not only a single man but every man, counts as a sovereign being; but it is man as he appears uncultivated and unsocial, man in his accidental existence, man as he comes and goes . . . in a word, man who is no longer a real species-being. (Marx, 1843: 50)

The constitution of the political state in the act of revolution separates civil society from the state, gathers together all forms of politics and domination and constitutes them as the sphere of the community in contrast to the specific life activities of the individual. This political revolution is authoritarian by its own logic because in order to effect political emancipation, the state will attempt to nullify the particular spheres of life and "to constitute itself as the real, harmonious life of man". Yet at best it can succeed for only a short period of time and only then by force, as the political declares a revolution against the social conditions upon which it is based, that is, the private life of civil society, to be permanent. That struggle is futile because, as Marx shows, the Jacobin Terror was necessarily followed by "the restoration of religion, private property, and all elements of civil society" (Marx, 1843: 47).

These considerations lead to four conclusions.

1. Only when real individuals reabsorb in themselves the abstract citizen, when individuals have recognized and organized their own powers as social powers – that is, no longer as a state community beyond isolated private individuals but in the form of conscious cooperation with others – only then "will human emancipation be completed" (Marx, 1843: 57). This is the production of the real, cooperative community without classes and without a state as the medium of public welfare lying above social classes and individuals.

2. Marx repeatedly restated this idea of reabsorption. Yet it is clear that this cannot strictly refer to reabsorbing the state and the political into society because, as a material foundation, civil

society is constitutive of the separation of civil society from the state. It must itself be fundamentally altered. Changing and overcoming the state requires, above all, a change in its social foundation. In the particular bourgeois manner in which they are articulated both civil society and the state are problematic: as spheres of particular, private individuals and as abstract community. Marx therefore concerns himself with overcoming the constitutive line that differentiates these two spheres from one another. But this differentiation occurs within society itself. As it is reorganized around the previously disavowed forms of social labor (that is to say, the privately appropriated surplus labor of waged and reproductive labor), the practices of political domination will gradually become superfluous:

> State interference in social relations becomes, in one domain after another, superfluous, and then dies out of itself; the government of persons is replaced by the administration of things, and by the conduct of processes of production. The State is not "abolished." It dies out. (Engels, 1882: 70)

The particular antinomies in the society in which the capitalist mode of production prevails are lifted: the specific and the universal; the tangible, living individual and the species-being (*Gattungswesen*); the private and the public.

3. Marx places human emancipation at the center of his thought. For him, the point is to overcome the fundamental conditions under which social classes have been formed throughout world history:

> When, in the course of development, class distinctions have disappeared, and all production has been concentrated in the hands of associated individuals, the public power will lose its political character. (Marx and Engels, 1848: 237–8)

Moreover, public power as the organized power on the part of one class for the suppression of another becomes superfluous itself. According to Marx, the proletarian class should no longer pursue the project of political emancipation and political revolution. Such emancipation would have authoritarian consequences without changing society's foundations. The revolution must come from below and be implemented as a social revolution that changes people's living and working conditions:

> A social revolution, even though it be limited to a single industrial district, involves the standpoint of the whole, because it is a human protest against a dehumanized life, because it starts from the standpoint of the single, real individual, because the collectivity against whose separation from himself the individual reacts is the true collectivity of man, the human essence. The political soul of revolution consists on the contrary in a tendency of the classes without political influence to end their isolation from the top positions in the state. Their standpoint is that of the state, an abstract whole, that only exists through a separation from real life, that is inconceivable without the organized opposition, the general concept of humanity and its individual existence. (Marx, 1844a: 126)

4. The problem is nonetheless that human emancipation cannot be achieved directly. Any appeal to the humanity of each individual will fade out; human rights do not extend beyond capitalist servitude because they defend the existing ownership structure. Given the actual basis of its existence and its symbolic significance in connection with all other social classes, Marx sees the working class as the one that must organize the transition, which he identifies as the "dictatorship of the proletariat" (Marx, 1875: 565). The working class is the universal class because it represents universal suffering. Marx sees the working class as the one that contributes in a particular way

to sustaining society through its labor. At the same time, the working class is subsumed within capital and its living labor power exploited and appropriated as the private wealth of a few people, who base their domination on that appropriation. If the working class wants to emancipate itself, it can do so only by emancipation *from* itself and from the social relations under which it is a working class at all, meaning only by abolishing the bourgeois society under which everyone else also has to suffer. "This dissolution of society, as a particular estate, is the proletariat" (Marx, 1844b: 73). The working class is therefore defined in a dual and contradictory way. On one hand, it gains its particular identity within the capitalist mode of production and it is – from the perspective of democracy theory – only one particular group with particular interests. On the other hand, it symbolizes something universal that, by its very nature, establishes the basis for its own transcendence, its existence as a radical Other, and the emancipation of humanity in general; a promise that cannot be kept in civil society. As a result, human emancipation means that there will be neither class nor any popular sovereign – positions that consist of private individuals who form the basis of the state.

These four conclusions also underpin Marx's analysis of the Paris Commune's measures in 1871. In that analysis, he introduces the first steps in the transformation of the division between politics and economics. Consequently, that analysis becomes one of the significant bases for the further "historical development of Marxist thinking about councils" (Bermbach, 1973: 19).

According to Marx, disappointing experiences with the republic as a form of government demonstrated that a republic must be a social republic. The Paris Commune put a social republic into practice by snatching the state apparatus away from the capitalist and landowning class and by "frankly [avowing] 'social emancipation' as the great goal of the Republic and [guaranteeing] thus that social transformation by the Communal organization" (Marx, 1871a: 497, 1871b: 541). The supporters of that process were no longer the various bourgeois class fractions but the "producing masses" (Marx, 1871a: 261). Unlike previous revolutions, the nation – the combination of workers, the petty and middle bourgeoisie and the farmers (Marx, 1871a: 259, Marx, 1871b: 214) – took "the actual management of their Revolution into their own hands . . . displacing the state machinery, the governmental machinery of the ruling classes by a governmental machinery of their own" (Marx, 1871a: 261) by establishing the commune on the workers' initiative. But at the same time, the commune was more than the replacement of one machine with another. The commune met to the goal of reabsorbing the state, as Marx put it:

> [The Commune] was a revolution against the state itself, this supernaturalist abortion of society, a resumption by the people for the people, of its own social life. It was not a revolution to transfer it from one fraction of the ruling classes to the other, but a Revolution to break down this horrid machinery of Class domination itself. (Marx, 1871a: 249; see also 241–2, 250–1)

To define the commune's political location, Marx resorted to Abraham Lincoln's definition of democracy as a form of government of the people, by the people, for the people. The main feature is that the people, and particularly the working class, actually govern themselves in the communes (Marx, 1871a: 261). But the commune is only the first step towards social emancipation. The communal form of political organization makes it immediately possible to make great strides for the "movement for [the working class] themselves and mankind" (Marx, 1871a: 254). But the commune is still a political form and not the "movement of . . . a general regeneration of mankind" nor the "abolition of all classes". This is because it represents a particular interest: the liberation of labor from the "usurpation of the . . . monopolists of the means of labour, created by the labourers themselves or forming the gift of nature" (Marx, 1871a: 252). The commune still means class struggle, "but it affords the rational medium in which that class struggle can run through its different phases in the most rational and human way" (Marx, 1871a: 253). Economic reforms, changes in the distribution and reorganization of production and the establishment of the conditions for "the spontaneous action of the laws of the social economy of free and associated labor" (Marx, 1871a: 253–4) all take time.

Marx identifies a series of decisions made by the commune. He names the suppression of night work for journeyman bakers and the transfer of closed workshops and factories to workmen societies as social measures (Marx, 1871a: 236, 1871b: 217). But the most important features for him were the political measures as he considered the commune as "a lever for uprooting the economical foundations upon which rests the existence of classes, and therefore of class-rule" (Marx, 1871b: 212). The "unproductive and mischievous work of the state" which absorbs "an immense portion of the national produce" was eliminated and, to the extent that it was necessary, transitioned into local and national administration. This meant replacing the costly military apparatus, the standing army that was separate from the people, regular officers, and expensive armaments with a popular militia. The independent police were abolished and the functions of safety and order were assumed the citizens themselves. This could have created a threat of capriciousness, but Marx emphasizes the context of democratic politics in which these measures were taken. Universal suffrage was expanded and served the people for the first time (Marx, 1871a: 251, 1871b: 210–11). The election of representatives was no longer restricted to voting once every few years, as it is in parliamentary systems. In its various districts, the commune elected its deputies to bodies of self-governance based on universal suffrage. The city councils assumed the tasks of legislation and administration. They were accountable and could be recalled at any time. Public positions were no longer the "private property" of a central administration that endowed offices with functional authority. All official functions were instead administered by communal functionaries and were under the control of the communes. The country's universal and vital functions presented no reason for developing a standing hierarchical civil service above society; instead it was also be administered by communal positions:

> The few but important functions which would still remain for a central government were not to be suppressed, as has been intentionally misstated, but were to be discharged by Communal, and therefore strictly responsible, agents. The unity of the nation was not to be broken but, on the contrary, to be organized by the Communal Constitution, and to become a reality by the destruction of the State power which claimed to be the embodiment of that unity independent of, and superior to, the nation itself, from which it was but a parasitic excrescence. (Marx, 1871b: 210)

State and official secrets were eliminated; the pay levels of communal councils corresponded to those of skilled workers (Marx, 1871a: 251–2, 1871b: 209.

From the perspective of democracy theory, it is particularly significant that the commune governed itself and that the elected committees combined both legislative and executive functions. The commune, which is to say its united deputies, "was to be a working, not a parliamentary, body" (Marx, 1871a: 537, 1871b: 209) with an elected, accountable, and recallable judiciary that was separate from it. From the perspective of liberal political theory, the combination of legislative and executive functions might appear to be a retrograde motion towards a more primitive moment than the separation of powers, which is expected to ensure a certain measure of freedom and democratic rights. By contrast, from a council democracy standpoint, the separation of powers is viewed as an anti-democratic principle and the "unification of all powers in the hands of the people" (Adler, 1919: 60–1) is seen as necessary. There is a whole array of arguments against the separation of powers.

1. The debate on democracy theory itself provides no clear explanation of how the separation of powers is to be composed. According to John Locke, the elected parliament is the people's highest representational body, but the people do not give up power (Locke, 1689: Book II, § 149). The power of the people therefore remains with the people – in contrast with the terms of Germany's *Grundgesetz*, or basic law (in practice, Germany's Constitution) – and is not divided between parliament, the executive and the judiciary.

2. Historical analyses of the debate over the separation of powers in the drafting of the Constitution of the United States show that it was devised by the bourgeoisie as a means to prevent expression of the free will of the people and with it the possibility that the people might initiate a constitutional challenge against constitutional institutions and, above all, private property (see Beard, 1913).

3. From a materialist political sociology perspective, the separation of powers is a way of allocating the power of the various factions of the ruling classes in the state apparatuses. In its totality, however, the state elaborates the total interests of the ruling classes in opposition to the subaltern class (see Poulantzas, 1974: 303).

4. The separation of powers exists only as a strategic factor in the exercise of state dominance. Factional and party interests permeate individual state bodies (for example, public prosecutors, judges and tax investigators are prevented by the various ministries from investigating politicians or employers: where necessary, the latter are transferred or even persecuted by means of the courts, the police or psychiatric institutions. On the other hand, representatives who are critical of the

police or even of the secret service are themselves subjected to surveillance; positions are filled in the military or the police force with an eye towards their party affiliations and parliamentary decisions on legislation or budgeting are oriented to the standards of the sitting government). Under the separation of powers, then, a government agency is independent only when official limitations and jurisdictions are strategically used on behalf of the particular interests of ruling class factions in political conflicts.

5. The separation of powers is regarded as a form of protection against a totalitarian infringement of rights. Yet the idea that the legislative branch may be checked and mediated by the executive is absurd, given that infringements of the rights of citizens are themselves filtered through these same executive bodies: the police, administrative authorities and the military. In fact, it is the separation of powers that makes independent bureaucratic procedures possible. The coincidence of legislative and executive powers in council democracy may give rise to fears that the weak control of the legislature over the executive would be weakened further, leading to capriciousness and political decisions implemented by means of violence. This is contradicted by the absence of a separate, permanent body with its own staff for the implementation of decisions; the fact that those who look after matters on behalf of the general public do not do so on a representative basis but are instead required to adhere to the decisions of the communal councils; and the fact that the people who make decisions, act and are elected directly from below, under conditions of public control. Capricious and violent actions would be less likely than under the current form of bureaucratic domination. Where it might happen, it would not be concealed by the official channels and secrecy of the rational-legal institutional state. Instead, it would be the subject of public scandal.

Additionally, there is no compelling reason for the separation of powers from the perspective of democracy theory. In Rousseau's conception, the popular sovereign and its will are inseparable (Rousseau, 1762: 170–1). In support of the separation of powers, it might be argued that the nation binds itself to its decisions through the separation of legislative and executive powers. This is because restricting the legislature to lawgiving and allocating implementation powers, that is, governance and administration, to the executive prevents legislators from being overly influenced by current situations. The general will is mediated by the executive. But democracy theory sees this as problematic. According to this logic, the popular sovereign is viewed as a temperamental little child, but what is left unexplained is why the popular sovereign should not be allowed to overturn its previous decisions precisely on the basis of new insights or a change of preferences. When the executive impedes it, that executive becomes a transcendent power and a political party, or a place of party formation, against the parliament. Both the empirical arguments as well as those arising from the discussion on democracy theory make clear that the separation of powers is only minimally useful. The fusion of legislative and executive powers prevents power groups from organizing within state bodies and increasing their power by expanding their purview. In Marx's conception of the commune, all committees are checked from below by the electors, the councils perform their duties publicly and without recourse to official secrecy, and the deputies are accountable and can be recalled at any time. Democracy is therefore a matter of creating the socio-political conditions that impede the development of political power. This is possible, in particular, because power that speaks in the name of the popular sovereign is no longer concentrated in a political location. I would like to briefly examine this critical point.

Marx's vocabulary is ambiguous: he refers to the "citizens" of the commune who are entitled to vote, but he also refers to the "workers" and the "popular masses". He does not explain how the relationship between these various categories is to be understood. The group that is entitled to vote would be a legitimate body in the context of a democratic process. Marx does not explain who is entitled to vote. Should all adults over a certain age be considered entitled to vote? Does that include migrants? Does it mean only workers or those who still own or had once owned the means of production, as well but who do not exploit the labor of others? Political democracies derive the power of the centralized state and the legitimacy of their organs from popular sovereigns. Marx was obviously not interested in greater legitimacy for the exercise of state rule but rather in overcoming it. Logically, therefore, he had to challenge the concept of the popular sovereign. He did not explicitly comment on this, nevertheless a Marxist approach would be as follows. The popular sovereign is a political body. It gains its status from the existence of the national state, to which the popular sovereign grants legitimacy. Although the popular sovereign is the final authority for the self-conception of the democratic republic from which all state power is derived, it cannot be substantiated. This is because the people who establish the state from which state power is derived must logically precede that state. But under pre-state circumstances, just who constitutes the people cannot yet be precisely defined. This is because affiliation with a people or citizenship is defined only by the state. The popular sovereign and the democratic state can only be established on a circular basis.

The concept of the popular sovereign is consequently revealed to be an irrational category that displays its irrationality when it is traced back to the establishment of the people based on pre-political ideas such as that of the people as a community with a shared ancestry, destiny, language or culture (see Balibar, 2002). In such cases, the people assume an entirely mythical character. From the perspective of Marxian theory, we can say that the bourgeois economy, as well as the democratically representative republic, are irrational-religious social forms, given that they both utilize a foundation that they cannot establish.

In the case of the economy, it is assumed that commodity prices are rational: prices must correspond to value. But the bourgeois economy can neither identify nor explain what that value is. The value of a commodity embodies the social context of private production and is derived, in bourgeois society, from the amount of labor time expended. But living labor power has as little intrinsic value as any other use value; thus, the value of labor as a commodity is an irrational expression that only has meaning under capitalist relations of production. The democratic republic as an irrational-religious form of universality above the will of the private individual must be established in the form of the popular sovereign. But that popular sovereign does not exist. It cannot be established but is instead created by the political state. By contrast, Marx argues from the perspective of humanity and in advance of humanity. He explicitly defined humanity as a category that is beyond social classes, politics and the state. The goal is the association of free individuals. Marx suggests that the political category of the popular sovereign is invalid. This marks a far-reaching difference of opinion in the tradition on the left. One tendency, following Rousseau's thinking, deals with the actual and unified popular sovereign that embodies the common will to produce the common popular totality (see Adler, 1919: 137–8). The working class, which, according to this tendency, represents the productive functions that secure the life of the society and makes up a (relative) majority of the populace, can be seen in this sense as the basis for a unified popular will. The other tendency no longer strives for such a common will because it sees that will as the basis for reproducing the state, politics, and government, all of which it seeks to overcome:

> Political democracy disappeared under the council organization because politics itself disappeared and merged with the social economy. . . . Councils are not government; the central councils never took on a governmental character because they

did not have access to organs that could impose their will on the masses. (Pannekoek 1946, 70–1)

Pannekoek (1946: 271) correctly asks whether democracy is even an appropriate term for the councils, given that the people govern themselves. But this people is no longer a political body because there is no state that unifies and governs it. A kind of widely dispersed, spatially boundless, and socially open horizontal network of associations developed with variously structured self-governance bodies made up of communes and production or distribution groups without taking the form of a people. It is therefore appropriate to speak of a multitude (see Hardt and Negri 2002: 377ff; see Korsch, 1920: 225). Jürgen Habermas criticized Hannah Arendt for conceiving of councils under which society would constitute itself as a political society and a totality through a regenerated citizenship (Habermas, 1992: 360). He believed that this was no longer adequate in light of the functional differentiation of modern society, given that it no longer has a center or a political apex, but he did hold onto a system of division of political power. The council system, by contrast, suggests an end to the arrogant spread of the political that positions itself as the entire society. The councils constitute a completely new kind of complexity in which the public merges with the private and political action merges with social action. These actions are decentered and decentralized, yet at the same time they can also be broadly interwoven both horizontally and vertically, as needed. There are no local hierarchical authorities.

Marx's analysis is vague on one critical point. He has little to say about how the state was reabsorbed into the real production of the community. His most important argument is that the popular masses, and above, all the working class, had taken the initiative and assumed the affairs of state themselves. In this respect, the commune was the "form at last discovered under which to work out the economic emancipation of labour" (Marx, 1871b: 544). As a result, the question of democracy became strictly a question of class theory. Social relations become democratic when the popular masses govern themselves. That is an important step, but it does not meet the demand made by democracy theory that everyone should participate in self-government. And participation was uncertain even for members of the working class because a communal worker government does not mean that the division of labor between economics and politics has been instantaneously overcome.

It is more likely that the members of the working class fulfilled, in a practical sense, a variety of functions. There were a lot of them, but they would have had to do everything: produce, make decisions and implement those decisions. The result would have been a heavy workload that they could not have maintained over the long term, if the commune had been given a long enough opportunity to experiment with different forms of self-government. The result may have been that individual people or groups would have become political experts in public administration within the bodies of self-governance, governing in the name of the popular masses and the working class. Permanent monitoring and eligibility would have gradually proven to be too time-consuming for the civic assemblies. Thereafter, independent forms of political decision-making may have resurfaced, which the participants might all have experienced with relief at an increase in efficiency and effectiveness that would have nonetheless undermined the claim to self-governance. Council democracy's supporters addressed these problems in the decades following Marx's death. I would like to address a few of their answers below, particularly those that arose in Germany.

Some aspects of the debate around council democracy

In the thinking about councils in the wake of World War I, the working class was conceived as the basis for state power and authority in a way that was similar to Marx's descriptions. There was, however, a significant difference. While Marx placed the councils at the level of the commune, the revolution in Germany initially involved workers' and soldiers' councils and, over the course of 1919, this was reduced to worker councils only. Accordingly, a flier dated 23 November 1918 that was published by the Executive Council of Greater Berlin Workers' and Soldiers' Councils – formally, until January 1919 the government of the German Reich – declared that "Political authority is in the hands of the workers' and soldiers' councils of the German Socialist Republic" (cited in Müller, 1921). Ernst Däumig described the council organization as "practical socialism", explaining that

> [e]ven with a republican facade, a council organization is a proletarian and socialist means or struggle, destined to remove capitalist production and the authority of the state based on capitalist production. The council organization strives for socialist production and self-managed communities. (Däumig, 1920: 51)

For supporters of the council idea, this displacement of the unit that constitutes the community onto the workers is the decisive perspective:

> Only the proletariat can carry the council idea, that is, all manual and intellectual workers forced to sell their labor to capital in order to survive. The council idea stands in sharp, and natural, contrast to the common democratic idea that perceives the citizens as a unified mass. (1920: 52)

Anton Pannekoek (1946, 269–70) believed that a large segment of Germany's workers during the revolutionary period did not understand this crucial perspective because for decades the social democrat-led labor movement had been oriented to democracy theory's goal of establishing a democratic republic and equal, universal suffrage. From that social democratic perspective, monopolizing power within the councils must have appeared to be a usurpation of the power to make political decisions. By contrast, according to Pannekoek (1946: 271), the workers would have had to "develop the deep conviction that the council organization was a much higher and more complete form of equality". One could say, he continued, that the council system is the highest form of democracy and the form "that belongs to a society that is master of its own production and life" (see also Adler, 1919: 144).

But in the context of democracy theory these ideas raise a difficult problem. Just as a determination must be made as to who is allowed the privilege of voting rights, now the question arises: who is a worker? This class theory question takes on far-reaching political significance. Are only manual laborers in large factories workers? That might mean that women, apprentices and migrants could participate in their decision-making, but what about engineers and office workers? A narrow definition would create the danger of excluding large groups of wage laborers and related union and socialist tendencies from participating in economic self-management. While Marx had a broad confederation in mind, Ernst Däumig (1920: 58) spoke of an alliance between manual and intellectual workers and included those who sell their labor to capital among the people who could participate in decision-making: engineers, technicians, accountants, scientists and others (see also Korsch, 1919b). Max Adler had similar groups of workers in mind when he spoke of the necessity of involving all "economically critical strata". Like Adler, Däumig was aware of the need to prevent the formation of a powerful minority that would resort to using the terror of one segment of the oppressed class against another segment, or one socialist tendency against another, in order to implement its own will. The terms had to be set such that they did, in fact, involve the majority of those who provide social labor and opposed the bourgeois minority. Moreover, it could not be assumed that the make-up of the class that was empowered to make decisions would be defined on a permanent basis. The goal of the councils was to reorganize production and society in such a way that everyone could take on a share of social labor. "With labor emancipated, every man becomes a working man, and productive labour ceases to be a class attribute" (Marx, 1871b: 544). To the extent that this is the case, previously excluded individuals would be able to participate in decision-making (Pannekoek, 1946: 272). This, however, leads to a problem. Defining technicians, engineers and managers as workers, which is supposed to prevent them from being excluded from the decision-making process, can also help to conceal lingering class differences. These categories of people could use their monopoly on knowledge and expertise to subordinate the production process and organize it in such a way that it suits their interests. That is why Gramsci and Korsch also demanded that the "previous bourgeois 'division of labor' between corporeal and mental production" would have to be overcome as the process moves forward (Korsch, 1919b: 173).

This question is closely linked to another problem that arises from the institution of the workers' and soldiers' council and the call for "all power to the councils". Max Adler, in particular, raises the question of whether or not workers as workers should have sole authority over production and social needs. In this light, councils should then be formed, as Hannah Arendt maintained, in every social sphere and profession: councils for construction workers, architects, students, uniform tailors, public officials and farmers. At this point the danger arises that the system of workers' councils might transform from an "instrument for the destruction of capitalist society into an institution for special interest groups within society" (Adler, 1919: 153). Moreover, he saw the risk that petty professional and status interests might form or stabilize. Councils should therefore not be misunderstood as a "long-term formal principle", he thought, because that would codify and perpetuate the class character of the proletariat, which would only bring back positions of power without changing the actual relations. If the workers had previously been aggrieved, they would feel like masters within the framework of council democracy (p. 149). Rather than the contempt of all named council theorists for the whole concept, as Arendt suspected, it is this concern for the reactionary possibilities that might be incorporated into council ideas that is the underlying reason why all the council theorists named here understood them as only a transitional form of struggle. Accordingly, Adler believed that the councils should not be composed of workers but of socialists. He recommended that only those who were explicitly committed to overcoming the class divide, the goal of socialism, should be eligible for election to the workers' councils, while professional perspectives and immediate interests should be of secondary importance.

If the workers' councils were to function only as workers' councils, the danger would arise that they would only represent the interests of certain businesses. From an emancipatory perspective, the councils should, in fact, not become firmly established. Individual workshops should be subordinated to the larger context in the interest of total social planning. To that end, the supporters of the council movement proposed an articulation of will formation and decision-making from below. The workers' and soldiers' councils would then form the units of political decision-making and action. As in the communal councils, they would also be democratically elected, accountable and recallable at any time. They would attend to legislative and executive duties. Bottom-level delegates would be elected directly: blue-collar and white-collar workers would elect works councils which, together with the managers, would monitor and organize the company's affairs. The self-employed and other professional groups that could not be included in companies would elect a common trade council on the district level. Bodies that would monitor production, the district group councils that would also appoint managers, would be elected from within the works and trade councils. A district group council would represent the companies in a given industry at the economic district level.

Richard Müller, the chairman of the Executive Council of Workers' and Soldiers' Councils of Greater Berlin and, along with Ernst Däumig, one of the theoretical leaders of the council democracy movement in Germany (see Bermbach, 1973: 10; Hoffrogge, 2015, forthcoming), identified fourteen industries, including agriculture, mining, the metallurgical, chemical and textile industries, banking and trade, state and communal officials and workers, and independent professionals (see Müller, 1921). For their part, the district group councils would form their own planning and decision-making committees called district economic councils and send delegates to the national group councils under which each industry would be organized on a national level. The national group councils would in turn be combined once again into the national economic council. For Müller, political (or even democracy-political) ideas were completely secondary. Above all, he emphasized the need to maintain production and to orient its organization to the general welfare. As such, he implied that what the council-democratic process should actually produce was a foregone conclusion: democratically aware coordination between the workers in the individual production and distribution centers and responsiveness to social needs. That means that at least three aspects of democratization that would have to be considered are not mentioned in Müller's model.

1.   The first aspect concerns individual workers' right to have a direct voice in a council democracy. To make that voice possible, the authority and supervision of the owners of capital would have to be overcome at the workshop level in three distinct areas: (i) control over products, production revenues and the use of those revenues; (ii) authority over the production process (including the means of production, work flow, pace of work and hierarchies) and (iii) determination of the conditions under which human labor is used (such as wages, hygiene and workplace health and safety) (see Korsch, 1919b: 92). Council democracy is linked to the goal of overcoming these three forms of authority on the workshop and company levels in such a way that the immediate producers can decide on what and how much, with what means of production in what way, and under what working conditions production takes place. This requires forms of democratic participation by

the immediate producers on these levels, yet surprisingly little has been said about this in the debate around council democracy. According to Müller, participation consists of electing delegates who in turn influence production and the election of managers through district councils; he says nothing about more far-reaching direct participation in decision-making on the company level.

According to Pannekoek, the leading body in the workplace is the totality of the collaborative workers. "They convene to discuss their issues and make their decisions in assemblies. That way anyone who participates in the work also participates in regulating social labor" (Pannekoek, 1946: 40). In the event that the number of workers was very large, assemblies would be formed on the departmental level and there would also be an assembly of central delegate committees. The delegates would participate in the discussions as simple members of their departments and establish a link between them and the committees. From Pannekoek's perspective, there were no leaders, but particular matters were passed on to individuals who were fully accountable for implementation. Korsch recommends that the mass of workers be "subjected in submissive dependence" to a single decision-making leader during the production process at work, but that they should be able to decide at any time who those leaders are and how long they should remain in that position (Korsch, 1919c: 179). This idea has the virtue of not interrupting the workflow, but there is a significant danger that the democratic decision-making process would again be separated from the immediate work process and the concrete labor would not be determined in mutual cooperation. From the perspective of democracy theory Korsch's idea can hardly be generalized.

2. Agreement between individual workshops on the industry, district and national levels should replace the blind coordination of the market and the decision-making of the owners

of capital. While social needs should be satisfied by deliberate planning and management, company egotism should be prevented:

> In the case of direct socialization, land and equipment are also merely lent to the working production participants at an individual workplace (branch of production). As the socio-economic basis of the entire process of production and consumption, they do not belong to any individual group of workers but to the combined community of each of the groups. (Korsch, 1919a: 90)

The factories "should function by combining [them], as the separate members of one body, into a well organized system of production" (Pannekoek, 1946: 33). Bookkeeping, statistics and accounting offices are all necessary, but it is more important that workshops participate in the decision-making of the higher rank-ing authorities than that they are simply informed through abstract indicators. The attention and knowledge of individuals, their com-munication and the agreement between workshops contribute to producing and regulating the socioeconomic context (pp. 37, 67). But the socioeconomic context is not the only thing that mat-ters. In *Capital*, Marx uses the concept of social industrial methods (*Betriebsweise*) to indicate the view that, under capitalist relations of production, nature is appropriated under the guise of a particular method that organizes the means of production in such a way that wage labor can be exploited as efficiently as possible, while also maintaining the possibility of monitoring it. One particular result is the concentration of the means of production and the discipli-nary means of organization. The labor movement hoped that this form of factory work would produce great strides in productivity, pushing the criticism of factory work (and, in fact, the organization of labor altogether) into the background. From the perspective of council democracy, however, the social industrial methods them-selves, meaning a particular kind of cooperation, would also have to be available. This would completely change the structure of industrial forms with respect to their size and the way that the division of labor is networked, restructuring production and service, workplaces, housing and the location of free time.

3. Even if the immediate producers coordinate the production processes so thoroughly that they form one collective social laborer, there may still be a basic conflict with respect to consumption. The producers may want to limit the scope of their output or direct a smaller share of the proceeds of their labor towards the community. Korsch assumed that the conflict of interest with consumers would become the object of explicit social coordination with the disappearance of the owners of capital, who had previously mediated between wage earners and consumers. Although he does mention this problem, his work does not offer any further proposals as to how such coordination from below may take place. It is only with the work of Michael Albert that the idea of council democracy is expanded to the sphere of consumption and coordination between producers and consumers (Albert, 2003; see also Demirović, 2007).

Council democracy constitutes the social, collective laborer as the community that is capable and authorized to make decisions and in which all pertinent decisions are made through universal participation. It is thus meant to reabsorb the sphere of the political into society and to make the struggle for a share of political power superfluous. New contradictions arise between producers and consumers, but there is yet another contradiction that democracy theory does not address. This has to do with antagonisms within the immediate producer class itself. Hannah Arendt believed that there were no conflicts between parties and their factions within the councils. Members of the council movement felt the same way:

> Since the council idea's goal is the liberation of the entire proletariat from capitalist exploitation, the council organization

cannot be the domain of a single party or a single profession but must include the proletariat as a whole. (Däumig 1920: 53)

Max Adler has something very similar to say:

> The workers' council comprises the workers of an entire workshop without consideration for the orientation of their party membership within socialism, meaning Social Democrats as well as Communists, etc., with no division into union and political orientations. Consequently, political interest is stirred much more quickly and earlier than before due to the creation of mass participation in the political discussion. Because each individual is a co-actor in this and recognizes his equal contribution in the day's results, the bond between the masses and those whom they have elected and who are under their daily, even hourly supervision grows tighter. (Adler, 1919: 149, 159)

In fact, as Adler observed, various tendencies and factions as well as conflicts in the councils did form and parties did push their own interests through. Däumig (1920: 83–4) believed that this was the result of a historical coincidence. The workers' councils did not arise from the proletarian revolution but rather "owed [their] existence to coincidental constellation of parties". He implies that there can only be a single, uniform will among the immediate producers. To the extent that this is not the case, he looks for the cause among the parties of the labor movement, but he does not account for the possibility that further, new forms of difference of opinion over every aspect of production might arise on the workshop level, between workshops or between producers and consumers. These are no longer conflicts between classes; they no longer need to assume the form of the political or the exercise of state authority, but they do raise questions about forms of coordination and decision-making that include everybody.

If collective decisions were to be made in the workshops and if only workers were able to participate in making them, then a great many people would be excluded. That exclusion is intentional as far as the segment of the populace that had previously controlled the social means of production, which is to say, a small minority. But there are also groups of freelancers, independent workers, small businesspeople, farmers and the unemployed. Moreover, there are those who perform housework (mostly women, based on the widespread division of labor) as well as retirees, long-term care patients, children and young adults. Given the large number of these heterogeneous groups, the supporters of council democracy are faced with the question of territorial representation, which, since the time of Locke and the development of the Constitution of the USA, has assumed its classical form in parliament. In the debate over council democracy, the significance of territorial representation is still considered controversial and, due to its historical development, ultimately undetermined.

Ernst Däumig (1920: 51) saw a clear alternative and pleaded for a council democracy that would be supported by workers' councils. However, he did not address the problem of interest groups and democratic circumstances in areas other than economics. Rosa Luxemburg, on the other hand, claimed that it was a false alternative. She argued against ignoring the parliament as a site of political debate, which she said would contribute to the left's self-marginalization (Luxemburg, 1919: 484–5). Hers was a tactical argument, but that does not rule out the idea that she saw the problem as one of how to move a broad public discussion, one that encompassed the whole of society, beyond economics. Max Adler, who linked membership in the workers' councils not only to one's status as an immediate producer but also to a belief in socialism, wanted to avoid the exclusion of all those not instantaneously committed to this goal of socialism by pleading for the continued existence of the national assembly.

For Richard Müller, the national economic council, which was "necessary to ensure and maintain economic life in its entirety", was to coordinate its responsibilities with the national assembly. Both bodies would respectively have to submit the laws and ordnances that they had passed to the other (Müller, 1919: 90).

He pays just as little attention as Adler to the resulting problem that this might result in a kind of double sovereignty (in economics with the functionally determined councils and in politics with the territorially based parties) and would therefore complicate relations of power and authority.

From a democracy theory perspective, the impression arises that the question of council versus parliament is a product of a particular political constellation. Marx saw the commune's councils as organs of territorial representation and execution. By contrast, subsequent council theories have characterized the councils as organs of workshop representation. This brings the problem of workplace self-management by direct producers to light. In this framework, the problem of the amount of time that must be spent on distribution and coordination, which Marx does not clarify, can be resolved directly in the everyday activities within and between the workshops. But the result is a distinction from the outset between the workshops and their social environment in the commune or the region such that the problem remains: how do people who live there participate in decision-making? That is no inconsequential matter. Many other issues, to which Marx gives appropriate attention, immediately arise on the communal decision-making level: public safety, traffic, waste disposal, medical care, childcare, education and culture. These cannot all be addressed within the framework of councils that are essentially responsible for economic questions of production, distribution and consumption. Processes of democratization and of democratic self-management can and should be organized in all of these fields so that the society is entirely democratized and broadly supports the production and distribution councils. But in the debate around council democracy, hardly any attention is paid to these social spheres or their democratization. The concept of the workers' council has its own dynamics and leads to an inescapable economism:

> Council organization is a real democracy, the democracy of labor, making the working people master of their work. Under

council organization political democracy has disappeared, because politics itself disappeared and gave way to the socially organized economic workshop. (Pannekoek, 1946: 70)

That is to say, if political democracy (in Marx's sense) should become superfluous, the assumption that the economic functions would be the only thing left of social life would become highly questionable. If the state's viewpoint with respect to society in general is reabsorbed into that society, the economy could no longer remain the economy but would instead become the real community in which people produce, organize, and manage their shared life.

Final comments

In his study of workers' councils, which summarized his own engagement with the council movement over many years, Pannekoek stated, "This new organization of labor we have to investigate and to clarify to ourselves and to others". Regarding the new way of living together in a society where people control their own relationships and mutually establish their spontaneously effective legalities in complete freedom, he wrote: "We cannot devise it as a fantasy. . . . It cannot, of course, be depicted in detail; we do not know the future conditions that will determine its precise forms" (Pannekoek, 1946: 39). He was confident that council democracy would be such a new form. The future is nonetheless so imprecise that that is never certain; but perhaps social principles, the existence of which Hannah Arendt as well as Marx and many others were convinced, allow us to say that councils will always form in the great upheavals in society and as long as humankind has not overcome the realm of necessity. This is not the only reason why it is worthwhile to consider further the concepts of council democracy as one alternative to capitalist socialization. There has never been a moment in history when an attempt at council democracy has had the opportunity to demonstrate its inherent emancipatory potential. They have instead been violently suppressed and their supporters persecuted in the name of democracy or socialism.

Criticizing the councils should neither give support after the fact to their defeat over history nor justify their repression. By the same token, however, it should not obscure them either. Criticism is meant to rescue the legacy of council movements, though it is nonetheless criticism. It points towards the possibility that the debate in the council movement reached a threshold at which it encountered considerable problems over any further implementation. The supporters of council democracy saw the councils as creating the conditions by which production could be managed and coordinated by the workers. In this way, state authority and its command over living labor power and its exploitation by the owners of capital were to be dismantled. Individual production and distribution sites would see themselves as elements of the collective labor. This, however, creates the problem of coordinating the individual units of that collective labor. They would no longer be mediated by the market or the state – coordination would be a service that every individual must perform together.

Astonishingly little has been written about this type of coordination with the exception of a single model of council institutions – one that is hardly distinguishable from later economic democracy proposals. Moreover, that one model, produced by the Executive Council of Workers' and Soldiers' Councils of Berlin, was merely formal. It does not address the question of worker self-management: they only have the right to vote for the people who manage and monitor the workshops. These problems are, in fact, no less than those of a parliamentary democracy. Over time, there is a danger that certain groups of workers, be they elected workshop managers, technicians or engineers, would gradually appropriate entrepreneurial power. What is to prevent the development of a new "hierarchic investiture" (Marx, 1871b: 543)? The specific operational form of the appropriation of nature on the workshop level, the relationship of the workshops to one another, and the social division of labor must be democratically decided and coordinated through universal participation. If no democratic answer is found for this problem, the result may be the development of power and conflict between various workshops, industries and sectors that would argue over raw materials, the type and amount of products or the amount of human labor power that is available. Over time, the scarcely controllable mechanisms of coordination through the market, state bureaucracy or the authority of experts could once again develop.

A second criticism is that the problem of coordination between producer and consumer is hardly discussed. Korsch developed the problem and pointed out the conflicting interests, but he did not produce an answer to the ensuing question of coordination. Only more recently has Michael Albert again taken up the problem of the democratic coordination of consumer need (including productive consumption) and production.

Thirdly, there is a problem of centering these models on work and professional life as well as the economism of many such attempts. Max Adler pointed out the dangerous, specifically corporative consequences that they might bring about. But apart from briefly mentioning them, he never addressed the fields of childcare, education, housekeeping or nurturing. If the market and the state disappear, then the paternalistic coordination mechanisms – which are essentially organized by specific powerful groups for their own particular interests – disappear with them. Consequently, the task of taking on full responsibility for resolving shared problems without being treated like children falls on individuals. That takes a lot of time out of individual lives. Individuals, of course, would gain much time by not being exploited any longer and by self-determining the time that is socially necessary for work, and their engagement in coordinating mutual living would become a component of the concept of work which, in that respect, would transform itself. However, the positively understood possibility of withdrawing from the community and a right to be lazy are part of the free development of each individual. How can the community limit itself and not demand that individuals continuously produce more, satisfy more consumption or become more committed?

References

Adler, M. (1919[1981]) Demokratie und Rätesystem. In Adler, M. *Ausgewählte Schriften, Norbert Leser and Alfred Pfabigan* (eds) Vienna: Österreichischer Bundesverlag.

Albert, M. (2003) *Parecon. Life after Capitalism.* London: Verso.

Arendt, H. (1963[2006]) *On Revolution.* New York: Penguin.

Balibar, E. (2002) Kultur und Identität (Arbeitsnotizen). In Demirovic, A. and Bojadžijev. M. (eds) *Konjunkturen des Rassismus,* Münster: Westfälisches Dampfboot.

Beard, C.A. (1913[2004]) *An Economic Interpretation of the Constitution of the United States.* New York: Dover.

Bermbach, U. (1973) Einleitung. In: Bermbach *Theorie und Praxis der direkten Demokratie.* Opladen: Verlag für Sozialwissenschaften.

Däumig, E. (1920[2012]) The council idea and its realization. In Kuhn, G. (ed.) *All Power to the Councils!: A Documentary History of the German Revolution of* 1918–1919. Oakland: PM Press.

Demirović, A. (2003) Revolution und Freiheit. Zum Problem der radikalen Transformation bei Arendt und Adorno. In Auer, D., Rensmann, L. and Schulze Wessel, J. (eds.) *Theodor W. Adorno und Hannah Arendt.* Frankfurt am Main: Suhrkamp.

Demirović, A. (2007) *Demokratie in der Wirtschaft. Positionen – Probleme – Perspektiven.* Münster: Westfälisches Dampfboot.

Engels, F. (1882[2008]) *Socialism: Utopian and Scientific.* New York: Cosimo.

Habermas, J. (1992) *Faktizität und Geltung. Beiträge zur Diskurstheorie des Rechts und des demokratischen Rechtsstaats.* Frankfurt am Main: Suhrkamp.

Hardt, M. and Negri, A. (2002) Globalisierung und Demokratie. In Okwui Enwezor U.A. (ed.) *Demokratie als unvollendeter Prozess.* Documenta 11_Plattform 1, Ostfildern: Hatje Cantz.

Korsch, K. (1919a[1980]) Sozialisierung und Arbeiterbewegung. In Korsch (1980) *Gesamtausgabe, Bd. 2: Rätebewegung und Klassenkampf.* Frankfurt am Main: Europäische Verlagsanstalt.

Korsch, K. (1919b[1980]) Die Sozialisierungsfrage vor und nach der Revolution. In Korsch, K. *Gesamtausgabe, Bd. 2: Rätebewegung und Klassenkampf.* Frankfurt am Main: Europäische Verlagsanstalt.

Korsch, K. (1919c[1980]) Die Arbeitsteilung zwischen körperlicher und geistiger Arbeit und der Sozialismus. In Korsch (1980) *Gesamtausgabe,*

Bd. 2: Rätebewegung und Klassenkampf. Frankfurt am Main: Europäische Verlagsanstalt.

Korsch, K. (1919d[1980]) Das sozialistische und das syndikalistische Sozialisierungsprogramm. In Korsch (1980) *Gesamtausgabe, Bd. 2: Rätebewegung und Klassenkampf.* Frankfurt am Main: Europäische Verlagsanstalt.

Korsch, K. (1920[1980]) Grundsätzliches über Sozialisierung. In Korsch (1980) *Gesamtausgabe, Bd. 2: Rätebewegung und Klassenkampf.* Frankfurt am Main: Europäische Verlagsanstalt.

Kottler, W. (1925) *Der Rätegedanke als Staatsgedanke. 1. Teil: Demokratie und Rätegedanke in der großen englischen Revolution.* Leipzig: Theodor Scott.

Locke, J. (1689[1993]) An essay concerning the true original, extent and end of civil government. In *John Locke: Two Treatises of Government.* London and North Clarendon: Everyman.

Luxemburg, R. (1919[1974]) Rede für die Beteiligung der KPD an den Wahlen zur Nationalversammlung, dies. In *Collected Works,* Vol. 4. Berlin: Dietz Verlag.

Marx, K. (1843[1977]) On the Jewish Question. In *Karl Marx: Selected Writings* by McLellan, D. (ed.) Oxford University Press: Oxford.

Marx, K. (1844a[1977]) Critical Remarks on the Article: 'The King of Prussia and Social Reform In *Karl Marx: Selected Writings* by McLellan, D. (ed.) Oxford University Press: Oxford.

Marx, K. (1844b[1977]) Towards a Critique of Hegel's 'Philosophy of Right': Introduction. In *Karl Marx: Selected Writings* by McLellan, D. (ed.) Oxford University Press: Oxford.

Marx, K. (1871a[1977]) First Draft of 'The Civil War in France. In Marx, K. and Engels, F. *Collected Works,* Vol. 22, Progress Publishers: Moscow, 1986.

Marx, K. (1871b[1977]) The Civil War in France. In Marx, K: Selected Writings, McLellan, David. (ed.) Oxford University Press: Oxford.

Marx, K. (1875[1977]) Critique of the Gotha Programme. In Marx, K: Selected Writings, McLellan, David. (ed.) Oxford University Press: Oxford.

Marx, K. and Engels, F. (1848[1977]) The Communist Manifesto In Marx, K: Marx: Selected Writings, McLellan, David. (ed.) Oxford University Press: Oxford.

Müller, R. (1919[1973a) Das Rätesystem im künftigen Wirtschaftsleben. In Bermbach, U. *Theorie und Praxis der direkten Demokratie.* Opladen: Verlag für Sozialwissenschaften

Müller, R. (1921) Die Entstehung des Rätegedankens. In Adler, P. *Die Befreiung der Menschheit.* Berlin, Leipzig, Wien and Stuttgart: Dt. Verlagshaus Bong.

Ness, I. and Azzellini, D. (eds) (2011) *Ours to Master and to Own. Workers' Control from the Commune to the Present.* Chicago: Haymarket.

Pannekoek, A. (1946[2008]) Arbeiterräte. In *Arbeiterräte. Texte zur sozialen Revolution,* Fernwald: Germinal Verlag.

Poulantzas, N. (1974) *Politische Macht und soziale Klassen.* Frankfurt am Main: Fischer.

Rousseau, J.-J. (1762[2011]) On the Social Contract. In *The Basic Political Writings,* Second edn. Indianapolis, IN: Hackett.

TWO

Contemporary Crisis and Workers' Control

Dario Azzellini

During the first decade of the current century factory occupations and production under workers' control seemed to be limited mainly to South America, with a few exceptions in Asia (Ness and Azzellini, 2011). It was beyond the imagination of most workers and scholars in industrialized countries that workers would or could occupy their companies and run them on their own. Nevertheless, the crisis that started in 2008 put workers' control back on the agenda in the northern hemisphere. Occupations of workplaces and production under control of workers sprang up in the USA, Western Europe and Egypt. This chapter describes some of these struggles and their common characteristics and differences. The crisis since 2008 triggered more factory occupations and workers' take-overs in Latin America; in Buenos Aires alone the number of companies under worker control grew from 28 in 2009 to 50 in 2013.

In the course of the current crisis, factory occupations occurred throughout Europe, especially in France, Italy and Spain, but also in other countries, including Switzerland and Germany and in the USA and Canada. Nevertheless, in most cases the occupation was a means of struggle and not a step towards workers' control. In some better organized cases workers achieved their demands, in others the occupations were a result of spontaneous indignation over factory closure or mass dismissals and the struggles fell apart without any concrete results. But for the first time in decades several struggles were also carried out with the perspective of placing production under workers' control. Some of these struggles gained a little international attention, like the Republic Windows and Doors factory in Chicago, USA, which opened in early 2013 under worker control, or Vio.Me. in Thessaloniki, Greece (see Chapter 10). Some, as with the Fralib Tea factory in Gémenos (France) gained at least some national interest. Most cases, however, are not at all well-known, such as Officine Zero in Rome and Ri-Maflow in Milan (Italy), Kazova Tekstil factory in Istanbul (Turkey) or Kouta Steel Factory, Tenth of Ramadan City (Egypt). It is likely that more struggles for worker control, for a self-administered workplace, are taking place which remain almost unknown to the wider public.

Compared with other historical moments when factory take-overs and workers' control were part of offensive struggles, the new occupations and recuperations are developing out of defensive situations. However, this has been true since the neoliberal attack on workers in the early 1980s, with very few exceptions like the recent struggles for worker control in Venezuela. As consequence of the current economic crisis, occupations and recuperations are accomplished by workers in reaction to the closure of their production site or company or the relocation of production to a different country. Workers are trying to defend their workplaces because they have little reason to hope to find a new job. In this defensive situation, workers not only protest or resign; they take the initiative and become protagonists. In the struggle and on the production site they are building horizontal social relations and adopting mechanisms of direct democracy and collective decision-making. The recuperated workplaces often reinvent themselves. The workplaces are also a site for build ties with nearby communities and other movements.

This description of contemporary take-overs includes certain features that are not necessarily shared by all such take-over of companies. While in fact it is fundamental to recognize the diversity of situations, contexts and modalities of workers' controlled companies, it is nevertheless important to understand workers' control or recuperation of workplaces as driven by socio-political considerations, not merely economic ones. Therefore it is necessary to use a basic set of criteria when discussing recuperated companies. Some well-intentioned authors calculate that there are 150 recuperated workplaces under worker control in Europe (Troisi, 2013). A closer look shows that very few of these can really be considered as recuperated and as under worker control. This total includes all workers' buy outs, of which most at best adopted the structure and functioning of traditional cooperatives. Many, if not most, have internal hierarchies and individual property shares. In the worst cases we find an unequal distribution of shares according to the company's social hierarchy (and therefore economic power) or even external investors and shareholders (both individuals and major companies). Such calculations reduce the concept of recuperation to the continued existence of a company originally destined to close that has merely changed ownership from one to many owners, some of whom work in the company. Companies following these schemes can hardly be considered recuperated in that they do not provide a different perspective on how society and production should be organized.

That contemporary worker-controlled companies almost always have the legal form of cooperatives is because the cooperative form is the only existing legal form of collective ownership and collective administration of workplaces. Usually, however, these are based on collective ownership, without any option of individual property; all workers have equal shares and an equal voice. One of their important and distinctive characteristics is that they question the private ownership of the means of production. They provide an alternative to capitalism based essentially on the idea of a collective or social form of ownership. Enterprises are seen not as privately owned (belonging to individuals or groups of shareholders), but as social property or "common property", managed directly and democratically by those most affected by them. Under different circumstances, this might include, along with workers, participation by communities, consumers, other workplaces or even in some instances, of the state (for example, in countries like Venezuela or Cuba). That workers control the production process and are decisive in decision-making usually also turns them into social and political agents beyond the production process and the company (Malabarba, 2013: 147).

Moreover, as Gigi Malabarba notes:

> It is essential that the forms of cooperative self-administration are strictly situated in a frame of a conflictual dynamic, in synchrony with the whole of social struggles, starting with workers' struggles together with pugnacious union militants: Our struggle for self-administration cannot be isolated. We cannot stop considering ourselves part of a more complex classist front. How can we alone achieve a law that really makes it possible to expropriate occupied spaces to give them a social use? Or in other words: how can we build social and political balances of power in order to stand up against the dictatorship of capital and achieve some results? This is the only way self-administered cooperatives and economic spheres based on solidarity can play a role in favor of workers' cohesion and prefigure an end of exploitation by capital, showing the contradictions of the system. This is especially the case in a period of deep structural crisis like the contemporary. (Malabarba, 2013: 148, translated by the author)

All the following examples of factories recuperated during the crisis share these characteristics.

Recuperated factories in France

Two cases of recuperated factories occupied by workers during the current crisis are known due to their persistent struggles. One is the

Pilpa Ice Cream Factory and the other is the Fralib Tea Factory. Both were closed by their huge multinational owners to relocate production.

Pilpa: La Fabrique du Sud

Pilpa was an ice cream producing company with 40 years of history in Carcassonne, near Narbonne, in southern France. It used to belong to the huge agricultural cooperative 3A, which sold its ice cream as famous different brands, among them the large French grocery store chain Carrefour. In September 2011 the plant was sold by 3A due to financial difficulties. The buyer, ice cream manufacturer Real Estate Investment Trust (R&R), (belonging to the US investment fund Oaktree Capital Management) was only interested in owning the famous brand names to add value to R&R (which would be sold by the investment fund in April 2013). In July 2012 R&R announced that Pilpa was to be closed and production relocated, with the 113 workers dismissed. The workers resisted, occupied the plant and started organizing a solidarity movement. Their goal was to save the production site (Borrits, 2014a).

The workers set up 24-hour surveillance to prevent the owner from dismantling the factory and removing the equipment. In December 2012 the workers gained a court order declaring the proposed R&R job protection plan and workers' pay out inadequate. While R&R formulated a new proposal, 27 workers decided on a plan to turn the former Pilpa into a worker-owned and worker-controlled cooperative under the name "Fabrique du Sud" (Factory of the South).

The new owner of R&R finally agreed in late spring 2013 to pay all workers between 14 and 37 months' gross salary and €6000 for job training. Moreover, it agreed to pay the cooperative more than €1 million in financial and technical assistance for job training and market analysis and to hand over the machines for one production line, on the condition that Fabrique du Sud would not operate in the same market. The municipality of Carcassone agreed to buy the land upon which the factory is built (Borrits 2014a). As former Pilpa worker and Fabrique du Sud founder, Rachid Ait Ouaki, explains, it was not a problem to agree not to operate in the same market:

> We will produce ice cream and yogurt, both eco-friendly and of higher quality. We will use only regional ingredients – from milk to fruit – and also distribute our production locally. At the same time, we will keep prices for consumers low. We will not be producing 23 million liters annually as Pilpa did, but only the 2–3 million liters we can distribute locally. We also have only 21 of the original workers who joined the cooperative, since we have to put even more money into it, including raising our unemployment benefits through a program for business creation, and not everyone wanted to take that risk. (Author interview, 30 January 2014)

As in other cases, the legal form the worker-controlled company had to take was that of the cooperative. Decisions are made by all the workers together and benefits were to be distributed equally among the workers, once production started in early 2014.

Fralib: the brand with the Elephant

Fralib is an herb and fruit tea processing and packaging factory in Gémenos, near Marseilles. The plant produced the tea sold under the famous *Thé Eléphant* brand created 120 years ago, as well as Lipton tea. In September 2010, the transnational food giant Unilever, the owner of Lipton, decided to close the plant in France and move production to Poland. The workers reacted immediately, occupying the factory and beginning a boycott campaign against Unilever. The union Confédération générale du travail (CGT), formerly close to the Communist Party, supported the Fralib workers. "The struggle at Fralib started on 28 September 2010. In 2010 we had 182 workers. Now we are 76 workers and still fighting", comments Gérard Cazorla, mechanic and union secretary at Fralib (Author interview, 31 January 2014). The workers want to restart production in the factory under workers' control and retain the *Thé Eléphant* brand, claiming it as regional cultural heritage. They want to switch to producing organic herbal teas, mainly linden tea, relying on regional production. As in most other cases, the self-organized struggle of the Fralib workers has three pillars: the project for production, public protest and the construction of a solidarity campaign, and a legal struggle against Unilever:

> We have militant production to make our struggle known and to support the solidarity campaign. We went through a long period without income and we had to live. What allowed us to live all that time was solidarity. I think it is important to make our struggle known in France, in Europe and in the world, and our production helps us. While our prior production was – let's say – industrial tea, now we produce organic linden tea. With that we show that the machines work and that we know how to make this factory work. That is important so the people can see that Fralib can work without bosses and without Unilever. (Gérard Cazorla, author interview, 31 January 2014)

On 31 January and 1 February 2014 Fralib housed the first European meeting of The Economy of the Workers. More than 200 researchers, supporters and workers from five European factories under worker control participated in the meeting inspired by and directly linked to the world meeting of The Economy of the Workers, which takes place every 2 years and had its third meeting in Brazil in 2013. Researchers from Argentina, Mexico and Brazil also participated in Marseilles, as did a worker from the Argentinean textile factory Pigüé. In honor of the meeting and with a nod to the Argentine movement of recuperated factories, the Fralib workers produced boxes of Argentine *mate* tea.

The workers succeeded in ensuring that the procedures to close them down and the company's social plans for compensating the dismissed workers were revoked several times by court order. Fralib closed officially only in September 2012. In March 2013 Unilever stopped paying the workers' wages despite a court decision that they had to continue paying them. In September 2013 the Urban Community of Marseille Provence Métropole bought the land upon which the factory is built for €5.3 million and paid one symbolic euro for the machines in order to support the workers' efforts. The workers know this is not enough to restart production and continue their struggle, as Cazorla explains:

> In January 2014 Unilever's social plan was revoked for the third time by the court. Now we are holding discussions with the Unilever directors while we are putting together our project. We need the rights to the brand, capital to buy raw material and the ability able to sell our products or we will not be able to produce and pay 76 workers. We want that money from Unilever as compensation for firing us. (Author interview, 31 January 2014)

After three and a half years of struggle the Fralib workers finally won against Unilever. Unilever settled the conflict by signing an agreement on 26 May 2014 establishing that the transnational food company would pay €20 million to the Fralib workers in the factory as compensation for closing the plant. The money from Unilever made it possible for the workers to reopen the factory as the SCOP TI workers' cooperative, producing high-quality organic herbal tea. The payment by Unilever included legally turning over the factory and factory ground to the workers' cooperative. One Fralib worker commented on the victory, saying "we stood up against billionaires, we were been told we were mad, but in the end our madness paid out!" (Borrits 2014b).

Italy: Officine Zero and Ri-Maflow

In Italy some 30–40 bankrupt small and medium enterprises have been bought out by their workers during recent years and turned into cooperatives. Even if some media compare them to the Argentine cases (Blicero, 2013; Occorsio, 2013), many are neither really under full and collective workers' control nor do they in any way envision an alternative to the capitalist system. The cooperatives work with a hierarchical structure and the change of the number of owners does not make a difference in how they function. Some even have only a minority of shares in workers' hands, while the majority is controlled by external investors and the managerial staff. Two recent cases, Officine Zero in Rome and Ri-Maflow in Milan, are different and fully comparable to many Latin American cases of workers' take-over.

Officine Zero

Officine Zero, former RSI (Rail Service Italia) and before that Wagons-Lits[1] (from France), was dedicated to the maintenance and repair of sleeping cars. When in December 2011 Italian train services decided to stop the night train service and invest in fast track trains, RSI closed. The work force at that moment consisted of 33 metal workers and 26 transport and administration workers. All were eligible for a special low unemployment income due to the abrupt closure of their company. But not all accepted the closing and 20 workers took up the struggle. Emiliano Angelè, who had worked since 2001 as a train mechanic for the company and was the union leader, explains:

> When we saw that all seemed lost since we didn't have any trains to build or repair, we locked ourselves inside the factory and occupied it in February 2012 as the first protest. But that was no use because we did not have any work to do,

so we tried different responses . . . traditional demonstrations, relations with politicians, with the union . . . but none of that could bring the work back to us. Right next to our company there is a social center. They saw us protesting and offered their support for our struggle. For a while they supported us in trying to get back to work in our branch. But after a while they asked us if the company's facilities couldn't be used for something else. We did not really know what for, but they presented an alternative idea based on the Argentinean experiences, where machines or facilities were used to produce or work something different from before. In September 2012 we started working again. We have equipment for carpentry, upholstering, welding etc. with welding equipment. You do not have to necessarily weld a train, you can weld anything. . . . The upholsterer, for example, who previously worked on the insides of trains, is now working on the interior of a boat. That is how we started putting ourselves back to work.

Together with the activists from the social center, "Strike", the workers started a laboratory on reconversion, organizing public assemblies attended by hundreds of people. The "crazy idea" of the Officine Zero was born. Precarious workers, independent workers, craftsmen, professionals and students joined the occupation. On 2 June 2013, Officine Zero was officially founded as an eco-social factory and presented to the public with a conference and demonstration. Officine Zero means zero workshops: "zero bosses, zero exploitation, zero pollution", as their new slogan says. The name also points out that they had to find a new starting point. The former RSI workers dedicate themselves mainly to recycling domestic appliances, computers and furniture. The mixture between old and new work forms, bringing together different precarious work situations, trying to overcome isolation and individualization is an important core idea of the project, as Emiliano Angelè explains:

In the former administration offices we built a co-working area. Architects, communication workers, filmmakers and others have their offices there and all cooperate with each other and with the workers. For example, I used to be a mechanic, but now I might help my colleague upholster the boat's interior and I also have access to work with these new forms. Moreover, we have opened a cafeteria in the former staff canteen. It is for all the people working there and for whoever wants to come from outside. That is the new project we call Officine Zero. It is a project with the goal not only to recuperate the workers who used to work there, but also to open the space to other workers and other forms of work. (Author interview, 31 January 2014)

The former company director's house, located on the factory grounds, is under construction to be transformed into a student dormitory (Mastrandrea, 2013). The workers are planning to hold workshops on recycling electronic equipment and renewable energies (Blicero, 2013).

From Maflow to Ri-Maflow

The Maflow plant in Trezzano sul Naviglio on the industrial periphery of Milan, was part of the Italian transnational car parts producer Maflow, which grew in the 1990s to become one of the most important manufacturers of air conditioning units worldwide with 23 production sites in different countries. Far from suffering consequences of the crisis and with enough clients to keep all plants producing, Maflow was put under forced administration by the courts in 2009 because of their fraudulent handling of finances and a fraudulent bankruptcy. The 330 workers of the plant in Milan, Maflow's main production facility, began a struggle to reopen the plant and keep their jobs. In the course of the struggle they occupied the plant and held spectacular protests on the plant's roof.

Because of this struggle Maflow was offered to new investors only as a package that included the main plant in Milan. In October 2010 the whole Maflow group was sold to the Polish investment group Boryszew. The new owner reduced the staff to 80 workers and placed 250 workers on a special income redundancy fund.[2] But even so, the new investor never restarted production and after the 2 years required by the law that preventing them from closing a company bought under these circumstances, in December 2012 the Boryszew group closed the Maflow plant in Milan. Before closing it down they removed most of the machinery (Blicero, 2013; Occorsio, 2013, Massimo Lettiere [Author interview, 31 January 2014]).

A group of workers in redundancy had kept in touch and were unwilling to give up. Massimo Lettiere, former Maflow worker and union delegate of the leftist and radical rank and file union Confederazione Unitaria di Base explains:

> We went on organizing assemblies over the Boryszew take-over. In some of the assemblies we talked about the possibility of taking over the plant and doing some work inside. We did not know exactly what kind of work we could do, but we understood that after such a long period of redundancy, the next stage for us would be unemployment. So we did not have any option and we had to try it. In the summer of 2012 we had already done some market studies and determined that we would set up a cooperative for recycling computers, industrial machines and domestic and kitchen appliances. (Author interview, 31 January 2014)

When the plant was closed in December 2012, the workers occupied the square in front of their former factory and in February 2013 they went inside and occupied the plant, together with precarious workers and former workers of a nearby factory shut down after fraudulent bankruptcy:

To stand and wait for someone to give you a hand is pointless. We must take possession of the goods that others have abandoned. I am unemployed. I cannot invest the money to start a business. But I can take a factory building that has been abandoned and create an activity. So our first real investment for the project is activity and political action. We made a political choice. And from there we started working. (Massimo Lettiere, Ri-Maflow, Milan, author interview, 31 January 2014)

In March 2013 the Ri-Maflow cooperative was officially constituted. Meanwhile ownership of the factory building passed to the UniCredit Bank. After the occupation UniCredit agreed to not ask for their eviction and permitted them free use of the building. The 20 workers participating full time in the project completely reinvented themselves and the factory, as Lettiere explains:

We started building a broader network. We had the Ri-Maflow cooperative with the goal of recycling as the economic activity. In order to gather money we built an association called Occupy Maflow, which organized spaces and activities in the plant. We have a flea market in one hall, we opened a bar, we organize concerts and theater . . . we have a co-working area with offices we rent. With all that we started getting in a little income and we could buy a transporter and a pallet carrier for the cooperative, refit the electricity network and pay ourselves some €300–400 each a month. It was not much, but added to €800 unemployment you have almost a normal salary. . . .

In 2014 we want to work on a larger scale with the cooperative. We have already started two projects and both are linked to ecology and sustainability. We have built alliances with local organic agricultural producers, opened a group for solidarity shopping and have contacted the agricultural cooperatives from Rosarno in Calabria, southern Italy. They are cooperatives paying fair wages. Three or four years ago there was a rebellion of migrant workers in Rosarno. They stood up against exploitation. We buy oranges from these cooperatives and sell them and we produce orange and lemon liqueur. We are also connected with a group of engineers from the Polytechnic University to do huge recycling projects. It might take some years until we get all necessary permits. We chose this kind of activity for ecological reasons, the reduction of waste, etc. and we have already started recycling computers, which is easy, but we want to do it on a bigger scale. (Author interview, 31 January 2014)

What can seem like a patchwork to traditional economists is in fact a socially and ecologically useful transformation of the factory with a complex approach based mainly on three premises: "solidarity, equality and self-organization among all members; b) conflictive relationship with the public and private counterparts; c) participation in and promotion of general struggles for work, income and rights" (Malabarba 2013, 143).

Greece: Vio.Me. – from industrial glue to organic cleaners

Vio.Me. in Thessaloniki used to produce industrial glue, insulant and various other chemically produced building materials. Since 2010 the workers agreed to be sent on unpaid leave every 4–6 weeks. Then the owners started reducing the workers' wages, but assured them it was only a temporary measure and they would soon be paid their missing salaries. The owners' main argument was that profits had fallen 15 to 20 per cent. When the owners did not keep their promise to pay their back wages, the workers went on strike demanding to be paid. As a response to their struggle the owners simply gave up the factory in May 2011, leaving 70 unpaid workers behind. Later the workers found out that the company was still making profits and the losses were due to a loan that Vio.Me. formally granted to the mother firm, Philkeram Johnson. In July 2011 the workers decided to occupy the plant and take their future into their own hands (see chapter 10 on Greece for more details on Vio.Me. in context). As Vio.Me.-worker Makis Anagnostou, from Thessaloniki, explains:

> When the factory was abandoned by the owners we first tried to negotiate with the politicians and the union bureaucracy. But we quickly understood that all we were doing was wasting our time and slowing down the struggle. It was a difficult time; the crisis was showing sudden and intense effects. The suicide rate among workers in Greece rose a lot and we were worried that some of our fellow workers might commit suicide. Therefore, we decided to open our labor conflict to society as a whole and the people became our allies. We discovered that the people we thought could not do anything in reality can do it all! Many workers did not agree with us or did not continue the struggle for other reasons. Among those of us with whom we took up the struggle, the common ground for our work is equality, participation and trust. (Author's interview, 31 January 2014)

Vio.Me. became known internationally and inspired several other workers' occupations in Greece, even if none was successful at retaining the workplace or production. The case best known internationally was the state-owned public broadcasting company, ERT (Ellinikí Radiofonía Tileórasi). After the government announced on 11 June 2013 that all public TV and radio stations would be closed (to be restructured and reopened with fewer workers, fewer rights and lower wages) workers and employees occupied the radio and produced their own program until they were brutally evicted on 5 September.

The Vio.Me. workers restarted production in February 2013:

> Now we produce organic cleanser, not the industrial glue we produced before. Distribution is informal. We sell our products ourselves at markets, fairs and festivals, and a lot of products are distributed through the movements, social centers and shops that are part of the movements. What we did last year is basically keep the factory active. We cannot yet say we have had a very positive outcome on production, distribution and sales. Earnings are quite low and are not enough to maintain all the workers. Therefore some of the workers have lost faith, or got tired and left Vio.Me. Recently our assembly decided unanimously to legalize our status by building a cooperative. The decision again gave us an impulse to continue. We consist of the 20 workers who signed the foundation act of the cooperative, but there are more waiting in the wings to see how things go. In the structure of the cooperative we also created the figure of the solidarity supporter, who is not a member of the cooperative as such, but supports it financially in exchange for our products. Solidarity supporters can participate in the workers' assembly and have an advisory vote in decision-making. They pay a minimum €3 a month and with that we pay the basic costs of the factory, like electricity and water. Having society on our side through this construction we feel stronger. (Author interview, 30 January, 2014)

Turkey: Kazova Tekstil – high-quality sweaters for the people

Kazova Tekstil is a textile factory in Istanbul, Turkey, in the Şişli district close to the famous Taksim Square. In late 2012 the owners explained to the 94 workers that they were passing through momentary financial problems and asked them to continue working even if their salaries could not be paid on time; they would get all their salaries paid later (Söylemez, 2014). The workers continued working for another 4 months and on 31 January 2013 they were given an unpaid week-long holiday by the owners. When they returned they found an almost empty factory. The owners, the Sumunçu family, had removed machines, 100,000 sweaters and 40 tons of raw material and left the workers not only without jobs, but also with 4 months of unpaid wages (Umul, 2013). Eleven of the 94 workers did not resign and decided to resist. They started marching every Saturday in the Istanbul city center with other workers demanding unpaid wages and respect for workers' rights (Erbey and Eipeldauer, 2013; Söylemez, 2014).

In April the workers decided to set up a protest camp with tents in front of the factory to prevent the owners from taking away the rest of the machines. In May their demonstration was attacked by the police with tear gas and water cannons, and at the end of the same month the Gezi resistance movement started and gave the Kazova workers strength and courage. The workers also participated in different assemblies and discussion groups and found huge support in the movement. Since they still had no response from the owners or the authorities, they began preparing to occupy the facilities and on 28 June they declared publicly: "We – the workers of the Kazova textile factory – have occupied the factory" (Söylemez, 2014; Umul, 2013). The workers prepared the factory for production and repaired three machines.

On 14 September 2013, the Kazova workers started producing sweaters and jerseys with leftover material. Each had a small label explaining "This is a product of the Kazova resistance!" (Söylemez, 2013; Umul, 2013). The production capacity at this point was 200 pieces a day. The cost of production for one sweater or jersey was around 20 Turkish Lira (approximately €7 or $10). Under the former owners the high quality sweaters and jerseys were sold for prices between 150 und 300 Lira (€50–100 or $68–135).

But the workers decided to sell their high quality products at a more affordable price and thus sold them for 30 Lira (€11/$15).

The Kazova workers started selling their products in front of the factory and in the different thematic and neighborhood meeting established after the eviction of Gezi Park (Umul, 2013). Nevertheless they were still not paying any salaries since they had to reinvest the money earned (Erbey and Eipeldauer). On 28 September Kazova organized a fashion show, but instead of skinny models the guests could see the workers themselves presenting their new production on the catwalk. After the fashion show, the famous Turkish communist band Grup Yorum gave a concert. A leftist journalist present at the show commented that it was a proletarian fashion show and that the proletarian's fashion was "occupy, resist, produce" (Erbey and Eipeldauer, 2013; Umul, 2013). The same slogan is used by recuperated factories in Latin America and comes originally from the Brazilian landless movement Movimento dos Trabalhadores Rurais Sem Terra.

In late October 2013, after 10 months of struggle, a court ruled that the former employers had to hand over the remaining machines to the workers instead of their unpaid salaries (Erbey and Eipeldauer, 2013). The machines were transferred to new facilities rented by the workers in the Istanbul Kağithane neighborhood. That allowed the workers to start paying themselves small salaries, the same for everyone. The workers see themselves as part of an international popular movement of resistance. As a sign of solidarity they produced jerseys for the Cuban and Basque Country soccer teams for a friendly game in Havana (Söylemez, 2014). On January 25, 2014 the Kazova workers opened their first retail store: "Resist Kazova-DİH Pullover and Culture Store" in the Istanbul Şişli district, where the factory used to be, and which also serves as meeting place. "Affordable sweaters for the people" is the Kazova slogan launched during the store's inauguration. According to the Kazova workers other stores in Istanbul and the rest of the country are planned (Söylemez, 2014).

The Kazova workers could count on massive solidarity from the neighborhood assemblies in the aftermath of the

Gezi Park movement. They also had the support of a small Marxist-Leninist group. But with time the support of the group turned into a take-over. Decision were not made by the workers but by the leftist group, which used the famous name Kazova for its own propaganda and did not seriously engage in attempts to restart production. Conflicts between the group and the workers took place until the workers, who still had the old machines in their possession, broke with the group in May 2014 and moved with the machines into a new facility in order to form a cooperative and restart production. Unfortunately the Marxist-Leninist group kept the name Diren Kazova and the shop. The Kazova workers, on the other hand, started collaborating with three graphic designers to develop new designs for pullovers and T-shirts and count on the support of the nearby Caferağa Social Center (occupied in the aftermath of the Gezi protests) in order to sell their products, which restarted in early November 2014. The newly formed cooperative is called Free Kazova Textile Cooperative. The pullovers Kazova produces are advertised as *patronsuz kazak* (pullovers without bosses). Their price at the time of writing was €18, compared with €100 for pullovers with comparable quality. After having sold successfully the first production stock the workers plan to strengthen their distribution system. The income is shared by all workers with only two different wage levels. At the beginning new workers earn a lower wage, until after a while they move to the same wage level as long time workers. Moreover the Kazova workers decided also to regularly put aside some money for solidarity with other struggles.

Egypt: steel and ceramics

In Egypt there are at least two factories under worker control: The Kouta Steel Factory in Tenth of Ramadan City, north of Cairo, and Cleopatra Ceramics, which has several thousand workers in two plants, one also in Tenth of Ramadan City and the second in Ain Sukhna. But it is not unlikely that there more factories have followed their example during the last few years of turmoil after

Hosni Mubarak's overthrow, the transition time until the election of Mursi and the short period during which Mursi was in power before the military toppled him. The overthrow of Mubarak on January 25, 2011 was preceded by a growing independent workers' movement that had been organizing more and more strikes and labor conflicts since 2003 (Ali, 2012). Workers' struggles suffered severe repression under Mursi and under the military regime.

The Kouta Steel Factory in Tenth of Ramadan City was abandoned by its owner a few months after he stopped paying the workers in March 2012. Previously, the workers at the plant had conducted several struggles and strikes through their independent union. When the owner fled, the workers began a struggle that included sit-ins and legal battles through the Prosecutor-General's office and the Ministry of Labor. The struggle culminated with an epoch-making decision by the Prosecutor-General in August 2012 approving their right to place the factory under workers' self-management and authorizing engineer Mohsen Saleh to manage the factory (Kouta Steel Factory Workers, 2013). The workers built collective decision-making authorities and elected a technical committee for the coordination of production.

To reassume production the workers had to negotiate with gas and electricity suppliers to reschedule the $3.5 million debt owed by the former owner. Moreover the workers, who had not been paid for months, had to cut their wages by half to buy production material. In April 2013 the Kouta Steel Factory started production under the management of the workers' technical committee. Shortly before that they sent a solidarity letter to the workers of Vio.Me. in Greece (Kouta Steel Factory Workers, 2013).

Cleopatra Ceramics is a tile factory formerly owned by Mohamed Abul Enein, who is part of to the Egyptian elite close to former President Mubarak. He was even a member of parliament for Mubarak's National Democratic Party. Abul Enein, who was widely known as a ruthless employer, closed two tile plants belonging to Cleopatra Ceramics without warning in July 2012.

When he reneged on agreements concluded after a factory occupation, workers travelled to Cairo, marched on the Presidential Palace and obtained a deal negotiated by Mursi. When this too unraveled, they stormed a government building in Suez, demanding punishment for Abul-Enein. Eventually they occupied the factory, resumed production on their own terms and sold their products directly to secure an income. (Marfleet, 2013)

Chicago: New Era Windows

On 9 May 2013, the New Era Windows cooperative on Chicago's Southwest Side officially started production under worker control. It began with 17 workers producing "professional grade energy-efficient windows at a revolutionary price point", as they say on their web site, and advise "Using energy-efficient windows is one affordable way to combat those high energy bills and taking a step towards long-term sustainability!" All decisions in the factory are made by the workers' assembly, which meets at least once a week. Every worker has the same vote. Armando Robles, New Era Windows worker, president of the local branch of the United Electrical, Radio and Machine Workers of America (UE) 1110, and among the driving forces behind the struggle during the last 12 years, explains:

> Right now things are slow but we know that in 2 or 3 weeks we will have lots of work. Now we are filling small orders and preparing the equipment for a larger production starting in two or three weeks. (Armando Robles, author interview, 2 March 2014)

To get to this point the workers twice had to occupy their former factory on Goose Island, the only island in the middle of the Chicago River. The second occupation in February 2012 ended with their being given 90 days to either find a new investor or buy the company. The workers did the latter. But they still had a great deal to accomplish:

> Since 2012, the workers have overcome enormous challenges. First, fighting for the right to be at the table to buy the business, then dismantling the factory and moving across the city to an affordable and appropriate space. Each of these steps the workers did on their own, and in the process they demonstrated the incredible potential that had never been tapped in their prior jobs. (*The Working World*, 2013)

In order to reduce costs the workers did almost everything on their own, taking out the machines they bought from the old factory and installing them and even the water pipes in the new place they rented to set up their cooperative (Cancino, 2013). To get to that point the workers of Republic Windows and Doors – mostly Latino immigrant and African American workers – had gone through a long struggle. In 2002 the 350 workers staged a wildcat strike since the union they were forced to join at the plant was not acting in their interest. The labor struggle against low wages, overtime and bad working conditions was not successful. But the workers started to organize and in 2004 they affiliated with Local 1110, a branch of the radical rank and file UE and got the company to sign a contract with UE (Lydersen, 2009). During 2007 and 2008 workers noticed that production was going down and that something was happening:

> By July 2008, the company had lost about $3 million in just six months. . . . Machines were disappearing, and workers wondering and asking became only vague answers. . . . Only later would they find out that the equipment was destined for the small town of Red Oak, Iowa, where Richard Gillman's wife Sharon had purchased a window and door factory. (Lydersen, 2009)

On 2 December 2008 the 250 workers under contract at that time were told by the manager that the plant would close 3 days later, on 5 December. The workers were not only left without jobs and income; their own and their families' health care protection would end within 2 weeks. Moreover, they would not get severance pay, or be compensated for their accrued vacation time and sick days. The short time announcement was also against the law. The union filed a complaint against the company for violation of the Worker Adjustment and Retraining Notification Act, a Federal law which requires employers with 100 or more workers to inform them 60 days in advance about mass layoffs. The union claimed the company owed the workers US$1.5 million in vacation and severance pay and demanded an extension of the workers' health care protection (Cancino, 2013; Lydersen, 2009).

The workers decided to add authority to their claims with a sit-down strike and occupied the factory. They demanded that the Bank of America and JP Morgan/Chase, which in the past had granted huge loans to Republic Windows and Doors, should pay the workers. After 6 days of occupation and 3 days of hard negotiations with both banks, they agreed to pay the workers, contributing $1.35 million and $400,000, respectively, although legally they had no responsibility for the workers. On 15 December, 2008, the company filed for bankruptcy. In December 2013 former Republic Windows and Doors CEO Richard Gillman was sentenced to 4 years in prison for stealing $500,000 from the company (*Chicago Tribune*, 2013).

In February 2009, California-based Serious Energy, specializing in highly energy-efficient windows and environmentally friendly building materials, bought Republic Windows and Doors promising to eventually hire back all workers and respect all previously signed union agreements. But it took several months before Serious Energy had hired only 15 workers and more than 2 years later the factory's peak occupation was 75 workers. By early 2012 the staff was reduced to 38 workers (Slaughter 2012). In the workers' words on the new cooperative's website:

Unfortunately, Serious Energy's business plan, which only involved the windows factory in a tertiary role, never functioned, and the company had to severely cut back on its operations, including closing the factory. Once again, the workers, despite their profitable work, found themselves being sacrificed in a financial game they did not control. (New Era Windows Cooperative, 2013)

The morning of 23 February 2012 the remaining 38 workers were told by a lawyer hired by Serious Energy that the plant would stop operations and close immediately, consolidating operations elsewhere. Police were already on the site urging the workers to leave. The workers decided in minutes that they would occupy again, without any preparation and lacking everything from sleeping bags to food. But this time they were not alone. Labor and community groups, as well as Occupy Chicago, mobilized to the factory and by the evening 65 people were inside the plant and 100 outside were delivering sleeping bags, pizzas, tacos and drinks (Cancino, 2013; Slaughter, 2012). The workers demanded that Serious Energy keep the factory working for another 90 days while their union would look for a new investor or the workers themselves would buy the plant. Well aware of the workers' history, Serious Energy agreed after 11 hours (Slaughter, 2012).

The workers' goal was to raise money and buy the factory to form a worker-controlled cooperative. But Serious Energy wanted to offer the plant to the highest bidder, meaning that the price would not be affordable for the workers. They had to fight for the right to be at the negotiating table to buy their former company. They succeeded by developing public and political pressure and formed a cooperative. Each worker contributed $1000 to the cooperative and the New York based non-profit organization, The Working World, which supports worker-controlled cooperatives in Argentina and Nicaragua with credit and technical assistance, provided a $665,000 credit line. With that the workers bought the equipment and moved it to their new rented facility in the Brighton Park neighborhood on Chicago's Southwest Side. The workers took cooperative management classes and prepared to administer the entire company (The Working World 2013). One year later, the former Republic Windows and Doors workers were producing windows under worker control.

Common challenges for workers' recuperations

Contemporary occupied or recuperated workplaces often face similar challenges, among which are a lack of support by political parties and bureaucratic unions or even their open hostility; rejection and sabotage by the former owners and most other capitalist entrepreneurs and their representations; the lack of legal forms of companies that match the workers' aspirations and the lack of institutional framework. They face obstruction by government institutions and have little or no access to financial support and loans and even less from private investors.

The general context that contemporary recuperated factories have to face is not favorable. The occupations are taking place during a global economic crisis. Starting new productive activities and conquering market shares in a recessive economy is not an easy task. Moreover, there is also less capital backing available for worker-controlled companies than for capitalist enterprises. Usually an occupation and recuperation of a factory takes place after the owner has abandoned the factory and workers, either by literally disappearing or by firing the workers between one day and the next. Such owners owe the workers unpaid salaries, vacation days and compensation. Before they close down the plant the owners often start removing machinery, vehicles and raw material. In such a situation, with the perspective of a long struggle without or with little financial support and uncertain outcome the best qualified workers, and often also the younger workers, leave the enterprise, hoping for better options or to find a new job. The remaining workers have to acquire additional knowledge in various fields to be able to control not only the production process in a narrow sense, but also to administer the entire company, with all that implies. But once the workers take over the factory, the former owners suddenly reemerges and wants "their" business back.

Contrary to the common belief that capitalists only care about business no matter how it is done and with whom, worker-controlled businesses face not only capitalism's inherent disadvantages for those following a different logic, but often constant attacks and hostilities by capitalist business and institutions as well as by the bourgeois state. Worker-controlled companies that do not bend totally to capitalist functioning are considered a threat because they show that it is possible to work differently. The Venezuelan worker-controlled valve factory Inveval, for example, had the experience that the valves it ordered from privately owned foundries were intentionally produced with technical faults (Azzellini, 2011).

In Europe, the Serbian pharmaceutical company Jugoremedija in Zrenjanin, the only worker-controlled factory in former Yugoslavia, was forced to declare bankruptcy in April 2013 after 6 years under workers' control. It is now under receivership and there is only a very small chance that the workers will regain control over their company. The workers started to self-administer their company in March 2007 after a hard struggle against privatization. In the following years Jugoremedija produced and sold its products with success. In 2013 the banks cut off credit although Jugoremedija had been paying and the debt was originated partly incurred by a former criminal shareholder. Therefore, the company had to declare bankruptcy (Author's interview with Milenko Sreckovic, 19 February 2014).

Common features of workers' recuperations

The few known existing cases of workers' recuperations described have huge differences. Some factories have modern machinery and are fully functional from the technical point of view. Others have been looted by the former owner and have to start from scratch.

Some factories have been given support by the local authorities, others by the unions. The common features are not a checklist for the authenticity of recuperated factories. The common features described are a repertoire of characteristics that are not necessarily all fulfilled by every recuperated factory. On the other hand, it is also not the case that every single characteristic taken out of context and separated from the others displays the perspective of seeking a different society beyond capitalism. It is the combination of several characteristics that turn the recuperations into laboratories and motors of the desired alternative future.

All recuperation processes and recuperated factories are democratically administered. Decision-making is always based on forms of direct democracy with the equality of vote among all participants, be it through councils or meetings. These direct democratic mechanisms adopted by worker-controlled companies raise important questions, not only about individual enterprises, but about how decisions should be made throughout the whole of society. In doing so, it challenges not only capitalist businesses, but also liberal and representative "democratic" governance.

Another obvious common feature is the occupation. Occupying a factory entails committing an act considered to be illegal and therefore to do so is to enter into a conflict with the authorities. It is a direct action by the workers themselves. They are not "representatives" nor do they wait for a representation – a union or party – or even the institutions of the state to solve their problem before they spring into action. As Malabarba correctly states: "The action has to be turned upside down: first the initiative, you occupy, and then you get in touch with the institutions that failed more or less consciously" (Malabarba, 2013: 149). Massimo Lettiere from Ri-Maflow explains:

> Illegality is a quiet elastic concept. We have thought about it. Laws are made in parliament and usually regulate things that have already happened. The only law that has defended the workers, which they passed for the workers, was Law 300

in 1970, The Statute of the Workers. Why did they make it? Because there was a movement and because the content was already in the metalworkers' national contract. The workers had already won that right, then the law has actually made what was in the contract worse. . . . The law has regulated a state of affairs that was already a fact. If someday there is a law on expropriation that establishes that when a company wants to de-localize production or fails it must be given to workers because they can get going, if we want a law on expropriation, we must first take the factory. You have to start from illegality. Once there is a movement of re-appropriation of the means of production there will be a law for us. We are beginning to build this path. (Massimo Lettiere, Ri-Maflow, author interview, January 31, 2014)

This is also confirmed by the Latin American experience. In Argentina, Brazil, Uruguay and Venezuela the workers have always been in front of political parties, unions and institutions in their practical responses to a situation. Expropriations, nationalizations, laws, financial and technical support always followed the workers' initiative and are a reaction to their direct action and struggle.[3] The same is true for the productive activity developed by the recuperated workplace: strictly following the law, waiting for all legal authorizations and paying taxes would simply mean the activity would never start.

Most factories have to reinvent themselves, often the previous productive activity cannot be carried out in the same way (because the machines have been taken away by the owner, because it was a highly specialized activity with very few customers, whom the workers do not have access to, or because the workers decided so for other reasons). In all the better documented cases we find that ecological aspects and questions of sustainability became central, be it an orientation to recycling, as in both Italian factories, changing from producing industrial glue and solvents to organic cleaners in Vio.Me. in Thessaloniki, or switching to organic products and using local and regional raw materials and also distributing their products locally and regionally, as in the two factories in France. The problematic is seen by the workers in the larger context of the future of the planet, as well as on a smaller scale related to health threats for workers and surrounding communities. The importance of ecological awareness is part of the new society envisioned by the workers, as are the democratic practices they put in place.

The struggles of the workers and the occupied or recuperated workplace have also become a space in which new social relations are developed and practiced: affect, reliability, mutual help, solidarity among the participants and solidarity with others, participation and equality are some of the characteristics of the new social relations built. New values have arisen, or at least values that are different from those characterizing the capitalist production process. For example, once the workers decide on it, safety on the job becomes a priority.

The recuperated factories usually develop a strong connection with the territory. They support the neighborhood and in turn are supported by it. They interact with different subjectivities present in the territory and develop joint initiatives. Connections with different social movements and social and political organizations are built and strengthened. All the factories mentioned in this chapter have developed direct relations with social movements and especially the new movements that were part of the global uprising since 2011. This is a clear parallel with Latin America where successful factory recuperations are characterized by having a strong foothold in the territory and close relations with other movements (Ness and Azzellini, 2011; Sitrin and Azzellini, 2014).

This anchorage in the territory also helps them to face another important challenge. Changing forms of work and production have radically diminished the overall number of workers with full-time contracts, as well as reducing the number of workers in each company. While in the past job and production processes automatically generated cohesion among the workers, today work has a dispersive effect, since workers of the same company often work under different contracts and with a different status from each other. Generally, more and more workers are pushed into precarious conditions and into self-employment (even if their activity depends totally on one employer). How can these workers be organized and what are their means of struggle? This is an important question the left must deal with to achieve a victory over capital.

Ri-Maflow and Officine Zero in Italy have built strong ties with the new composition of work practices by sharing their space with precarious and independent workers. In the case of Toronto we can see a different approach to counteracting the dispersive effect of work (see Chapter 3 by Elise Thorburn). Officine Zero declares: "We want to restart from the origins of the workers' movement by connecting conflict, mutual aid and autonomous production" (Blicero, 2013). Territorial organizing has been mentioned and even practiced more often during recent years. In Italy in 1997, Marco Revelli advocated in *The Social Left* (Revelli, 1997) a territorial organizing model based on houses of labor, like those that existed at the beginning of industrialization, connecting all workers in one district.

Workers from all recuperated factories name the Latin American, and especially the Argentine factory recuperations, as a strong source of inspiration.[4] Ri-Maflow adopted the slogan "Occupy-resist-produce" (Malabarba, 2013: 146). Republic Windows and Doors and Vio.Me. invited visits from workers from recuperated factories in Argentina before they restarted production. And it was once again Argentinean development assistance that encouraged the European meeting of "The economy of the workers" in the Fralib factory near Marseilles in early 2014.[5]

The workers of the recuperated factories recognize themselves in each other and consider themselves part of a broader movement. The Kouta Steel Factory Workers in Egypt sent a letter in support of the Greek Vio.Me. workers when they heard about their struggle (Kouta Steel Factory Workers, 2013). Makis Anagnostou from Vio.Me. declares: "The goal of the Vio.Me. workers is to create a European and international network with many more factories under worker control". There is good reason to believe that this goal will become reality.

Notes

1. Compagnie Internationale des Wagons-Lits (International Sleeping-Car Company), commonly called just Wagons-Lits, is Europe's oldest on-train catering, sleeping car and luxury train car company. It was founded in 1872 and was the historical operator of the Orient Express. In 1991 it became part of the French transnational hotel group, Accor.
2. The Cassa integrazione guadagni straordinaria, is a redundancy arrangement under which workers of closed down companies receive 80 per cent of their salary for a year. In certain cases it can be extended one more year.
3. With the exception of Venezuela, where some expropriations, nationalizations and political initiatives came from government institutions. Even so, the workers have to fight for real participation in workplace administration and for worker' control (Azzellini, 2011).
4. With the exception of Egypt, where it could not be determined from available data.
5. Andrés Ruggeri, militant researcher and director of a special research program at the University of Buenos Aires travelled around Europe and put different actors in the field of recuperated workplaces in touch with each other.

References

Ali, K. (2012) Precursors of the Egyptian Revolution. *IDS Bulletin*, 43 (1) 16–25.

Azzellini, D. (2011) Workers' Control under Venezuela's Bolivarian Revolution. Ours to Master and to Own. Workers' Councils from the Commune to the Present. In Ness, I. and Azzellini, D. (eds) Chicago: Haymarket.

Blicero (2013) Dalle ceneri alla fabbrica: storia di imprese recuperate. *La Privata Repubblica.* 24 October. Available at http://www.laprivatarepubblica.com/dalle-ceneri-alla-fabbrica-storia-di-imprese-recuperate/ (accessed 18 November 2014).

Borrits, B. (2014a) De Pilpa à La Fabrique du Sud. *Association Autogestion.* January 30. Available at http://www.autogestion.asso.fr/?p=3884 (accessed 18 November 2014).

Borrits, B. (2014) Victoire des Fralib. Une nouvelle histoire commence. *Association Autogestion*. 28 May. Available at http://www.autogestion. asso.fr/?p=4338 (accessed 4 December 2014)

Cancino, A. (2013) Former Republic Windows and Doors workers learn to be owners. Their co-op, New Era Windows, has had "ups and downs". Chicago Tribune. 6 November. Available at http://articles. chicagotribune.com/2013-11-06/business/ct-biz-1106-new-era-windows-20131106_1_armando-robles-17-workers-former-republic-windows (accessed 18 November 2014).

Chicago Tribune (2013) Republic Windows ex-CEO gets 4 years in prison. 5 December. Available at http://articles.chicagotribune. com/2013-12-05/news/chi-republic-windows-exceo-gets-4-years-prison-20131205_1_ricky-maclin-republic-windows-doors-vacation-and-severance-pay (accessed 18 November 2014).

Erbey, M. and Eipeldauer, T. (2013) Sieg der Ausdauer. Besetzung, Widerstand, Produktion: In Istanbul betreiben Arbeiter seit vier Monaten ihre eigene Textilfabrik. *Junge Welt*. 2 November.

Kouta Steel Factory Workers (2013) From the workers of Kouta Steel Factory in Egypt To the workers of Vio.Me Industrial Mineral Factory in Greece! Message of Solidarity. February. Available at www.viome. org/2013/02/from-workers-of-kouta-steel-factory-in.html (accessed 18 November 2014).

Lydersen, K. (2009) *Revolt on Goose Island: The Chicago Factory Takeover and What it Says About the Economic Crisis*. Brooklyn: Melville House Press.

Malabarba, G. (2013) L'autogestione conflittuale del lavoro. In Bersani, M. (ed.) *Come si esce dalla crisi*. Rome: Edizioni Alegre.

Marfleet, P. (2013) Egypt: the workers advance. *International Socialism*, 139, online version, 4 July. Available at www.isj.org.uk/?id=904 (accessed 18 November 2014).

Mastrandrea, A. (2013) Roma – Officine Zero, la fabbrica riconvertita. *Il manifesto*. Available at http://www.globalproject.info/it/in_movimento/roma-officine-zero-la-fabbrica-riconvertita/14424 (accessed 20 November 2014).

Ness, I. and Azzellini, D. (2011) *Ours to Master and to Own: Workers' Control from the Commune to the Present*. Chicago: Haymarket.

New Era Windows Cooperative (2013) Our story. Available at http:// newerawindows.com/about-us/our-story (accessed 18 November 2014).

Occorsio, E. (2013) Le fabbriche ripartono senza padrone. La Republica. Le Inchieste. 17 June. Available at inchieste.repubblica.it/it/repubblica/rep-it/2013/06/17/news/le_fabbriche_autogestite_ripartono_senza_padrone-61256995/ (accessed 18 November 2014).

Revelli, M. (1997). *La Sinistra Sociale.* Torino: Bollati Boringhieri.

Sitrin, M. and Azzellini, D. (2014) *They Can't Represent Us! Reinventing Democracy from Greece to Occupy.* London and New York: Verso.

Slaughter, J. (2012) UE occupies Chicago Window plant again, and wins reprieve. *Labor Notes.* 24 February. Available at http://www.labornotes.org/2012/02/ue-occupies-chicago-window-plant-again-and-wins-reprieve (accessed 18 November 2014).

Söylemez, A. (2013) Kazova resistance ends with victory. *Bianet.* 20 November. Available at www.bianet.org/english/labor/151460-kazova-resistance-ends-with-victory (accessed 18 November 2014).

Söylemez, A. (2014) Kazova factory to make jerseys for Cuba, Basque Country. *Bianet.* January. 22. Available at www.bianet.org/english/labor/152996-kazova-factory-to-make-jerseys-for-cuba-basque-country (accessed 18 November 2014).

The Working World (2013) New Era Windows. Available at http://www.theworkingworld.org/us/ex-republic-windows-and-doors/_(accessed 18 November 2014).

Troisi, R. (2013) Le imprese recuperate in Europa. comune info. 11 November. Available at comune-info.net/2013/11/le-imprese-recuperate-europa/ (accessed 18 November 2014).

Umul, F. (2013) Für ein Leben ohne Chefs! *ak – analyse & kritik,* 587, 15 October. Available at http://www.akweb.de/ak_s/ak587/07.htm (accessed 18 November 2014).

THREE

Workers' Assemblies: New Formations in the Organization of Labor and the Struggle against Capitalism

Elise Danielle Thorburn

The repeated global financial crises that have circumnavigated the globe since 2008 have signified both a crisis of capitalism and a crisis of the left. The imagined spontaneous and elementary communism that Hardt and Negri predicted of multitude did not arise. Multitude, for Hardt and Negri (2004), describes both the radical subject emerging in a moment of globalized and high-tech capital and the organizational possibility of this subject. Nevertheless, In 2008, at capital's moment of weakness, a multitude did not rise up to relentlessly attack the economic system, and the crisis of 2008 was not brought on, as autonomist theory has for so long had it, by the cycles of struggle waged by the working class. Rather, all was quiet on one front of the class war; labor engaged minimally while capital furiously raged against the working class, remolding the world in its own favor repeatedly over the course of half a decade. The working class plunged deeper into economic straits while the financial and capitalist class grew every second wealthier. Reverting to almost pre-New Deal era forms of labor relations, the world and capital changed since 2008 (especially in North America) and class composition changed with it. What was the Western industrial working class of the early 20th century was not the working class of the 1960s and 1970s; and the working class of that mid-century is not the working class of today, in the Global North.

The theory of class composition, developed by Italian autonomist thinkers in the mid-20th century, is a dissident adaptation of Marx's "organic composition of capital", and represents, at a theoretical level, a return to the central, historical importance of class struggle as waged by workers to processes of change. Whereas other Marxist theories may focus on the importance of capital, class composition begins from the perspective of labour. The theory refers to "the process of socialisation of the working class, and the extension, unification, and generalization of its *antagonistic tendency against capital*, in struggle, and *from below*" (Negri, 1991: xi). Class composition defines the power and organization of labor as it is configured antagonistically in relation to capital. Furthermore, it is the way in which the technical composition of labor (the capitalist organization of labor power) corresponds to various behavior patterns constituting particular openings among workers which then permit a reading of the forms of action and organization possible at various historical conjunctures (Cleaver, 1998; Negri, 1991; Nunes, 2007). The forms of struggle are thus expressed in terms of the particular composition of the working class. What this means for activists is that the tactics, strategies, and organizational bodies of class struggle change alongside changes in the composition of the working class. What I want to argue specifically, then, is that in the contemporary conjuncture of those modes of class struggle organization that previously prevailed (particularly the party model, both revolutionary and parliamentary, the vanguard and the bureaucratic trade union model) should no longer be considered either as the exclusive representatives of working-class political activity, or as the hegemonic form of working-class struggle. Rather, I want to point to an emergent political institution;[1] that of the assembly. I am not interested in drawing a surgical line between the compositions of the class and the tactics used – it is clear that there is a flow to history and one form, model and era bleeds into the other. Rather, what I am curious about, in terms of how we conceive of workers' control movements in the present, is where we see ourselves in the circulation of struggles. What I want to suggest is that we are in the embryonic stages of a re-composition of the working class in the Global North, after a long and decisive period of decomposition, and the general assemblies of the Occupy movement, the student and neighborhood assemblies of the Quebec student strike of 2012, as well as the model of the Greater Toronto Workers' Assembly (GTWA) (the example that I will interrogate in this chapter) and the assembly form in general, are indicative of new ways forward for workers' control movements. These emergent bodies are not brand-new institutions but owe much to past struggles, and can learn from their own histories.

As it is constituted today – especially in the various Occupy movements, square seizures, and public protests against austerity – the GTWA is explicitly *not* the similar to the stale representative politics of the general assembly of the UN, nor the parliamentary assemblies of various states. Seeking to deepen and develop democratic practices, the contemporary assembly rejects a politics of simple representation. The assembly, as discussed here, is not a party or a multitude or a swarm but, rather, a revolutionary organ of broadly defined workers assembled from below in a state of both resistance and creation. It is disciplined and networked, with a clarified sense of purpose, directionality and courage – the assembly comes from the cohering of multiple political tendencies to make up a new political form. Like Marx's non-party workers' party of *The Communist Manifesto,* for example, it could be called "a self-organised organ of distributed directionality" (Dyer-Witheford, 2011: 135). It operates to destroy or deconstruct the institutions of capital and create or construct new institutions of the assembled – new experiments in democratic infrastructure. Emerging experiments in the assembly or assembly politics bear out this call. It is unveiling itself as a novel form of organization and as the emergence of a radically new workers' subjectivity that pushes beyond the limitations of what Hardt and Negri have not unproblematically referred to as the multitude – the latest manifestation, they claim, of class composition in contemporary capitalism – or what Dyer-Witheford has called the global worker (Dyer-Witheford, 2010).

Because it is the context in which I live and work, I focus in this chapter on a particular experiment that took place (and in some ways continues to operate) in Canada, but I do not mistake the North American situation to be an isolated or even unique one. The model of the assembly, which was central to the organizing body of Occupy, to the student strikes in Quebec, and to my example of worker-community organizing in the GTWA as well as in worker and movement assemblies in the American South, is co-extensive with projects of a similar infrastructure in the squares of Athens, Madrid, Cairo, Quebec and beyond. The radical proliferation of assembly projects across the globe points to an emergent mode of organizing in a new era of class composition: one that begins to prefigure the possible infrastructures of the common and asserts a new organizational form that has historical precedents but is unique to this particular historical conjuncture. That the assembly as the organizing model of the common escapes the nexus of party/union that is particular to most leftist organizing throughout the history of capitalism is not to suggest that these models are dead, but that new experiments have become necessary to revive movement politics, create decisive models for democratic action and bring new subjects into revolutionary organizing. It is in this contemporary moment that old political concepts and practices, such as the vanguard party and the mass, may not be permitted to re-emerge as hegemonic and disrupt or co-opt struggles of the working classes from below.[2] This moment allows us to examine what Negri (1988) sought to illuminate in his discussion of the transition from the mass worker to the social worker in his analysis of class composition: a framework of incipient new values, existing at a mass level, able to repurpose dissent into a new model for the construction of a communist future.

In this article I propose that the assembly is an emergent mode of organizing in the contemporary class composition. In order to consider the prefigurative possibility that assemblies in general open up I look at the politics and practices of the GTWA[3] and attempt to discuss how it concretely operates and how we can theorize the possibility of new autonomist political movements out of these examples.

The GTWA offers an example of an embryonic and experimental political form. It is a project that brings together disparate actors and crosses previously un-crossable sectarian divides, as well as contends with the criticisms that arose in the aftermath of the anti-globalization movement. The struggle in which we currently find ourselves will continue with or without the workers' assembly, but if we build on the project, interrogate it and expand it as the possible political re-composition of the working class, we open up the possibility of bringing those struggles to the next level, a possibly revolutionary level.

The GTWA was formed in the fall of 2009 after a series of consultations with a variety of differently situated activists and organizers on the anti-capitalist and social movement left. These consultations, particularly between labour activists from an auto plant and organisers within the social movement-oriented Ontario Coalition Against Poverty, sought to illuminate the differences between various activist projects and labor. They asked how a stronger relationship of solidarity could be built between the two forces and examined the relationship between class and other forms of oppression and social determination. The aim was to build a different kind of organizational form; considered by many to be new, as the history of workers' assemblies are largely unknown and rarely discussed, which would create a new political space to the left of social democratic politics, but broad enough to encompass the radical left, from socialists to anarchists and labor activists to social movement organizers. It is anti-capitalist in general. It is a space of reflection and action for disparate and often disconnected actors, in which discussions could develop around the limits of fragmented struggles and work could be done to build a larger collectivity that might address these limits.

Membership in the assembly is open only to individuals, not to already existing organizations of union locals. Instead, one must freely enter into the assembly and work to organize in one's own workplace from there. There are no workplace committees or workplace representatives. Instead workers are constituted *as* workers and not related through their specific labour. This makes the GTWA different from historical assemblies, rooted as they often were in the specific workplace. Instead, the GTWA responds to the changing composition of the class and of labor in new forms of production and to the increasing use of high tech, decentralized workplaces by bringing together workers who would otherwise rarely meet in the flesh, and combining these workers with those in older segments of the labor force, where the spatial organization of work is still centralized and ordered in place.

The assembly seeks to do a number of things simultaneously:

1. Create and maintain an organization based on the common class interests of unionized workers, non-unionized, the unemployed, people in temporary and part-time jobs and other forms of precariousness, the poor, students, and community activists.
2. Develop a common basis for socialists, anarchists, communists, autonomists and others on the anti-capitalist left to work together in struggle, and contribute to building a strong, viable, anti-capitalist political movement.
3. Create a center of discussion, debate, analysis and struggle, help to build resistance to the crisis measures and contribute to moving struggle to higher and higher levels.
4. Support and participate in already existing movements, develop spaces for cross-organizational dialogue and become locations for union workers to partake in radical organizing outside and within their own union.
5. Broaden the understanding of workers' power, workers' control, working-class subjectivity and solidarity among young and old workers, new and seasoned activists.

While many of the assembly participants have been part of impressive movements and political projects that have had varying degrees of success, the time had come to acknowledge "that our capacities to resist have not matched what we are up against" (GTWA vision statement). Though it was actively under way, class warfare was not being fought effectively by those on the dominated end of society and failures abound throughout the left's past. The workers' assembly seeks to address these failures and offer a site for a sort of political consciousness raising among different workers, leading, it is to be hoped, to the growth of movements for workers' control.

Protracted internal debate is an essential component of an assembly. This commitment to debate and dialogue can make arriving at conclusions a slow process but does not have to derail the process of decision-making entirely. The meetings of the GTWA are forums for debates that are otherwise not held on the left in general. With just over 300 members, the assembly does not operate on the basis of consensus, and instead uses voting as its decision-making tool, but it does this in the most open and democratic way possible. The general assembly is the highest authority of the assembly and no decisions can be made or passed unless they go through discussion and debate and are voted on by the assembly as a whole. In this way, assembly politics can begin to actively rethink the dichotomy between vertical and lateral organizing, in favor of more hybrid models. This involves an open recognition that organizing to build an institution of workers' control requires working with diverse people and groups, while maintaining a commitment to continued struggle through practice, debate and action. An assembly, then, affords the strengthening of political communication in the best possible sense. If we are to see networking and dialogue as a series of situational negotiations based on the possibility of changing both one's own standpoint and that of another person's, an assembly gives a foundation for this reasonable and practical temporal togetherness without the need to draw clean lines of for or against, and make distinctions of good versus evil.

After 4 years the assembly reached its height at around 300 members and incorporated several autonomous yet connected committees and campaigns. It organized in a directly democratic and horizontal manner, with open voting structures and open committee work, and in which all authority rests with the assembly as a whole. The campaigns and committees do most of the assembly's work. These include the free and accessible transit campaign (struggling for free transit), the public sector defense committee (organized to deal with the round of privatizations currently hitting public sector workers in Toronto) and the feminist action committee (which brings a feminist perspective to analyses of capital, today particularly on the issue of subsidized day care). There is also a flying squad, a cultural committee and the coordinating committee, which acts as the administrative body. So, it is much more than simply process but rather at its best it is a living body engaged in the creation of revolutionary institutions of dissent and workers' power. It brings together those disparate and heterogeneous elements that Hardt and Negri describe as a multitude and attempts to create, through that diversity, a common context, if not an absolute consensus, around which to base the political actions it will take. The heterogeneity of the assembly – sectarian divisions, gender, race and class differences, for example – is never eradicated but rather used as a creative force. In this way, the assembly does what Hardt and Negri suggest the multitude will do: it demonstrates, in this case with great specificity, the coming to political subjectivity.

A precedent for the current rise in assembly politics does exist. There have been organizational forms which, in their very construction, resist the top-down politicking of parties, vanguards and parliamentarianism. Athenian democracy used the Ecclesia, an all-male citizen's assembly, and the workers' councils of the council communist movement were assemblies in form if not in name. More contemporarily, Spain in the late 1970s saw the rise of a workers' assembly movement that described itself as the "independent manifestation of the proletariat" (Amoros, 2011: n.p.) and served as a physical confirmation of the class struggle in that country.

Not simply a movement against Franco's dictatorship and its backward policies, nor a movement in support of Franco's replacement, the assembly movement in Spain was an "upraising against all forms of exploitation that escaped the narrow framework of bourgeois politics intended for the containment of the workers" (Amoros, 2011: n.p.) and catalyzed resistance to anti-Franco oppositions groups who attempted to impose, via incorporation in the liberal capitalist system, a more European form of social slavery. Rejecting vanguardism, electoral politics and trade union reformism, the then-emergent assembly movement sought to invoke instead practices of solidarity, self-defense, direct dialogue and the general strike as their specific methods of struggle, and offered a location for the exercise of democratic praxis on the left. Though at the beginning they were not a clarified movement, the assemblies soon forged ahead as institutions for the defense of workers' everyday interests and served as spaces for workers to discuss labor problems and strategize around employment issues. For a moment, workers' assemblies in Spain became a true power, independent and with enormous force, and full of apparent possibilities.

The Spanish assembly movement was eventually defeated but the idea never totally disappeared. Its red (and black) thread runs through the current re-emergence of assemblies as political decision-making bodies in a wide variety of occupations, demonstrations and actions taking place globally, but especially in the GTWA, a body that opens up the possibility of re-animating the assembly model as a viable political force – a new model of an embryonic and emergent political form – and also opens up new discussions on working-class politics and its imbrication in other political movements that are not historically considered workers' movements.

Here the work of the feminist action committee becomes important. Although it does not focus on internal politics, the committee has attempted to provide critical space to reflect on the patriarchal tendencies that operate even within left spaces, and to challenge politics that do nothing to diminish this base-level patriarchy. The feminist action committee has joined other feminist groups in the city of Toronto to participate in collectively building community accountability processes for dealing with sexual assault. As in all cities and political spaces, the left in Toronto has cases of sexual assault – patriarchal mores and oppression are perhaps the hardest obstacles to overcome – and no organization has been able to effectively deal with these issues alone. Therefore, people have begun come together across organizational lines to begin to build collective responses to patriarchal oppression. Sexual violence, intimate partner abuse and domestic assault are all workers issues, the feminist action committee contends, and must stand on an equal footing with other struggles for workers' control. As women are workers, workers' control is meaningless if it does not incorporate movements for women's control over their own bodies, and workers' collective control over their intimate spaces, homes and relationships. There is no separation, in the mind of the feminist action committee, between the productive and the reproductive sphere, the capitalist factory or the social factory. If workers' control movements seek to undermine and overturn capitalism, and if capitalism is a social relationship, then all social relationships within capitalism need to be consider part and parcel of working-class struggle. In this way, the feminist action committee, as part of the GTWA, expands our understanding of what workers' control can mean in all areas of one's life.

Another aim of the GTWA is to bring together different segments of the working class, segments that have been divided by "the pressures of neoliberal politics and labour markets" (Rosenfeld, 2011: n.p.); a division both physical and ideological. As the GTWA recognizes, many working-class communities in Toronto are isolated in the suburbs that ring the urban centers. Campaigns such as the free and accessible transit campaign actively make outreach efforts to the inner suburbs in order to interact with those whose lives are cut-off from political organizing in the center due to, among other things, poor transportation infrastructure.

These divisions that are also part and parcel of the new, post-Fordist workforce have created rancor within the working class itself, as workers are pitted against workers for jobs in times of austerity. For example, those perceived to be members of the labor aristocracy with union protection, who labor for higher wages and greater benefits, are taken to be an obstacle to the attainment of working-class wealth or to the political constitution of the lumpen-proletariat. They themselves therefore make up a different kind of perceived class enemy. In Toronto, for example, the demography of the working class is very mixed. The industrial base − mostly automotive manufacturing − has gone into dramatic decline; arising in its place as prime economic drivers are the financial sector, real estate and public services. The working class itself is divided into "highly segmented clumps of concentrated numbers: construction; upper-end manufacturing; lower-end manufacturing; servicing the financial services cluster, as well as the retail centers and the entertainment complexes" (Rosenfeld, 2011: n.p.) and those divisions are simultaneously highly racialized and gendered. Support for public sector workers is, at present, frighteningly low, largely as a result of this internal class war. Real wages across the city of Toronto have declined over the last decade (Hulchanski *et al.*, 2005) as much work is being continually outsourced, privatized and restructured.

Immigrants, who are very numerous in Toronto,[4] can make up key elements of the commercial capitalist class, but these communities also make up an "increasingly cheapened and precarious segment of the working class" (Rosenfeld, 2011: n.p.), this being doubly true in the case of migrant women. What we are seeing, then, is not the circulation of struggles, but rather their segmentation. The rights of employed people are counter-posed to those of unemployed people; low-waged workers without union protections are pitted against municipal workers with union backing and benefits, the squeezed middle-class is positioned against immigrants, the taxpaying private sector maligns and competes with the "parasitic" public service. The current momentum has not been towards a re-compositionary circulation of struggle, but of a de-compositionary antagonism of struggles, and this is a trajectory that the assembly movement – and the GTWA in particular – is making efforts to intervene in.

As unions move further into reformism, radical social movements have picked up the slack for those left out of organized labor. These movements have thus far been unable to create institutions that in any way rival the power, force, and coherency of trade unions for mobilizing class power. Thus, the fragmentation of the working class internally – as well its growing externalization from the sources of class advancement, wealth and power – make necessary the GTWA as a mode of organization, but also as a way for workers to frame their struggle. The GTWS provides a base organization that has a strong commitment to class analysis while simultaneously recognizing the differing experiences of those interpellated into the body of the working class.

The GWTA is attempting to work with existing labor organizations through the public sector defense committee, and with those not officially incorporated into unions, nor even necessarily having remunerated work via the fair and accessible transit campaign and the feminist action committee. It is thus taking the first steps towards creating an amalgam organization – and thus an amalgam movement – that is both centered in a class analysis of capital and able to see the tendrils of capitalist exploitation that radiate outwards, throughout the social factory – a classed, multitude with directionality and force.

It is equally important to devote energy to contemplating its own organizational form and defragmenting the ideological strands of the radical left if the assembly is to function as a relevant and serious threat to capitalist power. Organizationally, Leninism and the communism of old were able to build and maintain institutions based in primarily in the control of state power. Conversely, the aim of the assembly is to articulate a coherent, non-authoritarian communism; to create a structure capable of conducting discussions and negotiations, articulating a politics and deriving direction from and among its broad membership, all of which is necessary for such a long-term program. In the long term, this requires two things, that the assembly itself works towards (i) closing divisions and boundaries both between working-class people and between political sectarians, while maintaining heterogeneity and (ii) building lasting structures and institutions of the commons, in order to maintain a circulation of struggles long past the point of the successful invocation of revolution but throughout the very core of the new commons social future. Some of these tasks are discussed in the concept of multitude as elaborated by Hardt and Negri (2004) and by Virno (2004), though not without criticisms.

The concept of the multitude is meant to capture the political composition of the working class in biopolitical capitalism,[5] developed by Hardt and Negri in their three texts *Empire* (2000), *Multitude* (2004) and *Commonwealth* (2009). Critics of this the concept claim that the concept empties work, and especially reproductive work, of its gendered character, and that its connected notions of affective and immaterial labor posit a contemporary labor that requires emotions but not materiality (Federici, 2012). Federici excoriates this notion when she states that, for example, elder care "demands a complete engagement with the persons to be reproduced, a relation that can hardly be conceived as 'immaterial'" (Federici, 2012: 122). Furthermore, notions of the multitude as the composition of class in a contemporary regime of biopolitical production imagines that the technologies of the present movement create a spontaneous communism, ignoring the fact that

> the cooperation we can developed among ourselves, starting from those of us who must face the most vulnerable time in our lives without the resources and help they need, a hidden but no doubt widespread form of torture in our society. (Federici, 2012: 125)

The inadequacies of the concept of the multitude are manifold, then, and these inadequacies can lead us to consider more expansive and directed forms of struggle, such as those we find in the assembly. However, the concept can be fruitful for us in some ways: as

Virno (2004) and Hardt and Negri have made clear, in multitude there is no unity, no centrality, no homogeneity. Multitude is heterogeneous, the opposite of previous forms of vanguardist or revolutionary politics that relied on a homogeneous subjectivity around which their politics could cohere. The heterogeneity of the multitude differs, too, from the ethnically based movements in the Global South, which are able to often call upon a common, often indigenous, heritage.[6] Instead, the term multitude speaks to a divided, fragmented and differentiated populace working in vastly different sectors of the economy and living under different experiences of community. And even within the radical left, these fragmentations exist and were even exacerbated as activists worked through anti-globalization and anti-war movements, and ideological divisions became even starker. In a way that the multitude with its strict focus on absolute heterogeneity is unable to do, the GTWA seeks to bring together not only a fragmented working class but also a wildly fragmented left, with the aim of collectively creating a common project. Creating a form of unity, without necessitating absolute agreement, the GTWA opens up space for debate, critique and argumentation around particular political strands in a way that has heretofore been absent in Canadian radical left organizing. The assembly itself is made up of socialists who believe in utilizing parliamentary process and already existing political parties to achieve their aims, socialists who seek to create their own, alternative and openly socialist party, communist party members and anarchists, autonomists and social movement activists who want to see the assembly function as its own project. Debates rage within the workers' assembly about structure and practice, mostly centered around the future direction of the project: should the assembly intervene in electoral politics? Should the assembly transition into a party? Should it continue as an assembly and how do we know what this means? Should the assembly build a political platform? Should the assembly align with social movements? Should it become a more active force in organizing or should it focus on strengthening political debate and changing the political climate in the city? None of these debates have been resolved, but the important work is already there – creating the space for these conversations to take place. A common criticism of the politics of the anti-globalization movement is that difficult things were not debated, or if they were, the resolution was often left completely up in the air to avoid the oppressiveness associated with major-ity rules voting and imposing decisions (Ross, 2003; Nunes, 2007, Katsiaficas, 2002, 2006). The final result was indecision and it was frequently lauded as such – continuing, yet marginalized, debates around the efficacy and ethics of a diversity of tactics express this. The marginalizing of debate and conflict is something the workers' assembly seeks to tackle and, in its own way, resolve. At the most recent workers' assembly general meeting debates were long but never hostile, and many commented that after years involved in some variant of radical left organizing, this was the first time such an open and oppositional dialogue could take place.

Moreover, to the internal problems of purely horizontal organiz-ing models leading to the failure to promote or refusal internal debate can be added the external problem of negotiating and deal-ing with non-horizontal groups. This is an important consideration for organizing in the contemporary milieu as social movements, at least in Canada, are lacking in strength and low in numbers. Trade unions can still pull out the biggest numbers to demon-strations and events. The difficulty of placing horizontality and openness as both political means and ends leads to the question of how we relate to those who do not. Rejecting other political formations often means being closed and sectarian, and work-ing with them means "indirectly supporting hierarchical, vertical practices" (Nunes, 2007). This is a false problem as it relies on dichotomies and absolute terms. The assembly seeks to avoid such absolutes and to turn debates from a focus on ideology to a focus on the practical problems of struggle (rather than a strict theory of organization and revolution) with the hopes of eventually arriving at a practical solution. Although not without disagreement, the assembly works with and promotes the activities of horizontalist and anarchist-inspired groups and the activities of the relatively vertically organized unions and labor organizations, always with the aim of attempting to intervene in these groups and activities with the mandate of the assembly and its focus on capital and class power.

What this means is that there is an active rethinking of the dichotomy between vertical and lateral organizing in favor of more hybrid models; an open recognition that organizing to build a mass movement requires working with diverse groups, while maintaining a commitment to continue to struggle through practice, debate and action. The GWTA affords a strengthening of political communication for activists in the best possible way. If we are to see networking and dialogue as a series of situational negotiations based on the possibility of changing both one's own standpoint and that of the other person's, the assembly gives a concrete foundation and basis for reasonable and practical temporal togetherness, without recourse to spurious distinctions of good versus evil. As the assembly, through our debates we work towards an acceptance that planning, coherence, resilience and security does require some leadership structures to instill directional movement yet that these also have to be accountable to and take direction from open forums, always avoiding any implication of political domination or authoritarian tendencies. Coming to this has not been easy and how it will work out in the long run is still being sorted, but debates and disagreements about the specific political orientation of the assembly are fundamental and are part of the process of building coherent institutions of the commons.

By contrast, the anti-globalization movement was unsuccessful at creating long-lasting institutions, and to be fair, that was never its aim. As some have suggested (Katsiaficas, 2002, 2006; Nunes, 2007) the 1990s movements were often meant to be transient, spectacular and tangential and then dissipate. The main institutions that arose were largely in the ephemeral, virtual world of the internet. With its multipolar means of production and circulation, the internet was a way to massify information and open movements up to horizontality and transparency. As Nunes notes, "it is only within the horizon of a social life that has become networked that a politics of networking as such can appear" (Nunes, 2005: 301). Moving beyond the thrill of late-1990s organizing around the internet and the recent ecstatic claims of Facebook and Twitter revolutions that so ignored the low-tech actuality of the Egyptian and Tunisian revolutions, the assembly, as it exists, marks a turning point in the relationship between communication technology and radical political organizing. In its coffee house meetings, which take place monthly and offer space for members and the general public to discuss a specific theme or issue, in its campaigns and in its general membership meetings the GTWA attempts to create new spaces for people to meet in person, to create the persistence and physical connection that seem to be missing in the over-reliance on virtual communication. At the same time, the assembly pursues very sophisticated digital communication strategies, using the internet for flexible and quick straw polls and promotion, without forgetting the importance of face-to-face contact and debate. It is this strategy of melding the concrete and the virtual that operates to overcome the ephemerality of earlier politics. A simple expansion of existing networks, though, is not the main project of the assembly as it is currently operating in Toronto, nor is it an end in itself. The assembly offers something more than that and it grounds itself in a "thorough politicisation of social relations" (Nunes, 2005: 315).

Practically, what this may mean is a return to older forms of organizing and political action, some of which the GTWA has carried out. This could involve home visits, neighborhood organizing and community projects (Rosenfeld, 2011). Specifically, in the case of the GTWA's transit campaign these types of action have been put into practice. Members of the transit campaign participate in community and neighborhood organizing across the Greater Toronto area, with a focus on attending events in the far-flung suburban neighborhoods most lacking in accessible transport. Similarly, the public sector defense committee has engaged in door-to-door campaigns in its attempt to inform communities about and rally support for locked-out postal workers during a labor disruption in the summer of 2011. The assembly needs to carry out more actions, of course, some of which may entail practices that are disdained by strict horizontalists, like actively participating in the lobbying of city councillors, campaigning in support of certain laws (or for rescinding them) and even collaborating with different religious or trades union-based groups. These will be contentious projects, but ones that must be undertaken if a broad-based movement is to appear and the assembly is to offer itself as a long-standing institution of the commons.

Certainly, the biggest challenges for the GTWA are still to come. In terms of affecting actual policy and growing in membership, success is still up in the air. Even maintaining the current membership may be difficult as we begin to move into more contentious debates about direct action, for example, or towards creating a political party. But the struggle continues to create institutions of the commons that have longevity and the ability to imagine a post-capitalist future. The success of the workers' assembly remains to be seen, but at the very least it stands today as a laboratory of struggle, wherein a wide array of divergent radical politics are put into practice in the everyday constructions of our movements and our struggles.

Notes

1. In truth, we could say that the assembly is *re*-emergent, as assemblies are not a new form of organizing political struggle. There are, though, considerable differences between assemblies of today and their historical counterparts.

2. A partial list of very recent experiments in assembly politics could include the People's Movement Assemblies growing out of the World Social Forum and US Social Forum, the Southern Movement Assembly, the Southern Workers' Assembly, the People's Assemblies Network, alongside the better known Occupy assemblies, the student and neighbourhood assemblies in Quebec's Maple Spring and the assembly under discussion here, the GTWA. This list is in no way comprehensive but provides a sampling of assembly projects that have developed in the last decade alone, most within the last 12–18 months at the time of writing.

3. As they existed during the initial years of the Assembly's existence, 2009–2012.

4. Fully half of Toronto's population was born outside Canada, and 47 per cent of Toronto's population self-report as being part of a visible minority population. A visible minority is defined by Statistics Canada as "persons, other than Aboriginal peoples, who are non-Caucasian in race or non-white in colour" (Chui and Maheux, 2013).

5. Hardt and Negri (2000) see biopolitical production as the new nature of productive labor moving away from mass production in a factory setting and centered on immaterial modes of the production of surplus value, including intellectual and communicative labour power. This is important for conceptualising the new assembly movements because it signifies a new spatial locale for resistance. No longer situated exclusively in the factory, sites of resistance become the workers' very bodies, the home and the social realm. All labor, in a regime of biopolitical production, is immersed in the relational elements that define the social, but simultaneously activate the "critical elements that develop the potential of insubordination and revolt through the entire set of labouring practices" (Hardt and Negri, 2000: 28). It is both production and reproduction.

6. For a more elaborate explanation of this argument in action see Zibechi (2010).

References

Amoros, M. (2011) Report on the Assembly Movement. Available at https://libcom.org/history/report-assembly-movement-miguel (accessed July 2011).

Chui, T. and Maheux, H. (2013) Visible minority women. Statistics Canada. Available at http://www.statcan.gc.ca/pub/89-503-x/2010001/article/11527-eng.htm (accessed 4 December 2014).

Cleaver, H. (1998) The Zapatistas and the electronic fabric of struggle. Available at https://webspace.utexas.edu/hcleaver/www/zaps.html (accessed 4 December 2014).

Dyer-Witheford, N. (2011) Networked Leninism? The circulation of capital, crisis, struggle and the common. *Upping the Anti*. 13.

Dyer-Witheford, N. (2010) Digital labour, species-becoming, and the global worker. *Ephemera: Theory and Politics in Organisation,* 10 (3–4) 484–503.

Federici, S. (2012) *Revolution at Point Zero*. Oakland: PM Press.

Hardt, M. and Negri, A. (2001) *Empire*. Cambridge: Harvard University Press.

Hardt, M and Negri, A. (2004) *Multitude*. New York: Penguin.

Hardt, M and Negri, A. (2009) *Commonwealth*. Cambridge: Belknap.

Katsiaficas, G. (2002) *The Battle of Seattle*. New York: Soft Skull Press.

Katsiaficas, G. (2006) *The Subversion of Politics: European Social Movements and the Decolonization of Everyday Life*. New York: AK Press.

Negri, A. (1988) *Revolution Retrieved: Selected Writings on Marx, Keynes, Capitalist Crisis and New Social Subjects, 1967–83*, trans. Emery, E. and Merrington, J. London: Left Bank Books.

Negri, A. (1991) *Marx Beyond Marx*. Brooklyn and New York: Autonomedia.

Nunes, R. (2005) Nothing is what democracy looks like: openness, horizontality, and the movement of movements. In Harvie, D, Milburn, K, Trott, B, and Watts, D. (eds) *Shut Them Down! The G8, Gleneagles 2005 and the Movement of Movements*. Brooklyn and New York: Autonomedia.

Nunes, R. (2007) Forward how? Forward where? Post operaismo beyond the immaterial labour thesis. *Ephemera: Theory and Politics in Organisation*, 7 (1) 178–202.

Rosenfeld, H. (2011) Workers' assemblies: a way to regroup the left. *MRZINE*. Available at http://mrzine.monthlyreview.org/2011/rosenfeld280711.html (accessed August 2011).

Ross, S. (2003) Is this what democracy looks like? The politics of the anti-globalization movement in North America. In Panitch, L. and Leys, C. (eds) *Socialist Register*. Vol 39, London: Merlin.

Toronto (n.d.) Toronto facts. Available at http://www.toronto.ca/toronto_facts/diversity.htm (Accessed 18 November 2014).

Virno, P. (2004) *A Grammar of the Mulitude*. Los Angeles: Semiotext(e).

Zibechi, R. (2010) *Dispersing Power: Social Movements as Anti-State Forces*. New York: AK Press.

FOUR

The Austrian Revolution of 1918–1919 and Working Class Autonomy

Peter Haumer, translated by Joe Keady

In her book *On Revolution*, Hannah Arendt (1965: 256) writes that councils have formed spontaneously in every revolution since 1789 without any awareness on the part of the participants that it had happened before. Councils are generally characterized by their spontaneous development and their aspiration to be bodies of both struggle and order in an emerging society. They can be transitional or long-term forms of worker self-organization in the workplace or they can be more expansive, located within a territorial unit (such as city or country) for the initial purpose of controlling the conditions and production and labor or, among councils that act on a territorial level, living conditions as well. The underlying tension at the heart of all modern revolutions lies in the contradiction between worker self-organization and elite parties' claims to power. The councils were a mortal threat to the party system from the outset (1965: 253) and the conflict between party and council systems has been a decisive factor in every revolution of the 20th century. (1965: 265–6). This underlying tension clearly rose to the surface during the Austrian Revolution of 1918–1919, as it did in every European country where councils or similar bodies emerged over the course of World War I and its aftermath. The Habsburg monarchy, "the sick man on the Danube" (see Hanisch, 1978) and the Vltava, fractured into separate national components as a result of 4 years of mass slaughter. What remained was German-Austria, a state that no one wanted, one that was ruled on one hand by a bourgeoisie that initially lacked any state apparatus and on the other hand by a well-organized working class eager to dispose of its own social distress.

12 November 1918

The Vienna Workers' Council held a short meeting on the morning of 12 November 1918. It agreed to call for a mass demonstration and the Republic of German-Austria was pronounced in the course of that day. In the process, a gunfight inadvertently broke out in front of the Parliament building in Vienna. Someone lowered a roll-down gate that was misinterpreted as rifle fire, touching off heavy shooting that left two dead and many wounded. Communists and members of the Red Guards took advantage of the general confusion to occupy the editorial offices of the *Neue Freie Presse* in order to safeguard its equipment, but the offices were evacuated again at 8:45 that evening. Friedrich Adler rightly described the action as a "stupid operetta".

The revolution on 12 November 1918 came about under conditions of universal revolutionary crisis, yet its only outcome was a mass working-class movement. It was a result of the Central Powers' military defeat and the disintegration of the Habsburg monarchy into discreet nation-states. During that period, the "imperial and royal" system of rule collapsed and was forced to peacefully cede power to new authorities under social democratic leadership. Nothing that is ordinarily associated with the term "revolution" (such as insurrection, street fighting, barricades and bloodshed) was anywhere to be seen in November 1918, apart from isolated moments of unrest like the one described above.

Despite everything, however, the Austrian Revolution was driven by the working class and, to a great extent, was carried out using proletarian means and methods. The large-scale mobilization and politicization of working people and their active intervention gave the events a revolutionary character while, in a manner of speaking, simultaneously seeing through a comprehensive bourgeois democratic revolution. The bourgeois camp contributed nothing to it but rather begged the social democratic leadership to "save anything that can be saved" (Seitz, 1928: 518) and delegated to them the task of establishing a bourgeois democratic order, knowing full well that the working class was heading towards just the opposite: a transformation that would go beyond the limits of a bourgeois revolution.

"Up the socialist revolution!" read the banner that social democratic workers unfurled at the large rally on the ramp of the Parliament building on 12 November 1918. This socialist orientation directed at overcoming capitalist class relations subsequently grew stronger and dominated the thoughts and actions of the majority of the working class during the Austrian Revolution's social revolutionary period from February 1919 until late July 1919.

World War I and the labor movement

The outbreak of World War I did not come as a surprise to Austrian Social Democrats. They, like the other parties of the Second International, kept a close watch on the looming threat of war during the year leading up to it. But in discussions within the Second International, the Austrian Social Democrats proved to be very reserved, rejecting the demand that they call for a general strike in the event that war could not be prevented. Theirs, however, was by no means a social-patriotic or imperialistic argument. Instead it was based primarily on pragmatic considerations, such as the balance of power:

> On the day when the Serbian government's reply to the Austrian ultimatum was due, Austria's German Social Democratic parliamentary delegates issued a manifesto declaring that, 'We reject any responsibility for this war; we solemnly and resolutely place that responsibility on those who have incited and

want to unleash it.' The party leadership repeated that protest on July 28, 1914, the day the war began. (Deutsch, 1947: 54–5)

Unlike their German counterparts, the Austrian Social Democrats were spared a vote on war financing. While Germany's Social Democrats openly declared their support for the war by passing a bill establishing national war bonds in the Reichstag, the Austrian Social Democrats found a way to avoid being openly complicit with imperialist interests. The Social Democratic parliamentarians undoubtedly would have voted for war bonds had Parliament itself not been sent on vacation by Minister-President Count Carl von Stürgkh in the spring of 1914. Parliament was finally able to meet again regularly starting on 20 May 1917, but by that time the question of war bonds had long since ceased to be an issue. Opposition to the Social Democrats' imperialist policies was immeasurably weaker in Austro-Hungary than in Germany. Only the section in Reichenberg (present-day Liberec, Czech Republic) and its newspaper *Vorwärts* actively opposed the war.

During the major internal political changes of 1917, only one Austrian group was eager to exploit the crisis in the interest of revolutionary workers' struggle and topple the old power: the small yet active Organization of Left Radicals. The actual starting point for the left-wing radical group was the Social Democratic youth organization, particularly the local Leopoldstadt and Ottakring groups in Vienna. The leading figures in that circle were Franz Koritschoner and Leo Rothziegel.

A secret radical left action committee that included Koritschoner, Anna Ströhmer, Max Lazarowitsch and Karl Maurer as well as Russian immigrants Leo Piatigorsky and Matthäus Kasarnowski was formed in the winter of 1915–1916. When Friedrich Adler reactivated the Karl Marx Educational Association as an organizational center for the left-wing of the party in March 1916, the action committee joined it, linking legal with illegal work. They managed to increase the number of radical left supporters within the Karl Marx association from 10 to 22 people. The turning point for the radical left movement came in late 1916 as a result of Adler's actions. On 21 October 1916, the deathly internal silence in conjunction with the raging World War and the suffering of the working populace drove him to shoot Minister-President Count Carl von Stürgkh. He was sentenced to death on 19 May 1917 but was subsequently reprieved and sentenced to life in prison. The first major strikes finally started in Vienna and its surroundings in late May 1917.

World War I and the movement of workers

By the time Charles I was crowned Emperor of Austro-Hungary in late 1916,[1] there were already growing signs that the populace could no longer tolerate hunger and deprivation. Just how dramatically the situation had deteriorated became clear following the harvest of 1916. Heavy autumn rains that year meant that corn had to be ground while it was still very wet, causing vast quantities of an important food source to rot.

1917 was a year that was already thoroughly dominated by food substitutions. Long lists were published showing items that could be used to stretch flour further. *Kriegsbrot*, or "war bread", which was diluted with ground barley, corn, chestnuts and potatoes, would break apart into thousands of crumbs when it was sliced. It was made of oats and beans mixed with roots and grasses, acorns and sawdust.

Workers' material circumstances deteriorated significantly in 1916–1917. As a result, strikes in 1917 far exceeded those of 1915 and 1916 in terms of both size and intensity.[2] Offensive strikes, meaning industrial actions intended to extract new concessions, began to outnumber purely defensive strikes. The proportion of women who went on strike increased enormously. On average, 96.5 percent of the female employees at any given striking shop were strike participants. The number of successful strikes increased as well. In 1917, 17.1 percent of all walkouts were "completely successful", 70.7 percent were "partly successful" and 12.2 percent were "unsuccessful". Solidarity among workers grew and, for the first time, reached beyond the limited confines of the individual shop. Instead of isolated conflicts, there were more and more group strikes that simultaneously encompassed several companies. A common struggle began to take shape on a broad front.

The strike movement of 1917 reached its zenith in Vienna in late May. It started in the artillery arsenal, where 15,000 employees were concentrated during World War I. The moment that started it came when a debilitated worker fainted on the morning of 23 May 1917. All the workers in the arsenal were on strike by around noon. The strike spread to a series of other shops near the arsenal that same day. On 25 May workers in 47 metal works and 89 machine factories stopped working. Altogether, 42,000 Viennese metalworkers participated in the action. After negotiations between the Metalworkers' Union representatives and the government, the striking workers received wage increases of 5–20 percent in the form of wartime bonuses. The strike ended on 26 May. When Social Democratic representatives appeared in the arsenal shop to encourage the workers to resume working, they received an extremely unfriendly welcome and were called "traitors to the workers' cause".[3] Irritation with the appeasement tactics of the Social Democratic Party and the union leadership was being voiced openly for the first time.

Only a small portion of the workers in the militarized shops belonged to unions during the war years due to the unprecedented social restructuring of the workforce and the inclusion of women, youth and uneducated workers in the production process on a massive scale. The political police concluded that the strikes in the spring of 1917 were initiated by people who lacked any leadership and therefore any discipline. At the Social Democratic party conference in late October and early November 1918, Ferdinand Skaret complained that no more than 4–7 percent of the workforce in many shops consisted of established union members, with the rest coming in straight from the countryside, causing the Social Democrats to lose influence.

But the most interesting result of the spring 1917 strike wave was undoubtedly the fact that early forms of what would later become workers' councils arose in some of the armament factories. In particular, most of the striking shops almost simultaneously and independently of one another started to demand that shop stewards be commissioned to distribute food or monitor its distribution. Consequently, some factory boards were forced to agree to "recognize the shop stewards chosen by the workforce itself" (Neck, 1968: 7) after workers' and factory committees were established. The strike movement of the spring of 1917 marked the beginning of the revolutionary crisis in Austria.

From workers' committees to the first councils: the January General Strike of 1918

The radical left managed to establish a foothold in the major factories in the summer of 1917, particularly in the armament and munitions factories in the Vienna Basin. A few shop stewards who were dissatisfied with the Social Democrats' policies, including Eduard Schönfeld, secretary of the district health insurance fund for the city of Wiener Neustadt, made contact with the radical left on their own. In order to establish a solid foundation for these sporadic links with the industrial workforce, the radical action committee convened a secret conference of its supporters. It was held in the forest in St Egyden on 9 September 1917 with Eduard Schönfeld presiding as chairman. There were 35 delegates present, including workers from the Daimler engine works in Wiener Neustadt and from the Schoeller plant in Ternitz and also delegates from the Wöllersdorf munitions factory, from the Warchalowski aircraft factory in Ottakring and from the light bulb factory. This concentration of workers in St Egyden (located between Wiener Neustadt and Neunkirchen, roughly 40 miles south of Vienna) made it possible for the radical left to connect with a series of new large-scale factories. Shop stewards from shops the Traisen Valley in Lower

Austria (St Aegyd ironworks, Hohenberg file factory, Traisen steel foundry, and the Neumann company in Marktl) joined the action committee in the fall of 1917. Workers from Vienna's arsenal and Floridsdorf Fiat plant also joined the radicals.

Inspired by the Bolsheviks' seizure of power in the name of workers' and soldiers' councils in Russia, three leftist currents joined the radical group in late 1917: the syndicalists under Leo Rothziegel; the group around Arnold Baral, which had tended towards anarchism; and a radical faction of the Jewish socialist workers' party Poale Zion under Kohn-Eber. On 30 December 1917, the newly united revolutionary groups formed an illegal committee that called itself the Workers' Council, led by Koritschoner and Rothziegel. As a soldier, Rothziegel had contacts among radical-minded members of the military and managed to bring in platoon leader Johannes Wertheim, Corporal Haller, Second Lieutenant Fränkel and First Lieutenant Egon Erwin Kisch – and with that, the illegal committee expanded into a "workers' and soldiers' council".

Radical leftist and future communist Anna Ströhmer reported that the workers' and soldiers' council had decided to initiate a major strike in their strongholds in Wiener Neustadt, Neunkirchen and Ternitz at the end of January 1918. Dramatic developments in the peace negotiations in Brest-Litovsk and rumors of an impending reduction in the flour ration (which was confirmed in a report on 10 January in the *Arbeiter-Zeitung* [1918a]) induced the radical shop stewards from Wiener Neustadt and Ternitz to prepare for the strike to start earlier. The leaders of the workers' and soldiers' council in Vienna published a flier entitled *Working People!*:

We began agitating for the mass strike in every workshop, publicizing it in every barracks. Creation of workers' councils, sending workers' councils as a peace committee, immediate peace with Soviet Russia, armistice on all fronts: those were our demands. (Koritschoner, 1970: 10)

Otto Bauer described the start of the January General Strike as follows:

> When the flour rations were cut in half on January 14, 1918, the workers in Wiener Neustadt went on strike. The next day the strike spread. . . . The movement expanded sporadically from shop to shop, from town to town. . . . On January 16, the entire working population of Vienna joined the strike. On January 17 and 18 the movement spread to the Upper Austrian and Styrian industrial regions. On January 18, the Hungarian workforce also joined the strike. The enormous masses of striking workers, the wild revolutionary passion of their mass assemblies, the election of the first workers' councils in the strike assemblies – all of these things gave the movement a grandiose revolutionary character and stirred the masses to hope that the strike would rise immediately to revolution, that they would be able to seize power for themselves and force peace. (Bauer, O., 1965: 76)

On the morning of 17 January, the *Arbeiter-Zeitung* published a "Declaration of the Party Executive", which had a direct bearing on the Austrian council movement. It read:

> In order to guide the movement towards an orderly path, we call on the *shop stewards of the striking workers* to appear today, Thursday, at 9 a.m. at the local party offices of the districts in question and to elect district committees to see to the orderly conduct of the strike. (*Arbeiter-Zeitung*, 1918a: 1, emphasis in original)

The first meeting of elected district committee representatives (which means the first meeting of the central Vienna Workers' Council) took place that evening.

By 16 January, the council movement in Wiener Neustadt and the surrounding area could no longer be stopped. Similar efforts were underway that day in the strike assemblies in Vienna, including in Floridsdorf, where employees from all 60 striking shops met in the workingmen's club to elect a "permanence committee" to lead the strike. The Social Democratic party leadership knew that the radical current was influential among the councils that already existed in the southern Vienna Basin and that the council idea as such might assume a potentially revolutionary line of action directed against party and union leadership if matters were left to unfold on their own. For that reason, the party executive took over the vocabulary of creating "strike committees", which had been nothing more than a synonym for "workers' councils" at the start. It decided to direct the full force of its perfectly functioning organization towards influencing the election process and it was confident that, by doing so, it could limit the influence of the radicals, who were inexperienced and nearly unknown among the masses of workers.

At the party conference in October–November 1918, party secretary Ferdinand Skaret declared, "We must see to it that we establish close contact with the workforce. To that end, we are creating workers' councils" (Minutes of the party conference, see Garamvölgyi 1983: 56). While the notion of "creating" workers' councils by the party is purely euphemistic (most of the councils formed spontaneously), the Social Democrats undoubtedly placed themselves as taking charge of this council movement and thereby regaining influence among the workers. They hoped that, as a result, things "as we have seen them in January 1918" might be "if not stopped entirely, at least weakened for the future". (Skaret, minutes of the party conference, see Garamvölgyi 1983: 56)

By and large, we can say that disciplining the workers' councils by the party and their exploitation for the benefit of the party was a success. By the end of January 1918, the workers' councils were subordinated to the labor movement's traditional authorities and that would not change much during the winter of 1918–1919 when the council movement was reactivated and evolved. Workers' councils had to belong to the Social Democratic political and union organizations and subscribe to the *Arbeiter-Zeitung*. Although this made the purely Social Democratic workers' councils the scene of factional struggles between the radical left (which would later see its ranks recruited into the Communist Party of German-Austria (KPDÖ) and the Federation of Revolutionary Socialists "International", (FRSI), centrist (for example, Otto Bauer and Max Adler) and right-wing tendencies (Karl Renner, Karl Seitz and others), it never seriously jeopardized party unity. Moreover, the workers' council gained a popular and rousing unifying figure as chairman in Friedrich Adler after he was released from prison on 1 November 1918.

The January General Strike reached its high point on 19 January 1918. Some 750,000 strikers, of whom 550,000 were in the Austrian half of the Empire and 200,000 in Hungary. But at 3:30 in the morning on 20 January, the Vienna Worker's Council voted 308 to 2 to call off the strike, based on the urging of Social Democratic party leaders as well as a government statement that promised a lot but included no assurances. Tumultuous scenes followed in Vienna's strike assemblies as workers protested against ending the strike. Karl Renner was "arrested" by comrades in Wiener Neustadt as he tried to explain the rationale for it. On 22 January the strike began to break down in Vienna.

Future Communist Friedrich Hexmann was 17 when he took part in the January General Strike and we owe him a debt of gratitude for his vivid description of the experience:

> I think it was January 21, 1918 when suddenly everyone, the whole factory, gathered in the courtyard. How everyone fit I don't know. They were standing, packed together like sardines. We made telephones – field telephones – primarily for the front. It was a militarized factory and not always, but very often, there was an officer there. So the workers assemble and one man gets up, the works council, the shop steward, and speaks from a kind of stairway, saying, "*Strike! Enough! United strike!*" That spread like a fire throughout all of Vienna. . . .

The military put up a sign saying, "Strike Prohibited" or "Resume Work Immediately". If not, it would be punishable by however many years in jail up to the death penalty. But the office workers didn't go on strike. We had no idea how widespread it was. At night the strikers would always come together – not only from my factory but from others too – at an inn on Landstrasser Hauptstrasse that had a room in the courtyard. That room overflowed. The front court overflowed out onto the street, they were arguing inside, someone who had spoken there from a left perspective told me later. That was Arnold Baral, an anarcho-syndicalist. But he was organized, not some wacko, a go-getter who fit in with the radical left cause. They didn't want to let him speak, but the people called out, "Let the Russian speak!" He was Polish, but he looked like a Russian intellectual. A few people sang at the front. In the middle was an enormous pile of snow – it was one of the snowiest years. A few people climbed it and sang *Soldier of the Revolution*. So we just sang along. It was really easy to sing and so I forgot to ask, "Who are you and what is this?" and instead of the idiots there giving a speech and a lecture, we sang. And so I forgot to connect with the radical left.

I go the next day, there's a big crowd of people again. Not as many anymore, but the whole courtyard is full. Nothing is happening, suddenly a young man gets up – he could have been a student – and says, "Unfortunately, the speaker can't come. He's been stopped!" I don't know what happened to me – I think to myself, "That can't be. Hundreds of people and now they have no speaker? Someone should say something to the people". I pull myself together, barrel up the snow pile, and give the first speech of my life, without notes, without anything – later I couldn't speak without notes – I just spoke. So what did I say? What do you think? All the Bolshevik slogans that I had read in the *Arbeiter-Zeitung*: "For the eight-hour day! For immediate peace! Down with the monarchy! Workers,' peasants,' and soldiers' councils! Loot the storehouses of the bourgeoisie!" or – I didn't actually know who the bourgeoisie was then, I couldn't have said that – "Loot the cellars of the rich and distribute it to the poor!" (Hexmann, n.d.)[4]

From Hexmann's story, we can gather that the anarcho-syndicalist and member of the radical left Baral was still agitating for the strike to continue on 21 January and Hexmann himself was still advocating the strike and a revolution on 22 January. What is interesting here is that the bulk of the left-wing radicals had complied with the Vienna Workers' Council's 20 January decision and had likewise supported ending the strike. A pamphlet that the radicals published in August 1918 reads:

When the speakers who had to announce and justify the decision and also very cleverly managed to end it, we who were in the assembly appeared to be paralyzed by fear. It seemed inconceivable that a movement with such strength and such a high revolutionary spirit might come to such a pathetic end. Old, gray-haired workers sobbed out loud when they heard about the result of the strike, level-headed, serious men looked grim and resolute, dominated by the desire to push the movement forward despite the Vienna Workers' Council and not to accept its decision. Even the comrades on the radical left, who, after their own objective critique of the strike movement's "achievements", had recommended that the workers resume working given that, under the prevailing conditions for the workers at the time, an energetic and focused continuation of the strike was no longer possible, could not move the workers to start working again. The left-wing radicals themselves could not conceive of continuing the strike, given that there were too few of them and that they had lost their decisiveness and their focus due to the anarchist elements who had overwhelmed them during the movement. (Anon, 1918: 12)

And what were the "achievements" of this movement with a "grandiose revolutionary character" (Otto Bauer)? What did it help to achieve? "Nothing but a few promises from the government that weren't worth the paper they were written on and that were obviously broken two to three weeks later!" (Rosdolsky, 1986: 7).

On the councils that the January General Strike produced

When the strike ended in Wiener Neustadt, Neunkirchen and Ternitz on 24 January, the Vienna Workers' Council held a meeting in which it decided to continue to exist as a permanent institution.[5] The workers' council was intended to function as a kind of early warning system for the party executive over spontaneous rank and file movements in order to offset and prevent unpleasant surprises along the lines of the January General Strike. From January to November 1918, the workers' councils therefore had to either be overwhelmingly made up of members of the Social Democratic Party or under its intellectual influence. A significant element of these considerations was the fact that it was hardest to settle the strike in the area where a workers' council had arisen without the Social Democrats' guiding hand, namely, in Wiener Neustadt and its environs. The workers' council there was actually an autonomous body of workers for the purpose consistently carrying out the strike, a body where representatives who sympathized with the radical left could operate. Part of what Seitz and Renner had intended their proposals to do was therefore to rein it in with statutes so that it would be easier for the party leadership to control.[6]

The workers' councils of the January General Strike were fighting bodies designed to lead the mass strike; at the time, that was all that the workers themselves understood them to be. Progressing beyond this initial level of self-organizing would have required a fundamental shift in power relations, which is to say the destruction and paralysis of the state apparatus, which occurred only in November 1918. The January General Strike itself had many of the preconditions that could have led to a victorious outcome for this mass movement. While the Social Democrats had, on one hand, repeatedly rattled off the great dangers that continuing the struggle would bring, they also deliberately concealed and even sabotaged possibilities that opened up that might allow the mass strike to develop into the start of a revolutionary situation. So on 28 January a general strike began in Germany in which over one million workers participated and workers' councils were likewise elected. The naval arsenal in Pula[7] struck from 22–28 January and the Cattaro Mutiny[8] broke out on 1 February: sailors on 40 warships mutinied and elected sailors' councils.

The January General Strike had a tremendous impact on the Army:

> The discord among the troops expressed itself in a string of mutinies following the January General Strike. Slovenian troops mutinied in Judenburg, Serbian troops in Pécs, Czech troops in Rumburk, and Hungarian troops in Budapest. An arsenal workers' strike hit the navy in Cattaro during the first few days of February. Warship crews hoisted red flags, seized their officers, and demanded a peace agreement based on Wilson's Fourteen Points. (Bauer, O., 1965: 79)

Instead of uniting these struggles and possibly leading them to victory as a result, the Social Democrats did everything in their power to isolate them from one another.

So due to their defeat in the January General Strike, the self-organized councils could not develop any further towards structures that would challenge the power of capital and the monarchy and, ultimately, eliminate them. Demoralized by the devastating defeat and the wave of severe repression that followed, the workers' activities receded for a short time and the councils were subordinated to the structures and compulsions of the Social Democratic apparatus with relatively little opposition.

But the Russian Revolution, the Bolsheviks' appearance at Brest-Litovsk, with their resolute and uncompromising position against the war, the increasingly catastrophic state of provisions in the interior, the problem of nationalities that were suppressed by the Habsburg autocracy, and the Austrian workers' regenerating fighting capacity[9] had drained the monarchy and taken away its very foundation:

> *Reichsrat* [national parliamentary] representatives of every German electoral district met on October 21 in the conference hall of the Lower Austrian Landtag [state parliament]. The assembly unanimously came to a decision that, "The German people of Austria have decided to determine their own future state structure, to form an independent German-Austrian state, and to regulate their relations with other nations through freely made agreements". Accordingly, the representative assembly decided to constitute itself as a provisional national assembly and to elect an executive committee as a nucleus for the German-Austrian government that was to come. (Hautmann, 1978: 75–6)

Within 4 days, the dual monarchy was dismembered. The Czechs began breaking away from Austria on 28 October, followed shortly thereafter by the other nations. On 30 October a provisional government[10] in Vienna began looking after the remainder of Austria. A provisional soldiers' council was formed on the same day, also in Vienna. On 31 October the Red Guard was established in Vienna and freedom of assembly and association were restored; between 31 October and 3 November all political prisoners, including Friedrich Adler, were released.

From establishment of a bourgeois democracy to the social revolutionary phase

As a consequence of November 1918, the ruling classes, particularly the Austrian bourgeoisie, had to accept an extraordinary decline in power. Shocked by the sudden disappearance of the authoritarian monarchist state and temporarily robbed of their traditional means of domination, the bourgeoisie had to let the Social Democrats act. The bourgeois camp's weakness allowed working–class organizations to significantly increase their power; the council movement, which, in the spring of 1919, had become an actual mass organization with an electorate of over 800,000 and tens of thousands of active workers' council representatives, became the starting point for a qualitative expansion of their effective reach.

The Social Democratic Party, which in 1 July 1913 had 87,929 members within the territory of the future Republic of German-Austria, reached a membership of 322,826 by 1 July 1919. In Vienna, where the number of party members had declined during the first 2 years of the war from approximately 40,000 to 10,000, it grew to 20,000 by November 1918 and approximately 80,000 just 6 months later. The number of members of the Social Democratic unions, which amounted to 295,147 in German-Austria at the end of 1918, rose to 662,854 by 30 June 1919 and 772,146 by the end of that year.

Moreover, with the disintegration of the Imperial Army and the formation of the Volkswehr (popular defense), a new and influential movement, that of the soldiers' councils, joined the workers' councils' side. In the initial phase of the Austrian Revolution, until February/March 1919, the soldiers' councils were in fact the most forward-looking part of the council movement. That is because the Social Democrats had fewer opportunities to exercise political influence on the soldiers' councils, which were governed by an element of spontaneity during November and December 1918, than on the workers' councils, which by large maintained party discipline. But the situation was changing: the unity that the statutes had established between the workers' councils and the Social Democratic Party was increasingly eroding. With the establishment of the Communist Party on 3 November and the Federation of Revolutionary Socialists on 28 November 1918, new workers' parties emerged that, unlike the Social Democrats, pursued social revolutionary goals.

The Social Democrats soon learned that, despite their small membership, the KPDÖ and the FRSI were too big to ignore. Both parties had an influence among the members of the Volkswehr in Vienna that could not be underestimated and they were even able to support an armed formation, the Red Guard. While the soldiers' council movement was open to them and they were able to claim a mandate in the Vienna soldiers' council in the November 1918 elections, they were nonetheless denied access to the workers' council movement. Only the deterioration of the economic and political contradictions into a revolutionary crisis, which ended the relative peace among the workers starting in February 1919 and strengthened the social revolutionary movement, would induce the Social Democrats to reorganize the workers' councils and to open up to the KPDÖ, FRSI and other socialist groups.

The soldiers' councils

Like the Habsburg monarchy itself, the imperial and royal Army also disintegrated into its national components. As in the Russian and German revolutions, soldiers' councils were elected in the German-speaking units. The soldiers' councils were elected to represent the soldiers again while the new, small military force, known as the Volkswehr, was being created. The Social Democrats were a significant factor in creating the Volkswehr, which was ensured through their close connection with the labor movement. Rather than use the cadre of the Imperial Army as a basis for creating the Volkswehr, Julius Deutsch, then the Social Democratic Under-Secretary for the Army, was able to rebuild it from scratch.

On 3 November the government consented to the creation of the Volkswehr, which was to be composed of volunteers. Soldiers' councils were elected on the same day in every barracks in Vienna. The results were Social Democratic victories in almost all Viennese units. The representatives were "not always old, proven comrades . . . but often just young people who were all the more radical for it and who had only just found their way to us" (Deutsch, 1947).

In Linz and Klagenfurt, the soldiers' councils removed their garrison commanders and the Klagenfurt council mandated that every order from the Carinthian High Command be countersigned by a member of the soldiers' council:

> In Klagenfurt, the provisional state parliament had to accept the soldiers' council's demand that officers were to be elected. The chairman of the Villach council was a reserve second lieutenant, a left socialist; the officers there had to remove their rank insignia. Council chairmen in several smaller towns in Carinthia returned Russian prisoners of war. Officers' messes were abolished. But above all, the soldiers' councils insisted on using the right that was granted to them to elect their officers and refused non-elected officers and military officials access to the barracks and offices. (Carsten, 1973: 65)

The Vienna soldiers' council formed its own executive committee, which was fully under left Social Democratic influence. Its chairman was Capt. Dr Josef Frey, the commander of a Volkswehr battalion who, according to the *Arbeiter-Zeitung* of 3 December 1918, intended "to turn the Volkswehr into a fighting, proletarian, revolutionary army" and the soldiers' councils were to see to it "that this fighting army can only be used for revolutionary – not reactionary – purposes". The Viennese Volkswehr was a relatively strong and well-disciplined unit of roughly 16–17,000 men comprising 88 infantry and eight machine gun companies with five batteries and 20 pieces of artillery. They undoubtedly represented a force that was capable of ending domestic unrest or an attempted coup.

A unit that soon became known as the Red Guard was formed during the first few days of the revolution. The two founders, First Lieutenant Egon Erwin Kisch and Corporal Haller[11] were informed by the Council of State on 1 November that there were no objections to the creation of a Red Guard outfit. On 4 November 1918, after the Red Guard had already joined the Volkswehr, it began moving into the Stiftskaserne military barracks and started propaganda activities. The strength of the Stiftskaserne Volkswehr Division (Red Guard) fluctuated between 400 and 500 men.

Although it was left of the Social Democrats, the Red Guard was politically heterogeneous and should not be regarded as an extension of the Communist Party. About half the unit was made up of reliable Social Democratic comrades and the commander, Josef Frey, was a left social democrat, so it should come as no surprise that a series of often significant political-tactical differences of opinion with the KPDÖ arose. They agreed on the goal of pushing the bourgeois democratic upheaval towards a proletarian revolution, but they did not agree on how that should happen. On 28 November 1918, these differences with the KPDÖ led to the establishment of a second revolutionary party, the FRSI, in which members of the Red Guard held leading positions.

The FRSI and the council question

During its brief existence[12] the FRSI developed interesting solutions to a number of issues around the failure of social democracy and its open commitment to a bourgeois-democratically managed form of capitalism. Johannes Wertheim, a founding member of the Federation, describes its first steps:

> In early November 1918, a group of young men and women who had spread anti-militarism and pro-Bolshevik propaganda

during the war and especially during the January General Strike got together to publish a weekly newspaper called *Der Freie Arbeiter*. Its first edition came out on November 9. They used it to continue their agitation and, in the beginning, they wanted to impact on the soldiers who were returning home as well as members of the Red Guard, which was just forming at the time and for which they introduced a separate insert with the same title. But they soon began to do educational and organizing work among the unemployed, which was a constantly growing mass of people. The FRS International formed at an open assembly on November 28, 1918 in the large hall at the inn Zum Feldmarschall Laudon on Hernalsergürtel street. (Wertheim, 2003:17–18)

The Federation had only a few hundred registered members (such as Julius Dickmann, Rothziegel, Kisch, Hilde and Johannes Wertheim; the author Franz Werfel was a sympathizer) and they assumed that new forms of struggle would have to be established with the onset of a new period in the Austrian labor movement. It strictly rejected the "party hackery" of a "secret conventicle" of Communist Party leaders. Julius Dickmann[13] was the real mentor of the FRSI and in November 1918 he disapproved of the establishment of the KPDÖ, charging that it would become just another party like the Social Democrats.

Given that Dickmann rejected the party system while also recognizing that a council system anchored in individual factories around the country would not survive if it remained uncoordinated – in short, that it needed an organization that would bind the will of the masses together and coordinate their revolutionary activity – he saw Berlin's revolutionary shop stewards as a model that might provide a solution. Dickmann wrote the Federation's second leaflet *How Are We Different from the Communist Party?* under his pseudonym Ernst Jung (1919). It stated that

The overwhelming majority of workers' council delegates [in Germany and particularly in German-Austria] are allied with the Social Democrats. The main task of revolutionary

socialists in our country right now is less to outwardly assert
soviet power and more to achieve a majority within the soviets. Just as individual parties have fought for political influence
on parliamentary terrain until now, so will the conflicting proletarian tendencies struggle for leadership on the terrain of the
workers' councils.

But political parties are entirely ill-suited to this struggle.
Their structure corresponds entirely to the parliamentary
system. Given that this is based on the local composition of
citizens by residential district, each party seeks to make up its
membership locally. But these local organizations of members
are only incidental and artificial. They easily lose their cohesion when they are not held together by any external party
apparatus. The party's internal conditions have to be regulated through cleverly devised statutes and the party leadership
can very easily dominate the disjointed mass of its members.
Unlike parliamentarianism, sovietism is built on the factory
system. The council system takes hold of workers directly in
their social role in the midst of their drudgery. The production process itself ensures the workers' firm cohesion; external
apparatus is entirely superfluous. A revolutionary organization
directed at securing a majority in the workers' councils needs
neither statutes nor authorities. Its leadership cannot be independent of the masses that are bound together in the labor
process. The carpet will immediately be pulled out from under
it if it should oppose the masses. We must aim toward such a
revolutionary federation based on factory divisions if we want
to snatch leadership of the workers' councils from the Social
Democrats . . . and our loose organizational structure will
make that transition substantially easier.

Dickmann describes how that loose organization came about in the
same pamphlet:

From the start, the Federation's founders refused to bind
the workers to any single program. They called public

assemblies with the agenda "What Are the Workers to Do?" Every worker and soldier could have his say and express his views. . . . In the course of the discussion, the assembly participants became acquainted with the idea of a federation that would unite every revolutionary tendency. Nobody who just honestly wanted to get involved in the work of liberation was excluded. How that appeared in the individual minds of the future state was, for the moment, irrelevant. That is how our Federation came from among the masses. Whether it wanted to be big or small, weak or powerful, it was and is a product of the workers themselves. And with that, our proletariat had taken its first step toward independence.

One of the Federation's main tasks was to continue to maintain contact with the Social Democrats. It was completely clear to them that establishing an Austrian council republic would be pointless without the support of the Social Democratic workers. Although they fundamentally rejected parliamentarianism, they were nonetheless positioned to call for votes for the Social Democratic candidates in the National Constitutional assembly elections of 16 February 1919:

> We do not want to be accused of having ruined the possibility of a Social Democratic majority by withholding our votes, all the more so given that we cannot see any significant action around the class struggle by dropping a piece of paper in the ballot box. We therefore recommend that our comrades cast their votes for the Social Democratic candidates and await the evidence that the largest possible representation of Social Democratic deputies in parliament will, as we have predicted, be unable to do socialist work. (F.R.S. Internationale, 1919)

Social Democracy and the Austrian Revolution

The elections on 16 February[14] were a victory for the bourgeoisie, based on the very fact that they took place at all. While, as previously, it had no instrument of power with which to fight the workers' radicalism and to decisively push back the workers' councils, those embryonic organs of worker power, it could nonetheless rely on the Social Democrats, who could assert their dominant position among the workforce. Workers still pinned their hopes for a revolutionary society on the Social Democratic Workers' Party (SDAP) and at the time the workers' councils were still their executive bodies. Nonetheless, the Social Democrats could not simply do as they pleased. Moreover, their objectives were far too disconnected from the current mood among the workers.

The party conference in late 1918 empowered the faction to participate in forming the first government and set the subsequent goals for Social Democratic activities in the new state: establishing a republic and annexation to Germany. The annexation idea was one of the Social Democrats' main arguments against the immediate call for council power. Nobody could ignore the fact that German-Austria was not viable. The supplies of coal, the most important industrial energy source at the time, and food were, to a large extent, not guaranteed. The material problems were too large to be resolved simply with allusions to a possible revolution and the expropriation of the bourgeoisie.

The Social Democrats' second major goal, the construction of a bourgeois democratic republic and its defense against all attacks from the right as well as the left, arose from the logic of annexation. If the bourgeoisie were to be expropriated and worker power established, then the Entente would impose an economic blockade that the neighboring countries would certainly adhere to. The working class of German-Austria would then be condemned to starvation and reactionary forces would have an easy time with them. For that reason, they did not dare risk a step too far towards socialism. That was the only way that the powerless republic could ensure help from the other capitalist countries.

On that basis, it is clear that Otto Bauer's socialization plan, which he had proposed to the party executive on 19 December should be characterized as merely partial socialization. At the same time, it was a stepwise process combined with the need to reimburse the old property owners, a process that avoided substantially attacking the power of capital so as to forestall burdening the already suffering populace with still more deprivation due to struggles with foreign and domestic sanctions. Yet the workers were increasingly tumultuous in their demand that businesses be socialized and they took matters into their own hands more and more frequently: direct action and wildcat socialization increased.

Spring and summer 1919: once again, the revolution is just around the corner

> The revolutionary postwar crisis in Austria reached its high point between March and July 1919. On March 21, following the Hungarian Republic of Councils' call, the proletarian revolution pushed its way right up to the gates of Vienna and the Wiener Neustadt industrial region. On April 6, the revolutionary central council in Munich proclaimed the Bavarian Soviet Republic. The question of whether German-Austria would follow the example of both of its neighbors to the east and to the west now took center stage, dominating the political scene. All other problems paled in comparison. (Hautmann, 1987: 288)

The workers were growing increasingly impatient and considered themselves once again forced to take matters into their own hands. Socialization was progressing too slowly for them; they saw too little of social democracy and social justice. A few examples illustrate the situation. The Krupp plant in Berndorf, where only business-friendly company unions had been tolerated before the war, erupted in serious unrest in March 1919 after a worker was fired for communist activities. Several public officials and a manager were injured during the violent confrontation that followed and peace could only be restored through the mediation of high-ranking union representatives. Krupp had to allow factory committees (works councils) to be established and authorize union organization. On 14 March, the Mitterberger Kupfer ADD DEF factory in the village of Mühlbach am Hochkönig was temporarily taken over by a "workers' council" that also included two office workers.

On 7 April, the Seegraben coal mines and Austria's largest iron ore plant, Alpine Montan in Donawitz, were spontaneously socialized. The SDAP's *Arbeiterwille* (Worker's Will), published an article titled "Workers' Movement in Donawitz and Seegraben, Leoben" reporting on a major disturbance that day when flour and grease were distributed, which ultimately lead to a workers' assembly that resolved to remove the plant's manager. "The decision was immediately enacted and a four-member executive board was formed consisting of two engineers, a Social Democratic worker, and a Communist" (*Arbeiterwille*, 1919a).

The situation, including that of union representatives, was finally discussed in depth at a shop stewards' meeting in the Donawitz plant. The assembly took note of the Social Democratic board member's report that the new board asked the head of the socialization committee, Otto Bauer, to take over the process of socializing the plant. In a resolution, the office staff aligned themselves with the workers with respect to the question of socialization:

> The overwhelming majority of the office staff has declared itself willing to work, to the best of its knowledge and ability, on the major project of impending socialization side-by-side with the workers for the good of us all and for the good of the nation. It has done and will do this in the conviction that it is marching with serious and sober-minded men. (*Arbeiterwille*, 1919b)

Here as well, works councils and complete freedom to unionize, among other things, had to be granted after lengthy negotiations involving unionists and Social Democratic members of parliament as well as government officials and industrial inspectors.

Otto Bauer warned against syndicalist actions, claiming that an employee take-over of a factory is far from being socialization. Given that he considered socialization impossible at that moment, he tried to stave off the outraged workers and staff in Donawitz with the impending democratization of the plant.

The military contracting company Aviatik was also wildcat socialized, as was the Steyr weapons factory, amid growing signs of an incipient spontaneous shop floor council movement. The *Arbeiter-Zeitung* reported on 8 July 1919 that the Lorenz-Werke (radio manufacturer) had decided to socialize in a full workforce assembly to which a leading Communist had also been invited.

Despite this wave of "syndicalist actions", and although a communist revolution was expected at any time, official strikes in German-Austria reached their lowest levels in the early post-war era in 1919. However, industrial production came to its absolute low point that year as well. While the number of striking workers in Germany reached its highest level of the entire inter-war period in 1919, the number in Austria declined to a modest 70,000. In 1920 it was back to 199,000 and in 1921 it was 302,000. In 1919 there were 83 strikes, one lockout, and 92 other labor conflicts (Klenner, 1951: 507).

The precarity of the food supply made it completely clear to the industrial workforce that production had to be maintained, at least within the narrow scope of the provisions that were lacking. Social Democratic and union leaders did everything in their power to direct the inevitable social disputes towards channels other than a strike movement and the workers followed their leaders in that they concentrated the bulk of their activities on the workers' councils or the local council movements. This can be understood as an economic choice and an entirely reasonable one, given that the workers' councils offered far better and more efficient possibilities for alleviating the food shortage than factory strikes did.[15]

This associated revival of the council movement starting in February 1919 led to an increasingly widespread dispersal of workers' councils and allowed them to exercise their supervisory and leadership functions with self-confidence. The political system in German-Austria was called into question not only by the council republics in Bavaria and Hungary, but also by the development of the class struggle within the republic.

An evolving dual power

In 1919 armed power was still by and large in the hands of the working class. The various military units consisted of class-conscious workers who were, for the most part, more radical than the workforce because they were aware of their power. At the time, nobody would dare mount a military challenge to the Volkswehr.

The bourgeoisie and cooperative Social Democrats had not yet managed to send the workers back into the factories. The workers' councils partly replaced the collapsed state apparatus and partly operated in parallel to the remaining or already revived authorities. The councils were occupied with the housing question and the supply problem. They applied their authority and their strength to confiscating and commandeering what they needed and in doing so, the council bodies' significance and power went far beyond Vienna:

> The workers' councils in Upper Austria played a critical role in providing for the unemployed and providing housing. They had a significant influence on the food supply for workers in Upper Austria and on the pricing of all consumer goods. The workers' councils' political clout among administrative district heads, whose offices housed the district workers' councils, was not negligible; even in the state capital the district counselor could not make any significant decisions for the workforce without the workers' council's consent. (Braunthal, 1919: 7)

Workers' councils in Vienna operated in the same way as in Upper Austria and councils had a dominant influence on public events in Lower Austria and Styria as well.

The vast majority of the workers' council members came from the ranks of the Social Democrats and considered themselves party supporters, yet due to the objective situation as well as the dynamics of their activities, they consistently pushed beyond social democracy in terms of both individual political issues and on a general political level. Conflicts continually erupted in the Social Democratic camp in the debates concerning the SDAP's governing policies, the coalition, establishing the workers' councils' relationship with the state apparatus, and the issue of support for Soviet Russia and Hungary, and so on. Social Democratic workers' councils often consciously sided with the KPDÖ or the FRSI on various issues against their own party comrades. That tendency would reach its high point in July 1919 most of the Vienna district workers' council joined the communist minority on the question of the nature of support for the threatened Hungarian Republic of Councils. On 17 July, 142 workers' council members voted for a general strike on Monday, 21 July in support of Soviet Hungary. A total of 104 workers' council members were in favor of the Social Democrats' proposal to hold a demonstration that Sunday.

This development also had its organizational fallout:

By the time of the second Austrian council congress in early July 1919, some nationwide workers' councils had already held separate discussions under the rubric of 'the left.' But in the process, the revolutionary comrades also recognized that some people who identified as 'left' also rejected actual consistent, revolutionary politics. At a meeting of the Vienna district workers' council in October 1919, members presented a declaration that included the foundations of the new left. The declaration contained the signatures of some 80 outspoken Social Democratic members of the district workers' council. This new left went by the name of the Social Democratic Working Group of Revolutionary Workers' Councils and initially limited itself to workers' council activities. The first edition of their weekly newspaper *Der Arbeiterrat* [The Workers'

Council] was published on December 20 and with that the new left went public inside the party. (Rothe, 1920: 326)

A form of dual power began to develop in German-Austria in the spring of 1919, yet the possibility of a socialist revolution was not immediately apparent. Although the KPDÖ's membership had grown to 40,000 and while, along with the FRSI it represented 10 percent of the workers' council delegates, it was not in a position to push the differentiation process among Social Democratic supporters forward due to its putschist politics, which did not shy away from terrorist actions.[16] As a small, active minority, it wanted to force a council republic even against the will of the majority of the workers. Even the FRSI, with its more realistic outlook, was increasingly overwhelmed in the KPDÖ's putschism. It was also weakened by the fact that one of its more far-sighted representatives, Leo Rothziegel, had gone to Hungary on 2 April along with other 1300 Austrian volunteers to provide military support for the Hungarian Republic of Councils.[17]

On 15 March the Social Democrats formed a new coalition government under Karl Renner, this time with the Christian Social Party alone. Most of the working class believed that collaborating with the bourgeoisie in this coalition would make rapid progress towards socialism more difficult while the Social Democratic leaders were able to wash their hands of it:

> The coalition with this bourgeois party, the Social Christians – the struggle against which had been previously important in German-Austrian Social Democrats' domestic policies – is seen by the majority of the party comrades as a bitter necessity to which one can only submit reluctantly, unwillingly, and never without complaint. . . . In every party organization, in the workers' councils, and among the intellectual workers there are individual comrades or larger or smaller groups that "reject" the coalition policy, that "do not see" its successes, and that demand "more revolutionary' tactics". (Bauer, H., 1919: 455–6)

Instead of taking this discomfort as a starting point by turning its attack on the bourgeois cabinet members, the KPDÖ opted not to modify their ritual demand for a declaration of a council republic. The slogan "All power to the councils!" had undoubtedly lost none of its timeliness, but combining it with an orientation towards removing the Social Christians from the government appeared to be what the moment called for. The KPDÖ, however, did not recognize that the Social Democrats, despite their outstanding reformist "achievements", were driven into a dilemma due to the objective conditions and the radicalism of the working class. And while it simply intensified its criticism of the Social Democrats for their participation in the coalition, it no longer took the illusions of the Social Democratic masses into account. Demanding a single-party socialist government supported by the workers' and soldiers' councils would have been a shameful capitulation for the KPDÖ.[18]

Swan song

On 1 May 1919, the Soviet Republic in Munich was crushed and on 1 August the Hungarian Republic of Councils followed suit. Unification of a potential Austrian council republic with the Hungarian republic and consequently with Soviet Russia was a lost cause. The Treaty of Saint-Germain-en-Laye prohibited unification with Germany. German-Austria became the state that nobody wanted. As a consequence, the council movement increasingly relinquished its claims to power and was therefore condemned to a slow decline. Its formal conclusion came at the end of 1924 when the workers' councils in Austria were disbanded. The *Republikanischer Schutzbund* (Republican Protection League), the SDAP's military formation during the First Republic, developed from what was left:

> [In March 1919] the government was constantly facing passionate demonstrations by returning soldiers, the unemployed, men crippled in the war, etc. It was facing a Volkswehr that

was filled with the spirit of proletarian revolution. It was facing serious, ominous conflicts in the factories and on the railroads. And the government had no means to exert its power: The armed forces were not an instrument that it could use against the proletarian masses filled with revolutionary emotion . . . No bourgeois government could have coped with these issues. It would have been defenseless against the mistrust and hatred of the proletarian masses. Within eight days it would have been toppled by unrest in the streets and its leaders arrested by their own soldiers. Only social democrats could have handled these incomparably difficult tasks. They were the only ones who the proletarian masses trusted. (Bauer, 1965: 140)

But the Social Democrats were only able to manage it because they had promised to successively socialize the means of production during the tumultuous months of 1919. Key industries (coal, ore, iron, steel, and so on) were to be the first affected by these measures. "To that end, the state levied a progressive wealth tax on all capitalists and landlords in order to use the revenue to compensate the expropriated heavy-industry shareholders" (Bauer, O., 1919: 6). And finally, while socializing the banks "could not be the beginning of the greater socialization project, it would have to be its conclusion and its crowning achievement" (Bauer, O., 1919: 25). But these promises of socialization quickly proved to be no more than hot air and the attempts at socialization that were made in 1919 left hardly a trace in the subsequent history of the labor movement. "In a year and a half, the Socialization Office, led by farmers, had socialized nothing. It was a big business for non-socializing" (KPDÖ 1920: 341).

In return for relinquishing the intensely demanded socialization, Austria's blue-collar and white-collar workers were granted the right to elect works councils. For that reason, the Works Councils Act was issued on 15 May for all German-Austria. That law kept up the appearance that German-Austria was still on "the road to socialism" because, as Otto Bauer put it, any socialization would have to start with "democratizing the workplace constitution".[19] Yet after the Works Councils Act, nothing much else happened.

Works councils in German-Austria were to be elected at least once annually by the entire workforce. All employees at a workplace had active (from 18 years of age) and passive (from 24 years) voting rights. Works councils could be recalled at any time, although only en masse and not as individuals. The works council members, who had a certain degree of protection against unfair dismissal, had monitoring functions (such as payment issues, occupational safety and access to balance sheets), consultation rights (for example, work regulation and workplace social services) and mediation functions (like workplace discipline).

On one hand, the works councils did contribute to effectively improving conditions for workers and office staff on an everyday basis, yet it was also the works councils that made it possible for workers to return to the factories and to accept exploitative conditions once again. The works councils were the strongest weapon in the fight against the "lack of interest in working".[20] So, for example, there was no more piecework after the collapse of the monarchy. With its poor production capacity, the collapsed economy had no basis for piecework pay and workers were strong enough to implement the old union rejection of piecework pay ("piecework is murder") in their everyday operations. When the economy began functioning again in 1920, piecework pay was intensely taken up again, now suddenly imbued with an educational function through the works councils' cooperation. Once the works councils were involved in the calculation, workers could convince themselves of "the appropriateness of the proposed rate" so "the piecework system lost a great deal of its threatening character" (Bauer, O., 1919: 106).

The works councils operated in the tense atmosphere of class struggle. If on one hand they could express the struggle for worker control over production, then capital and social democracy, on the other hand, rapidly tried to make them the new guarantors of industrial tranquility. It is therefore no surprise that, when works councils spontaneously reformed in many places after 1945, often taking over "abandoned German property", both workers and employers' representatives rushed to legally regulate the works councils and render them toothless once again.

The workers' councils of the Austrian Revolution did not arise out of nothing. They were preceded by the shop steward structures of the Social Democratic unions, the complaint and review committees that the increasingly discontented workers were granted during the course of the war and finally, the strike committees that had to be created to implement the strike movements for bread and peace that the unions and the Social Democrats did not participate in. The future might not be very different if workers again had to resort to self-organization. It is therefore quite reasonable to have a look at the contemporary works councils system and the dynamics it might activate. Again and again, individual works councils play a progressive role in contemporary class struggles, but they are only able to do so when they, deliberately or not, return to their own roots, overcome legal regulations, shake off their claims to representation, and attempt to express the working-class' tendency towards self-empowerment as part of a new, self-organized labor movement.

Notes

1. Kaiser Franz Joseph died on 21 November 1916.
2. While the number of workers who went on strike had declined to 7091 in 1915 and increased only minimally to 14,841 in 1916, a total of 163,215 workers struck in 1917.
3. During the strike radicals distributed fliers outside the arsenal calling on the strikers to demand immediate peace negotiations. One passage says, "Learn Russian! Learn from Petersburg!"
4. Friedrich Hexmann was arrested on that same day, 22 January 22. The Viennese police had already started arresting the leaders of the radical left on 21 January. He would meet Baral, who had also been arrested, in Vienna's regional court and from there joined the radicals.
5. "The need for constant contact between the executive leadership and the labor movement and for a body representing the totality of Vienna's

workforce that is directly connected with the individual factories is explicitly emphasized" (*Arbeiter-Zeitung*, 1918a).

6. At a meeting on 19–20 January Renner was the first to suggest that "the representatives be considered permanent" (*Arbeiter-Zeitung*, 1918b). This was aimed at, among other things, "influencing the unorganized" *Arbeiter-Zeitung*, 1918a).

7. Pula is in present-day Croatia, but at the time was part of the Habsburg monarchy.

8. Cattaro is present-day Kotor, Montenegro, but at the time was part of the Habsburg monarchy.

9. A new wave of strikes arose from 17 to 26 June following a reduction in bread rations. At its peak, 48,406 workers took part in that struggle in Vienna.

10. The provisional government consisted of members of the Social Democratic, the Christian Social and the German National parties.

11. Corporal Haller, whose real name was Bernhard Förster, came from Galicia. He was arrested in mid-November 1918 and deported from Lower Austria.

12. In 26 May 1919 the expanded Federation council decided to merge with the KPDÖ.

13. Jonas "Julius" Dickmann, born in Chortkiv, Galicia, was a deaf man who published a few articles in the Social Democratic Workers' Party's theoretical newspaper *Der Kampf* and in the SPD's theoretical paper *Die Neue Zeit*. He was a white-collar worker and an autodidact. On 26 May 1919 he also joined the KPDÖ and published an article in the *Rote Fahne* in the fall of 1919. In 1927 he edited his own newspaper *Die Wende – Neue Marx Studies* and sporadically published articles in *La Critique social*, edited by Boris Souvarine. After the Anschluss in 1938 he was arrested by the Gestapo, deported to the Izbica Ghetto in Poland and died on 15 May 1942.

14. With 69 of 159 seats in Parliament, the Social Democrats were the dominant party.

15. The 3-day strike from 26 to 29 March 1919 by more than 10,000 railroad employees, which brought the country to the brink of absolute chaos, made the feasibility of actually carrying out a strike even in that difficult situation absolutely clear, particularly given that it led to a sympathy strike in Wiener Neustadt for the striking railroad workers and the Hungarian Republic of Councils on 29 March.

16. For example, communist and workers' council member Johann Lumpi, along with a few supporters, wanted to blow up Vienna's Nordbahnbrücke, a rail bridge over the Danube. Their attack failed.

17. Rothziegel died on 22 April in a battle with Romanian forces in Vámospércs.

18. The coalition came to an end on 11 June 1920, which the workers unanimously welcomed. Bauer (1965: 234) wrote that "The workforce received the news of the coalition's collapse with cheers".

19. The workplace constitution regulates the election and work of the enterprise councils.

20. In 1919 Otto Bauer identified a tendency among the workers "to refuse to work for capitalism".

References

Anon (1918) Der Januaraufstand der österreichischen Arbeiterschaft und der Verrat der sozialpatriotischen Führer: 12. Zurich.

Arbeiterwille (1919a) 10 April.

Arbeiterwille (1919b) 13 April.

Arbeiter-Zeitung (1918a) 17 January.

Arbeiter-Zeitung (1918b) 21 January.

Arbeiter-Zeitung (1918a) 27 January.

Arendt, H. (1965) *On Revolution*. New York: Viking Press.

Bauer, H. (1919) Aussprechen, was ist. Zur Gründung der "neuen Linken". *Der Kampf*, 15: 455–6.

Bauer, O. (1919) *Der Weg zum Sozialismus*, Vienna: Verlag der Wiener Volksbuchhandlung.

Bauer, O. (1965) *Die österreichische Revolution*. Vienna: Verlag der Wiener Volksbuchhandlung.

Braunthal, J. (1919) *Die Arbeiterräte in Deutschösterreich*: Vienna: Verlag der Wiener Volksbuchhandlung.

Carsten, F.L. (1973) *Revolution in Mitteleuropa 1918–1919*. Cologne: Kiepenheuer & Witsch.

Deutsch, J. (1947) *Geschichte der österreichischen Arbeiterbewegung*. 3rd expanded edn. Vienna: Verlag der Wiener Volksbuchhandlung.

F.R.S. Internationale (1919) Die F.R.S. "Internationale" und die Wahlen. (Entschließung), *Der Freie Arbeiter*, 2, 3: 21.

Garamvölgyi, J. (1983) *Betriebsräte und sozialer Wandel in Österreich 1919/1920*. Vienna: Verlag für Geschichte und Politik.

Hanisch, E. (1978) *Der kranke Mann an der Donau*. Marx und Engels über Österreich. Vienna, Munich and Zurich: Europa Verlag.

Hautmann, H. (1978) *Die verlorene Räterepublik*. Vienna, Munich and Zurich: Europa Verlag.

Hautmann, H. (1987) *Geschichte der Rätebewegung in Österreich* 1918–1924. Vienna: Europa-Verlag.

Hexmann, F. (n.d.) *Erzählte Geschichte: Arbeiterbewegung* 1918–1934. Available at http://www.doew.at/erinnern/biographien/erzaehlte-geschichte/erste-republik/friedrich-hexmann-linksradikaler-bin-ich-erst-im-gefaengnis-geworden (accessed 20 November 2014).

Jung, E. (1919) Was unterscheidet uns von der kommunistischen Partei? *Der Freie Arbeiter*, 2.

Klenner, F. (1951) *Die österreichischen Gewerkschaften* 1. *Band*. Vienna: Verlag des österreichischen Gewerkschaftsbundes.

Kommunistische Partei Deutsch-Österreichs (KPDÖ) (1920) Thesen für die wirtschaftlichen Forderungen der deutschösterreichischen Arbeiterschaft, *Kommunismus*, 3 April: 341.

Koritschoner, F. (1970) Der Jännerstreik und seine Vorgeschichte. *Theorie und Praxis*, 2–3, 8–13.

Neck, R. (1968) *Arbeiterschaft und Staat im ersten Weltkrieg* 1914–1918 1/2, Vienna: Europa-Verlag.

Rosdolsky, R. (1986) *Die revolutionäre Situation in Österreich im Jahre* 1918 *und die Politik der Sozialdemokratie*. Vienna: No publisher.

Rothe, F. (1920) Die Arbeitsgemeinschaft revolutionärer Sozialdemokraten Deutschösterreichs, *Der Kampf*, 6, 326.

Seitz, K. (1928) Vor zehn Jahren, *Der Kampf*, 21 (11) 518.

Wertheim, J. (2003) *Die Föderation revolutionärer Sozialisten "International"*. Vienna: Arbeitsgruppe Marxismus.

FIVE

Chile: Worker Self-organization and *Cordones Industriales* under the Allende Government (1970–1973)

Franck Gaudichaud, translated by Joe Keady

From the creation of the *mancomúnales* and the resistance societies of the late 19th century to the coup d'état on 11 September 1973, including the emergence of the Central Única de Trabajadores (Workers' United Center) (CUT), the labor movement became one of the central nationwide drivers behind Chile's historical development, particularly through its powerful labor union movement (Barria, 1963; Frías, 1993). The history of the Chilean labor movement, and particularly its union struggles, is also permanently branded by its oscillation between periods of autonomy and subordination to state institutions, the political parties that participate in them and, at various times, partial alliances with or opposition to segments of the ruling classes. Historically, the two major labor parties have been the Partido Comunista (Communist Party) (PC) and the Partido Socialista (Socialist Party) (PS). They have always attempted to guide the socially transformative power that they attribute to the proletariat (above all, the working-class miners and workers in large-scale industry), trying to orient the movement according to their objectives and political struggles (Angell, 1972). In order to analyze the collective actions and attempts at worker control that developed during the era of Unidad Popular (Popular

Unity) (UP), that is to say, under the government of socialist president Salvador Allende (1970–1973), it is necessary to understand the dialectic relationship between the labor movement, the Chilean state, and the political parties as well as the consequences of its articulation in terms of alliances and social contradictions.

1000 days that shook the world

This essay primarily addresses the most crucial period of the class conflict during the UP era. But it is important to briefly note a few elements of the global political context as well as the objectives of Allende's leftist government and his "Chilean way to socialism". What was novel about the Chilean way proposed by the *compañero-presidente* Allende (Amorós, 2008) was its reassertion of the importance of respecting the then-current institutions, universal suffrage and the 1925 Constitution and its affirmation that a transition to socialism was possible without destroying the bourgeois state, neither through armed confrontation nor popular insurrection. That transition was seen as a gradual political-institutional path towards transforming the relations of production based on a mobilization of the majority of the people and the unity of the left, but without interrupting the current legal order: the parliament's prerogatives and the private property of the "non-monopolistic" economic sectors' would be respected, and the military would be seen as constitutionalist (respectful of the constitution and of representative democracy) and respectful of lawful activity. In that way, the reformist project could be seen as a prolongation of Chile's Popular Front of the 1930s and 1940s in another context and with a more radical impulse. When Allende won the 1970 presidential election, an entire left-wing coalition gained access to executive power, particularly the Communist and Socialist parties (the latter of which the president was a member), which is to say two political entities with solid working-class roots and a long-term view combining participation in the popular movement and in parliamentary life. With only 36.6 percent of the votes, Allende had defeated the right-wing (Allessandri, 34.9 percent) and Christian Democratic (Tomic, 27.9 percent) candidates in a one-round direct election. From the beginning of the transformation process, the supporters of the leftist government had a congressional minority. They were forced to sign a statute of constitutional guarantees with the center-right (Democracia Cristiana, or Christian Democrats) (DC) and had only very limited control over other powers (judicial, military, media, economic, and so on.).

The UP's objective was to facilitate national industrial development, modernize the rural regions, drive the redistribution of wealth, and make Chile independent of US imperialism. The Allende government immediately began nationalizing the main natural resources (starting with the world's foremost reserves of copper, which were in the hands of "yankee" businesses[1]) and 91 large monopolies (most of which were controlled by foreign capital) while implementing agrarian reforms, thus stirring up tremendous popular enthusiasm. The plan likewise provided for various social measures on an unprecedented scale aimed at extensively democratizing the country's socioeconomic structure (Programa de la Unidad Popular, 1969). What the left called "the new economy" based on the construction of an Área de Propiedad Social (social property area) (APS) was to be created by nationalizing the mining sector, the banks and several industrial monopolies. According to this idea, the APS was to be converted into a strategic sector of the economy and initiate an interesting system of worker participation. But in spite of its initial accomplishments and in the face of resistance from the ruling class, the APS gave work at first to only a limited sector of wage laborers (approximately 10 percent of the industrial working class, for example). Nonetheless, the vertiginous rise in workers struggles during that period shook the whole of Chilean society. The UP era is without a doubt the period when a new moment of struggle from below appeared, putting pressure on Chile's institutions: both the parties and the apparatus of the large CUT, the country's only national labor union confederation and an essential tool for constructing class in the 20th century.[2]

In doing so, the labor movement wove together contradictory political tendencies that clashed with one another (particularly among the communist, socialist and DC leadership).

The ninth national CUT conference in February 1971 was, above all, an occasion to reiterate the support of the center (led by communists and socialists) for the government's nationalization policy and the call for a working-class mobilization around the "battle over production", a slogan used primarily by the PC and Allende. Likewise, the question of worker participation in managing companies in the APS was also discussed extensively. The conference's conclusions led to the writing of the "basic standards of participation", composed jointly by the CUT and the government. Although that participation initially only included a minority of wage earners, it was undoubtedly adapted to worker mobilization and social transformation elements that were to unleash a powerful process from below. The testimonies allow us to analyze the social geography of each company and to understand the concrete landscape of the social dynamics. They also confirm the effectiveness of worker participation and control in a number of factories. Juan Alarcón, a syndicalist communist who worked at the SUMAR-Algodón textile factory, where the union membership exceeded 1500 people, emphasized the achievements of that era:

> We formed a company administration committee made up of workers, of technicians and professionals, that allowed everyone who was able to help make the company work to be included. The workers who participated were chosen because they knew the production system and they also knew the gaps in production . . . which is to say that it was a big responsibility that we always took extremely seriously. There were also the security committees to watch after the company, the production committee, departmental delegates, etc. (Gaudichaud, 2004: 95–6)

These stories show a real workers' epic, a participatory battle for control over production and command of the company. This is the heart of a true "popular festival" of members and wage laborers who were putting their dreams of social revolution and joy into practice. On a local level, these day-to-day struggles were simultaneously a product and a consequence of the worldwide class conflict. Political power relations within a company or the degree of worker radicalization or awareness in a number of workplaces led to a real clash between the traditional leadership and the will of the rank and file to go further in the process of economic and political democratization. According to researchers Juan Espinoza and Andrew Zimbalist, the highest degree of participation was driven by the most radical members, the ones who were called the *polo rupturista* (rupturist pole),[3] meaning the left-wing of the PS or the Movimiento de Acción Popular Unitaria (Popular Unitary Action Movement) (MAPU), the Izquierda Cristiana (Christian Left) (IC),[4] as well as the members of the Movimiento de Izquierda Revolucionaria (Revolutionary Left Movement) (MIR), an extra-parliamentary party that was critical of what it perceived as Allende's reformism. They were the same members who would later defend the idea of popular power and call for an expansion of the nationalized sector, occupying factories and forcing the government to intervene by naming a public administrator. By mid-1973, more than 200 companies had been nationalized or had experienced interventions by the government, often after a seizure or strike, which is to say many more than the 91 companies that the UP had initially anticipated. That dynamic can be seen in a textile company like Yarur, studied closely by the historian Peter Winn when its 2000 workers took over the mill on 25 April 1971 amid cries of "Nationalization!" which they achieved, beginning a new story:

> The seizure and socialization of the Yarur mill marked the end of one historical era for its workers and the beginning of another. The change was symbolized by the banner, hung over the entrance, made of factory cloth dyed in the national colors and bearing the proud message – "Ex-Yarur: Territory

Free of Exploitation". It signified the end of capitalism in one of its most repressive redoubts and signaled the start of a transition toward socialism at the Yarur mill. (Winn, 1986: 209)

Yarur would become a pioneering company, the first to initiate a worker co-management system under the control of its general assembly. As Winn shows, Yarur's workers adapted the CUT government's co-management system in order to implement a mode of operation that was even more democratic and participatory. Within 17 months they managed to show the concrete possibility of socialism: from the plant's "production committees" to the administrative council, the workers' assemblies were able to intervene and make decisions. Half the management (apart from the union leaders and government representatives) was elected by an annual vote in an assembly. That is how Emilio Hernández, a worker and leader of the resistance against the demands of the former owners, the Yarur family, was elected to the company's administrative council. A coordinating committee made up of delegates from each production committee, board members, and union leaders organized an open forum every 15 days and acted as a link between the rank and file and the management. The workers' transformation into administrators of their means of production was a moment of collective and individual transformation, apprenticeship, education and a great deal of debate as well as difficulties, mistakes and conflicts. Yarur would become an example for many people, including the socialist minister Pedro Vuskovic, who understood the tremendous potential behind the textile workers' praxis.

Nonetheless, as class conflict intensified, the popular government found itself increasingly trapped within an institutional framework, losing all the effectiveness of its own plans in addition to the priorities it had set for its activities, namely structural reforms driven from below, due to consideration for the liberal constitution of 1925 (and the military). As historian Mario Garcés notes:

> The people were counting on the government as an ally in their struggles, but the government was very quickly hemmed in by traditional powers, external as well as internal, so the popular movement found itself stuck with the dilemma of following the government's rhythms and pacing (that is to say, perpetually blocked institutional change and political negotiations that were increasingly difficult to settle) or having confidence and accelerating its autonomy trainings in order to strengthen and expand its positions of power within society. (Garcés, 2003)

In response to the violent offensive by the elites and the owners of the means of production, the Nixon administration's destabilization operations and the Allende government's increasing difficulties (being fiercely attacked from both inside and outside the country), the organized sectors of the labor movement sought out new forms of collective self-organization. In that way, the Chilean Red October was a genuine trial by fire.

The Chilean Red October: worker self-organization and popular constituent power

The large-scale lockout in October 1972 was a key moment in the history of UP and the Chilean way. During the first period of the new government, the ruling classes attempted to make the most of the UP's short-term economic program in financial and political terms (by using the black market, speculation, sabotage and the increase in production costs). After implementing that policy, the offensive against the UP shifted to a higher level: social confrontation and a widespread economic boycott. This opposition movement that October resulted in a corporatist conflict with truck owners, gradually uniting the employers' associations (particularly the Sociedad de Fomento Fabril (Association for Industrial Promotion) and the Confederación de la Producción y del Comercio (Confederation for Production and Commerce), independent professionals (such as lawyers, doctors, engineers and architects), and right-wing political parties under the banner of the Confederación de la Democracia (Democratic Confederation). It was a show of force on a national scale that relied on the active support of the US government (Church Report, 1975) and developed in a context of increasing terrorist actions by extreme right-wing organizations, such as Patria y Libertad (Fatherland and Liberty), and opposition parliamentary pressure to remove provincial ministers and governors from office (Samaniego, 1996). In order to remain within the bounds of the law and uphold its theory of the constitutionality of the armed forces, the government issued an appeal to the military to control the situation and declared a state of emergency. The CUT likewise called on workers to be vigilant and to participate in voluntary provisioning work, initiating collaboration with the drivers who were not on strike. The response to the employers primarily came from the rank and file, however. Carmen Silva, then a member of the Socialist Party, emotionally recalled the strength of popular self-organization in Santiago's *cordones industriales*, saying:

> It was wonderful – almost all of the factories in Santiago were operating without owners! The workers started up the most sophisticated things, designing shoes . . . and in the end we sold those things on the market. Personally, I organized mobilization, making a list of trucks by industry to deliver products, seeing how many workers were in the factories, going to look for them . . . And all of this lasted for over a month. (Gaudichaud, 2004: 343)

One of the most innovative acts of that working-class response was therefore the creation of unitary organizations that crossed previously existing divisions, operating across a territorial base and allowing different unions to work together in a particular industrial sector. Depending on the size of the social factions joining together, the extent of their actual power and the orientation provided by the present members, these organizations called themselves *cordones industriales* (industrial belts), *commandos comunales* (community commando units) or *comités coordinadores* (coordinating committees). In the industrial sector, these horizontally organized groups would respond to the lockout en masse with a series of factory occupations in accordance with the workers' mobilization in the main companies in the APS. Thus, the workers in that sector managed to continue production (albeit incompletely), running the factories without their owners, usually with the help of few managers and on completely new foundations, including questioning the division of labor, the factory hierarchy and the legitimacy of the managers' leadership:

> "We began commandeering buses with handguns, with pistols", recalls Mario Olivares, a worker member of the MIR, "and we drove them into the factories in the workers' hands". That way we guaranteed that production wouldn't be interrupted. We also looked for the workers and transported them. . . . We started talking about real workers' power. . . . We may not have had the clearest ideology, but we were demanding more participation everywhere, not just in production!" (Gaudichaud, 2004: 179)

Above all, that crucial moment for the UP showed both what the workers' and people's movements could do and the deep decentralization of political activity as well as openly raising the question of the relations of production again. There was therefore a clear tendency to break with the traditional ways of thinking about doing politics: the term "popular power", on the demand of a segment of the Chilean left, was transformed into a transitional reality. We can say that a participatory power was born, arising from the rank and file, what we call popular constituent power, fed by a segment of the organized workers who temporarily took part of their society's management into their own hands. This phenomenon is not exclusive to the Chilean experience. On the contrary, it is one of the universal characteristics of any process of worker control, be it latent or widespread (Zavaleta Mercado, 1974).

What was specific to Chile, however, is that this experience, which was not anticipated by the political parties, did not happen in opposition to the government but in order to defend it. On a subjective and ideological plane, most of the labor movement still regarded the executive headed by Salvador Allende as the incarnation of "their" government and a possible project of social transformation. These forms of worker solidarity already existed prior to the month of October, but that was when it became possible to say that *cordones industriales* in themselves, existing as an objective reality of the urban landscape on the periphery of the major Chilean cities (essentially Santiago and Concepción), appeared as *cordones industriales* for themselves, which is to say as a form of class organization that is conscious of that fact and of its power to mobilize horizontally and coordinate within a specific territory (Thompson, 1968).The most important precedent was the creation of the Cordón Cerrillos Maipú (Cordero *et al.*, 1973). It is undeniable that the initiative behind the *cordones* was not spontaneous but rather the result of an accumulation of experiences in struggle and day-to-day events, what English historian E.P. Thompson (1968) calls "class experience". And in a municipality like Maipú, that accumulated experience is central.

The Cordón Cerrillos had been established in June 1972 following a series of industrial strikes in which workers, particularly metalworkers, demanded their right to be part of the state sector. For that purpose, they did not hesitate to occupy the Ministry of Labor, headed at that time by the militant communist and former CUT leader Mireya Baltra. One week later, the workers in some 30 companies were coordinating their movement through the Workers' Struggle Coordinating Commando Unit of the Cordón Cerrillos-Maipú. Subsequently, the roads into the town were regularly blocked in order to pressure the government, which was trying to ingratiate itself with the DC once again by setting limits to the nationalized sector. It is no surprise that the town of Maipú was the first to recognize these forms of direct democracy. In the first place, this is because it lies in an area with one of the highest concentrations of industry in Chile, dominated by mid-sized but dynamic factories such as Fensa and Perlack, which were left at the margins of the UP's project. Secondly, the workers' demands progressively aligned with the significant *campesino* land-occupation movement in Maipú as well as in the neighboring towns of Barrancas and Melipilla. Finally, we likewise see that the residents of Maipú were also mobilized during that period, albeit more timidly than in other parts of the capital, particularly regarding transportation and public health problems.

The *comités coordinadores*, *cordones industriales* and *commandos comunales* proliferated throughout the country as a result of the Chilean Red October. The first were in Santiago (for example the Cordón Vicuña Mackenna, Cordon O'Higgins or the Comandos Comunales Estación Central and Renca), but they also arose in the region around Concepción, the port of Valparaiso, the electronics industry in Arica, and in the city of Punta Arenas in the extreme south of the country. According to our research, there were slightly more than 50 coordinating committees throughout the country in October 1972 (including 20 in the capital). It is estimated that the various coordinating committees of popular power represented between 60–80,000 mobilized people nationwide in 1973.[5]

As attested by Luis Ahumada, a socialist activist from Santiago, the role that non-working-class members played is important here:

> I think that the most important thing that we promoted through the Cordón Vicuña Mackenna was achieving wall-to-wall solidarity. It was something that, although it's true that that it is inherent among workers, we contributed to making that solidarity manifest in concrete terms. (Gaudichaud, 2004: 307)

The *cordones industriales* were created based on the territorial coordination of several dozen factories (which were often seized) and most of them assembled union delegates from mid-sized companies along with some representatives from large companies in the APS. From the evidence that we have been able to gather, a review of the newspapers and the debates from that period, the achievement of this "total" democratization of the *cordones* was not a result of the desire to be structured from the bottom up through the systematic election of delegates in assemblies and the rejection of appointees from the party leadership, although delegates from the *cordones* were in fact elected in several factories in worker assemblies. It was essentially the work of the union leaders and PS and MIR members who participated and passed down information to their factories, where the communist and DC union leaders were often rejected. Javier Bertin, then an MIR member in Cerrillos, recalls that real experiences of worker control were scarce and that the *cordón* was essentially a way of coordinating mobilization:

> The cordón was officially set up by union leaders. Anyone who wanted to be a member of the cordón was a member of the cordón in his own right and there was an executive committee that called meetings and coordinated and its president was Ortega and there were other comrades including Santos Romero. But the cordón did not have a regular function in the sense of periodic meetings or planning work. Instead, the cordón would react to what had already happened. So there was a conflict. Some of the comrades would talk about a conflict, so that is where the cordón was activated: a meeting would be called, where would be an assembly of leaders, and a mobilization would be decided on. Essentially the cordón would meet to decide on mobilizations and union leaders and political party representatives would participate in it. (Gaudichaud, 2004: 365)

So only a fraction of the worker members – albeit a fraction that was quite significant in terms of its activism – would participate in the assemblies. It is still very difficult today to know the exact degree to which the *cordones* functioned organically, together with their numbers, and the extent to which they actually represented the workers in the areas they developed. According to our calculations, a *cordón* like Cerrillos never had the capacity to directly convene more than 8000 workers, when it was imagined that it coordinated more than 30 companies and tens of thousands of workers. In terms of worker participation and the democratization of the relations of production, our field research has shown that it was the factories that were occupied by their workers and integrated into *cordones* that were best able to establish forms of actual worker democracy. They knew how to encourage and deepen the system of participation that the UP had proposed, go beyond the traditional union framework, expand the security squads and factory defense, and establish provisioning systems with the local councils in the surrounding town. This relationship between the labor and *poblador*[6] movements was also vital. The development organizations of industrial worker power based on autonomous foundations correlated with the creation of a popular alliance in the slums, particularly around the subject of provisioning. The ruling classes openly used poverty to destabilize the UP's economic policies. One of the methods for confronting the black market was the creation of juntas de abastecimiento y de control de precios (supply and price control committees) (JAP) by the government's Dirección de Industria y Comercio (Office of Industry and Commerce). They tried to involve the slum residents and small merchants as participants to reveal the black market's illegal practices. Some local experiences of collective self-organization against the black market through the JAPs produced substantial results. During moments when the crisis was at its worst, the companies in the APS and the *cordones* delivered their products directly to the JAP, organizing fairs where they could sell them directly and, they even organized parallel forms of "popular" provisioning outside the official channels with the aid of *poblador* organizations and the support of nearly autonomous neighborhoods like Nueva La Habana (controlled by the MIR) (see Cofré Schmeisser, 2007).

All these struggles from below can be viewed today thanks to the magnificent documentary trilogy by Patricio Guzmán (1972) on *La Batalla de Chile* (The Battle of Chile).

The social mobilization that October revealed the UP's weakness against such challenges, but it also revealed the fragility of the actions undertaken by organizations as important as the CUT at that moment. The official reaction from its main office came late, voting in particular for a resolution to reinforce unity and create coordinating committees. That call went out on 21 October, after unity and those committees already existed among the rank and file. While it is undeniable that the initiative behind the *cordones* was not spontaneous but rather the result of an accumulation of praxis and hard work by members and unions, in October 1972 a segment of the labor movement regained an autonomy that it had partly lost and far surpassed the political will of the parties. In practice, the government's calls for a battle over production meant more factory occupations and operating them under worker control. José Moya, a worker for the Industria de Radio y Televisión company and MIR member, recalls that

> It was a very rich period when a lot of people who sympathized with the UP were rebelling against it and joining in organizing the cordones. The UP did not look favorably on the organizing the cordones. I can remember assemblies where people from the CUT came to discuss things with the *cordones* and in the end had to leave with their tail between their legs. (Gaudichaud, 2004: 125)

In other words, if this movement was always mobilized in the name of defending the government, it also set its own conditions: the unification of workers across different branches of production, the unification of segments of the CUT with unaffiliated areas of light industry, the unification of economic demands at the heart of a more radical political project than merely the defense of the government. This was confirmed when the *comandos comunales* and the *cordones industriales* presented a list of the people's demands: the *Pliego del Pueblo* or the People's List. That document re-presented numerous demands (in education, health, supplies, production, and so on) and showed the direct ideological influence of the MIR members. In particular, it proposed

> That all industries should produce for the people and under the people's control, the establishment of worker control in the industries in the private sector, and that the ones that have been occupied during the strike should be transferred to the Área Social. Finally, the Pliego del Pueblo called for the construction of popular power and of an assembly of the people Santiago, October 1972. (Comandos Comunales y Cordones Industriales de Santiago, cited in Farias, 2001: 3272)

This overflowing dynamic is what researchers like Peter Winn or Miguel Silva call revolution from below. This potential orientation on the part of the *cordones industriales* clearly shows that they raised a whole series of crucial problems that still remained for the left over the process of transitioning to socialism, particularly the question of popular power and the role of the parliamentary state during that process. There were also lengthy discussions about relations between the government, the CUT and the *cordones industriales*. Above all, it must be noted that there were many organic links between the two latter organizations, given that most of the unions that participated in the meetings of the *cordones* were also CUT member organizations.

The *cordones industriales* and the fate of the left

Initially, the PC looked on the *cordones industriales* and the new organs of popular power with open hostility. Luís Corvalán, Secretary-General of the party, harshly condemned the *cordones industriales* in several declarations. They were presented as organisms that existed solely in the "agitated mind" of the leadership on the far left of the MIR (despite that organization's greatly reduced clout in industry) (Corvalán,1978: 160–8). The PC maintained a mistrustful posture towards those movements until the coup d'état and tried to integrate these new expressions of popular power under the control of the CUT, where the PC was the primary political force. The party was afraid that parallel organizations would develop that would weaken the CUT (Escorza and Zeran, 1973). Salvador Allende publicly supported this position several times. The PC even tried to directly organize parallel *cordones* that were linked to the CUT, based in the factory Textil Progreso del Cordón Vicuña Mackenna, an initiative that was amply denounced as a divisionist maneuver by the leadership of the Cordón Vicuña Mackenna (1973). According to Guillermo Rodríguez, an MIR member at the heart of the Cordón Cerrillos:

> It is worth emphasizing that during the final weeks before the coup, people in the PC began taking up more radicalized positions, particularly among the young Communists and the people who edited *Puro Chile*, the newspaper that started to raise the issue of popular power from that perspective. (Gaudichaud, 2005: 99)

On the contrary, however, Neftali Zuñiga, worker, PC union leader and manager ("supervisor") at the large nationalized textile company Pollak, emphasized the irresponsibility of many of the *cordones'* leaders and the "vice of absenteeism" that they contributed to with their repeated street mobilizations. According to him:

> If the leaders of these *cordones industriales* had had more of a vision, they would have had to take the role that they had achieved seriously enough to demand their production sheet from the companies in the Área Social. . . .

> What did the *cordones* do? They went to the factory to say, "Comrades, we have to march to keep up the pressure because we want to fight" . . . But leading the people into the street for parades was not defending the companies because they stopped the machines! (Gaudichaud, 2004: 292)

Some of the socialist and MAPU members also shared this opinion, in opposition to the cry "Crear, crear, poder popular" (Creating, creating, popular power) that emanated from the streets of the country, a slogan that they considered empty and problematic for the development of the Chilean path to socialism (see testimony of Fernando Quiroga of the PS in Gaudichaud, 2004: 357). Clearly the emergence of the *cordones* and their calls for factory seizures, control over production or the construction of barricades in order to force the expansion of the nationalized sector was openly opposed to the tactics of the PC, the main force in the government. As a result of the agreements that the UP adopted in 1972 at meetings in Lo Curro and Arrayán, Allende and the PC defended the idea of temporarily stopping the process in order to "consolidate" the reforms. Without a congressional majority, Allende tried to maintain common ground with the DC so that he could govern and isolate the most radical right-wing factions. The guarantees that the DC demanded were clear: ownership of the means of production had to be respected and the occupied factories had to be returned. But that congressional project heightened tensions between the government and the *cordones*, which showed their disagreement with a large mobilization. According to them, the PC and the "reformist segments" of the UP were acting against the "revolutionary process" (*Tarea Urgente*, 1973). This marks the return of the fratricidal opposition between the two poles of the left: the "rupturists" around the MIR, part of the PS, and pro-socialist Christians, versus the "gradualists" around the PC, part of the PS and Allende. This growing division manifested itself in two reductive slogans: "Consolidating to Advance" versus "Advancing without Compromising". Above all, the most influential members at the heart of the *cordones* were in fact from the left-wing of the PS, MAPU and MIR.

Nonetheless, the *cordones industriales*' provincial coordinating committee, which was established in 1973, always recognized the CUT as the highest workers' organization at the national level. At the same time, it also claimed the "autonomy necessary to fulfill its role as leader of the various allied social sectors of the proletariat in the struggle for socialism" (*Tarea Urgente*, 1973b). This declaration encapsulates the position of the socialist members of the left-wing of the party (such as the leftist Christians, for example). They were the ones who retained the greatest union influence on the leadership of the *cordones*. In 1973 the presidents of all of the *cordones* in Santiago were socialists.[7] The party's great flexibility (it was the party that made the most political progress among the working class during the UP era) explains its openness to pressure from the most radical industrial rank and file (Sarget, 1994). Some syndicalist socialist defended the idea of the *cordones*' autonomy with respect to the CUT and the government. Those factions, such as the MIR, also criticized the military's growing involvement in the government and the calls to return the occupied factories. A few weeks before the coup, Armando Cruces, president of the *Cordón* Vicuña Mackenna, stated:

> Comrade Allende, president of the republic, reformist, member from my party, gives in to the enemy all the time. He flip-flops a lot. Moreover, the PC has shown that it was completely in favor of "social peace" in Chile and it pulled that same president of the republic along with it. (Cruces, 1973)

Nonetheless, the PS leadership in the *cordones* often adopted an ambiguous stance towards the CUT and the government; a stance that was taken by its Secretary-General Carlos Altamirano Orrego. So, in some cases, it was the same syndicalist socialists from the

CUT who were calling for the creation of *cordones industriales* in the provinces (Valparaiso, for example) and, barely a month before the coup, Hernán Ortega repeated his proposal to integrate the CUT into the leadership of the *cordones*, recognizing that "to the extent that the CUT can accept a new structure and set itself toward new tasks, our coordination will no longer have any reason to exist (*La Aurora de Chile*, 1973).Without a doubt, this controversy on the left regarding the role of the CUT and the *cordones* shows the difficulty in finding a space for the forms of self-organization and popular constituent power proposed by UP within the project of statist and institutional transition. In February 1973, major union leader, CUT founder and Christian revolutionary Clotario Blest issued a warning criticizing the union movement for being too dependent on government leadership and the heads of left-wing parties (*El Pueblo*, 1973).

In January 1973 the government was able to reclaim control over the situation by creating a civic-military cabinet. Despite protests from the *cordones* against the government, their leadership stayed in the hands of UP activists who limited themselves to expressing doubts about the direction that Allende had taken. The Tanquetazo, a military uprising led by Lt Colonel Roberto Souper, took place on 29 June 1973. It was, in a way, an abortive trial coup. As in October, resistance from the *cordones industriales* was essential to the counteroffensive. The CUT issued a call to them that day and in fact sent delegates to each one (Ortega, 1973).

It was also in June 1973 when the PC officially recognized the *cordones* and called on its members to integrate in them. The communists' proposal was still that the *cordones* should become part of and be directed by the CUT while recognizing their right to preserve their own structure. That will to harness the *cordones* and popular power had previously been reflected in October when the PS and the PC invited the *comandos comunales* to place themselves under the authority of the *intendentes*, or regional governors.

Towards the coup: "the workers were demanding weapons"

> Before we were afraid that the process of moving towards socialism was being compromised by a centrist, reformist, bourgeois democratic government that tended to demobilize the masses or lead them to take anarchic insurrectionary actions out of an instinct for self-preservation. But now, looking at the most recent events, we are no longer afraid of that. Now we sure to be on a path that will inevitably lead us to fascism.

That is how the Santiago regional coordinating committee of the *cordones industriales* addressed the Chilean Head of State, President Salvador Allende, on 5 September 1973. It is from a letter that was published 6 days before the coup d'état that ended an extremely important experiment in the history of the international workers' movement. The letter ends as follows:

> Be advised, comrade, that with all of the respect and confidence that we still feel for you, if you do not carry out the program of the Unidad Popular, if you do not trust the masses, you will lose the only real support that you have as a person and as a governor and you will be responsible for leading the country not toward a civil war, which is already well under way, but toward the cold, planned massacre of the most conscious and organized working class in Latin America. (Coordinadora Provincial de Cordones Industriales de Santiago: 1973)

Finally, despite their numerous achievements in terms of participation, the control of production in some factories, partial self-management of supplies and defense of the factories, the *cordones industriales* remained at an embryonic stage. It is true that the powerful and often contradictory relationship between the Allende government and the more organized factions of the labor movement allowed the process to move forward and the Área Social to expand. But the strategic orientation on most of the left and the government's difficulties with an enraged opposition, both internally and externally, explain why the members of the UP and the CUT attempted to maintain control "from above" (as in Peter Winn's expression; "revolution from above" or Miguel Silva's "reforms from above") over this rash of constituent self-organization. The *cordones* were never large permanent assemblies of company delegates or actual Chilean-style soviets, as some historical accounts of the UP would have it. In the end they were, above all, a coordinating committee of revolutionary union leaders who were able to mobilize a significant number of the workers in an area and, with highly regional enrollment, make them participants in a crisis situation. Under those circumstances, the *cordones industriales* did not have the political-military capacity to resist a coup d'état and link their resistance with that of soldiers who supported the process. With the Arms Control Law passed by the congress, the military began its repression of the *cordones* from the start of 1973: the increase in the number of raids had allowed them to assess their strength. On 11 September only a few groups of trained militants were able to confront the coup while most of the working class lacked weapons and, above all, a political alternative (*Garcés,* and Leiva, 2005). Based on the categories established by political scientist Charles Tilly, we can say that this exceptional socio-political process led to a revolutionary situation characterized by various forms of self-organization and popular constituent power, but not to a revolutionary outcome (Tilly, 1978). "The workers were demanding weapons", recalls the communist former labor secretary Mireya Baltra, who was on her way to the Cordón Vicuña Mackenna on the day of the coup. Echoing this, José Moya describes waiting in his factory:

> We spent the whole night of September 11, 1973 waiting for weapons that never came. We heard shots from the side of the San Joaquín cordón. They had weapons there – at least at the Sumar textile company. Our dream was that at any moment,

weapons would arrive and we would do the same thing they were doing. But nothing ever happened. (Gaudichaud, 2003: 18)

Contrary to General Augusto Pinochet's propaganda, there was never an army of "cordones of death". In fact, apart from a few isolated acts of resistance (in the Cordón Cerrillos, for example), "popular power" quickly submitted under the relentless boots of repression.

The day of the coup there were dead bodies in the street. "They even brought them from other places and shot them there", says Carlos Mújica, MAPU worker from the Alusa metalworking plant:

And there was nothing we could do about it! I think that was the hardest thing about the period from 1973–74. Later, in 1975, the secret service came looking for me at Alusa. They arrested me and brought me to the famous Villa Grimaldi. That's where people went to the grill, meaning an iron bed where they would apply an electric current to your legs. . . . They knew that I was a sector delegate. (Gaudichaud, 2004: 149)

So the dictatorship defeated popular power at the same time that it brought down Salvador Allende's government. Forty years later, that collective memory remains: under Chile's current neoliberal consensus, a new generation is starting to vindicate the memory of the popular struggles of the 1970s.

Notes

1. The US-controlled copper mines were nationalized following a unanimous vote by the Chilean congress. It was the Chilean government's first act of sovereignty in the face of imperialism – as well as the first step toward a secret plan by the Nixon administration and the CIA to intervene against Allende (Church Report, 1975).
2. In 1970 the CUT brought together upwards of 700,000 workers and 4500 labor unions. Among them, 47 percent were part of the mining and

industrial working class, 40 percent were white-collar workers and 23 percent were rural workers. In total, 29 percent of all waged workers in the private sector were unionized in April 1971 (over a total membership of 38 percent).

3. Most historians of the UP distinguish between a gradualist pole around Allende and the PC and a rupturist pole.

4. The MAPU and the IC were two factions that rebelled from the DC and were integrated into the Allende government.

5. The newspaper *Chile Hoy* (1972) placed the number of *comités coordinadores* that were created nationwide during the month of October 1972 at 100). More reliable internal MIR documents, however, indicate there were 52 coordinating committees.

6. In Chile the term *poblador* refers to the urban poor or working-class urban areas and their organizations.

7. That influence becomes clear when we consider that the presidents of the *cordones* who signed the Declaration of the Coordinadora provincial de Cordones de Santiago were all PS members.

Acknowledgements

This article is based on doctoral research in political science, and was presented in 2005 with the help of advisor Michael Löwy at Paris 8 University, and was published as a book in 2013 as *Chili 1970– 1973. Mille juiors qui changèrent le monde* by Presses Universitaires de Rennes, France. This essay re-addresses part of chapter four of the anthology Pinto Vallejos, J. (ed.) 2005, *Cuando hicimos historia. La experiencia de la Unidad Popular*, Santiago, LOM, pp. 81–105 and the introduction to Gaudichaud, (2004) *Poder popular y cordones industriales: Testimonios sobre el movimiento social urbano chileno (1970–1973)*, Santiago, LOM.

References

Amorós, M. (2008) *Compañero Presidente. Salvador Allende, una vida por la democracia y el socialismo*. Valencia: PUV.

Angell, A. (1972) *Politics and the Chilean Labor Movement*, Oxford: Oxford University Press.

Barria, J. (1963) *Trayectoria y estructura del movimiento sindical chileno*. Santiago: INSORA.

Church Report (1975) *Covert Action in Chile* 1963–1973. Washington: United States Department of State. Available at https://www.fas.org/irp/ops/policy/church-chile.htm (accessed 20 November 2013).

Coordinadora Provincial de Cordones Industriales de Santiago 1973[2004]) *Carta de la coordinadora Provincial de Cordones Industriales de Santiago* (Letter from the Santiago Regional Coordinating Committee of the *Cordones Industriales*) to President Salvador Allende, September 5, in Gaudichaud (2004) *Poder Popular y Cordones industriales. Testimonios sobre la dinámica del movimiento popular urbano durante el gobierno de Salvador Allende.* Santiago.

Cofré Schmeisser, B. (2007) Historia de los pobladores del campamento *Nueva La Habana*, 1970–1973, Universidad ARCIS. Available at https://www.archivochile.com/tesis/01_ths/01ths0004.pdf (accessed 20 November 2013).

Cordero, C., Sader, E. and Threlfall, M. (1973) *Consejo comunal de trabajadores y Cordón Cerrillos-Maipú: 1972. Balance y perspectivas de un embrión de poder popular.* Working document no 67. Santiago: CIDU.

Cordón Vicuña Mackenna (1973) Alerta trabajadores: a parar las maniobras divisionistas. *El Cordonazo*, 3, 12. Santiago.

Corvalán, L. (1978) *Chile: 1970–1973*, Sofía: Sofía Press.

Cruces A. (1973) Habla la revolución chilena: ¡en Chile no debe quedar ningún explotador! *Avanzada Socialista*, 72: 2–3.

El Pueblo (1973) Entrevista a C. Blest. *El Pueblo*, 28, February. Santiago.

Escorza, G. and Zeran, F. (1973) Los comunistas y los Cordones. *Chile Hoy*, 61, 16 August. Santiago.

Farias, V. (2000–2001) *La izquierda chilena (1969–1973): documentos para el estudio de su línea estratégica.* Six vols. Berlin: CEP.

Frías, P. (1993) *Construcción del sindicalismo chileno como actor nacional.* Santiago: CUT-PET.

Garcés, M. (2003) El movimiento popular, la Unidad Popular y el golpe. *Punto Final*, 552, September. Available at https://www.puntofinal.cl/552/movimiento.htm (accessed 20 November 2014).

Garcés, M. and Leiva, S. (2005) *El golpe en la Legua. Los caminos de la historia y la memoria.* Santiago: LOM.

Gaudichaud, F. (2003) L'Unité populaire par ceux qui l'ont faite. *Le Monde Diplomatique.* Paris. 18–19 September.

Gaudichaud, F. (2004) *Poder Popular y Cordones industriales. Testimonios sobre la dinámica del movimiento popular urbano durante el gobierno de Salvador Allende.* Santiago: LOM.

Gaudichaud, F. (2005) Construyendo poder popular? El movimiento sindical chileno en el periodo de la Unidad Popular. In Pinto, J. (ed.) *Y hicimos historia. La historia de la Unidad Popular.* Santiago: LOM, 2005, pp. 81–106.

Guzmán, P. (1973–1975) The Battle of Chile. (*La Batalla de Chile* (I – II – III). Chile/Cuba/Venezuela Available at http://www. patricioguzman.com/index.php?page=films_dett&fid=1 (accessed 20 November 2014).

La Aurora de Chile (1973) A propósito de los Cordones y la CUT. 33, 26 July. Santiago.

Ortega, H. (1973) Interview. *Chile Hoy*, 59, 27 July. Santiago.

Samaniego, A. (1996) *Octubre 1972: triunfo y derrota de la unidad de los trabajadores*, Investigación DICYT-USACH. Mimeo: Santiago.

Sarget, M.N. (1994) *Système politique et Parti socialiste au Chili: un essai d'analyse systémique.* Paris: L'Harmattan.

Tarea Urgente (1973) Declaration by the Coordinadora provincial de Cordones de Santiago (Provincial Coordinating Committee of the Cordones of Santiago. 10, 27 July. Santiago.

Thompson, E.P. (1968) *The Making of the English Working Class.* Harmondsworth: Penguin,

Tilly, C. (1978) *From Mobilization to Revolution.* Reading: Addison-Wesley.

Winn, P. (1986) *Weavers of Revolution: The Yarur Workers and Chile's Road to Socialism.* New York: Oxford University Press.

Unidad Popular (1969) Programa de la Unidad Popular (1969) 17 December Santiago. Available at www.abacq.net/imagineria/frame5. htm (accessed 20 Novenber 2014).

Zavaleta Mercado, R. (1974) *El poder dual en América Latina.* México: Siglo 21 Editores, col. Mínima.

SIX

"Production Control" or "Factory Soviet"? Workers' Control in Japan

Kimiyasu Irie

Introduction

The revolutionary labor movement in Japan had almost vanished in the middle of 1930s. The Japanese Communist Party (JCP) had been outlawed by in the prewar period and was thoroughly destroyed by police repression. In March 1928 and April 1929 the police led two major crackdowns against leftist and workers' organizations. It targeted mainly the JCP by mass arrests of its main members, who were usually violently tortured. Party members had to work underground. The Japan Council of Labor Unions was one public organization under the control of JCP. The unions were the symbolic representation of left labor movements. Though they had suffered a crushing blow from their repression, the surviving leaderships of JCP immediately reconstructed the Japanese Trade Union Council. But for a long time it could not truly recover. With the beginning of Sino-Japanese war (1937–1945), Japanese trade unions (from moderate forces to the right wing) were forced to reorganize as industrial patriotic organizations (*dainippon-sangyo-hokoku-kai*), which were propped up by the Japanese government. Under the wartime system, the organization helped in increasing productivity, supporting strong cooperation between workers and management. This corporatist system oppressed class struggle and concentrated on production.

The purpose of this essay is to depict the rise of workers' control in Japan after World War II and provide some theoretical perspectives. The struggle to control production (*seisan kanri toso*) post-World War II Japanese meant varying degrees of worker control of some or all phases of production, the evolution of which will be explained. The struggles rose one after another and became very influential. Japanese workers, emancipated from the militarist-fascist regime after the war, had a feeling of freedom, partly due to the US democracy that gave the Japanese people a sense of democratic values. Furthermore, the JCP was legalized and gained mass support in many trade unions. Production control was not the JCP's idea but it became its basic policy. As a consequence the struggles reached a new climax.

Japanese workers massively endorsed the politics of the production control. The collapse of the war economy severely paralyzed production and reinitiating production was a shared goal for workers. Strikes were also not a useful instrument in the face of paralyzed production. Production control was a means of solving various contradictions and could democratize the extremely hierarchical internal structure of companies. The workers attained a decisive influence on production plans, wage levels, time administration and other matters. But the production control faced limits. Even if the workers also immediately established and participated in management councils, they could not completely deprive the management of rights over the management of staff or employment policies.

At the climax of the production control, Japanese trade unions started the Japanese Congress of Industrial Organization (CIO) October Struggle in 1946. It was substantially an extension of production control. The Japanese CIO aimed at reorganizing workers of every company, factory and workplace into one industrial union in a unification of the labor front to increase their numbers. The JCP was at the center of this initiative. Though this might seem to be red unionism, the main organizational feature of the Japanese CIO was a body of loose council systems. It was not a top-down decision-making system. This chapter presents four cases of the production control.

The rise of post-war labor movement

Chinese and Korean workers

At the end of the war, the Japanese people had fallen into a state of lethargy after the shock of defeat. Japanese society came to a standstill that lasted about 2 months. The General Headquarters (GHQ)[1] early occupation priorities were to disarm the Japanese Army and to weaken thoroughly the Japanese militarist regime to prevent the country from further threatening the Allied Forces. Then democratization imposed by the Allied Forces began to democratize Japanese political, legal, economic and educational institutions. The industrial patriotic societies founded before the war were dissolved on 30 September 1945 by the direct order of US President Harry S. Truman. Additionally, various oppressive laws from the prewar period, such as the enforcement of the Maintenance of the Public Order Act and the Preventive Detention Act, were abolished on 4 October 1945.

Under these new circumstances the Japanese working class began to change. The uncertainty that Japanese working-class people faced in their daily life – unemployment, wage cuts or no pay, food shortages and rising inflation – threatened them directly. As a result, they were compelled to organize struggles in various ways. October 1945 became the month of the labor offensive. The number of trade unions exploded. Since the Japanese government had not released imprisoned communists, some Korean communists in Japan[2] (such as Kim Doyon, Paku Onchoru and others) founded The Alliance to Promote the Liberation of Political Prisoners on 24 September and immediately obtained the release of several Japanese communists. But Justice Minister Iwate insisted, "I will not consider the liberation of political prisoners now" (Taisuke, 1993: 37). GHQ considered this unacceptable and ordered the Japanese government to free the remaining political prisoners. About 3000 political prisoners, most of them communists, were released by 10 October.

On 18 September Chinese prisoners of war at the Mitsubishi Bibai Coal Mine in Hokkaido rose up to protest against unfair and cruel treatment. The Chinese workers' struggle influenced other coal mines in Hokkaido and struggles erupted as well in the Mitsui Bibai and Hokutan Yubari mines (with mainly Korean workers). After the end of the war the cruel working conditions that Chinese prisoners had to face had not improved. Security measures were severe in the coal mines, shortages of food and clothing was common, workers were under strict supervision and were prohibited to move. Therefore, Chinese Communists (*hachiro-gun*, the Chinese communist army fighting Japanese imperialism) were at the front of the struggles in the coal mines. The Chinese insurrection soon inspired the Korean workers and they began to sabotage their workplaces.

According to government statistics of June 1945, the total number of coal mine workers was 396,712, and about one-third (124,025) were Korean. There were 2.1–2.4 million Koreans in Japan at that time. Most were brought to Japan against their will by the wartime labor mobilization program and others were economic refugees. Korean workers in Hokutan Yubari Coal Mine filed a labor dispute on October 8, 1945. Encouraged by the organizers, 6000 Korean workers went on strike in the first large-scale post-war labor dispute. Their demands were for (i) immediate repatriation to their native country, (ii) improvement of food distribution and (iii) the abolition of the wage gap between Japanese and Korean workers (Katzuo, 1971: 24–8; Taisuku, 1993: 22–8).

The Yomiuri dispute

GHQ's policy at the beginning was the top-down program of democratization, so they did not always support the self-organized labor movement. When GHQ ordered the abolition of the industrial patriotic societies it expected the leaders to remain as activists and reorganize the unions. GHQ considered Japanese workers to be backward and incapable of creating a labor movement by themselves. The Japanese proletariat was considered to be too debilitated and intimidated.

It was during the Yomiuri newspaper company dispute that Japanese workers first rose up to action. During the war, the Japanese press was under the total control of the government. The media praised and glorified war and expressed no criticism of the government. The labor conflict broke out on 13 September 1945 with Yomiuri's editorial department demanding an "investigation into war crimes" and the "democratization of the company".

The pressure on company president Matsutaro Syoriki for a response escalated, in fact, into a confrontation between capital and labor. After a month, the Yomiuri workers formed a society for the study of democracy. The society demanded the resignation of the president and all executives and department directors, together with recognition of the trade union. But the management leaders refused to comply with the demands and fired five of the society's leaders. In response to this repression the struggle expanded into a company-wide conflict. At a mass rally, the central slogans of the Yomiuri workers were: "Overthrow Syoriki!" "Management Executives Depart!" "I have been working for 30 years, but how much does this company pay me?" (Taisuke, 1976: 42).

On 23 October 1945 the workers formed a union. The struggle committee stressed that the union's form should be grounded on the principle of free association. Kuninobu Watahiki, an anarchist worker in the Yomiuri printing plant, said, "We have to learn from the history of the letterpress printer's union before the war". At that time the main ideology of factory workers was anarchism, namely, voluntarism and mutual aid. The anarchists rejected Red trade unionism like the Profintern[3] and were opposed to rules imposed by communist or socialist parties. Some anarchists had continued their struggles against managers in wartime, and secretly formed a mutual aid group. The anarchists in Yomiuri had insisted on organizing the union immediately and their position was supported by the radical socialist labor-peasant group, *rono-ha*[4] (Taisuke, 1976: 22–3). However, the lecture groups (*koza-ha*),[5] which were close to the JCP, opposed the immediate constitution of a union and insisted on first organizing groups across the company and only then on building the union only as second step. They justified this by the backwardness of Japanese workers and the fear that the privileged consciousness of the journalists would create antipathy and break the unity of the union across the company. In the end those fears did not come to pass and the Yomiuri Union played an important role as precursor of Japanese workers' self-organized unions.

As a reaction to the organizing, company President Syoriki fired Tomin Suzuki, who was appointed chairperson of the Yomiuri Union and became chairman of the chief struggle committee. He was a liberal not a Marxist, and a very determined leader of the committee. Suzuki was eager to thoroughly investigate war crimes, so Syoriki did not allow him to continue working at Yomiuri.

At a mass rally on 24 October the workforce announced the existence of a struggle committee based in every section of the workplace, and proclaimed workers' control of the newspaper. The next day, 25 October, Yomiuri workers started to exercise that control. At the same time, the Yomiuri Trade Union was recognized and, with the newly won right of collective bargaining, collective agreements and union's participation in management were secured. It was after this that the workers in Japan picked up the struggle called the production control. The Yomiuri newspaper company conflict was the first in which workers organized a struggle committee on their own initiative and formed a union during the struggle. Minister of the Interior Iwao Yamazaki commented on the struggle saying, "The special political police was still active, it would arrest, without mercy, those communists who had carried out anti-imperial family propaganda" (Taisuke, 1993: 7).

Yomiuri's President Syoriki had worked in the state police bureau during the war. In the newspaper company he set up a despotic-bureaucratic work regimen. He intensified control over employees and even put some under direct surveillance. Syoriki regarded the company as his personal property. Announcing "I will close Yomiuri Press, if I cannot deal with it without hindrance", he created anger among the workers (Round Table Conference of Labor and Agriculture, 1947: 38). The workers intended to overthrow the non-democratic work regime and turn their company into one that would fit into a democratic society.

The workers also recognized that press reform had to be the first step in a general democratization. During the war Yomiuri Press had adopted a market-driven approach marked by populism and sensationalism, with its only purpose being that of mass consumption, and its manipulated information supported militarism. Therefore, the workers declared that control over the editing section was crucial. They demanded thorough investigations into war crimes. In other words, the new union finally advocated getting rid of the imperial system (*tenno-sei*). In Japan, this position has always ultimately been a radical one. Production control in Yomiuri was originated by workers with no prior experience in labor and leftist movements, except for a small number of anarchists.

The organization advancing the production control struggle was the committee. The committee was the organ for decision-making and also the executive. All departments and sectors, from the editorial board committee to the committees of the different production unit (office work, typesetting, lead plate and so on) were subordinated to the chief struggle committee. Nevertheless, the Yomiuri workers were not able to form a management committee. Yomiuri Union adopted a closed shop system, to which all employees except for the executives belonged. Its manifesto was: "We intend to participate in management, remove old dark evils and promote the democratization of the press" (Taisuke, 1976: 50).

Kyuichi Tokuda stated in the JCP's organ, *Red Flag* (*Akahata*):

> The capitalists have sabotaged everything. That is because they have profited greatly and have enough food, and are conspiring with the military authority and bureaucracy. As the prices increasingly go up due to inflation, it will be to their advantage to delay production. If we carry on like this, we will suffer shortages of everyday necessities. Consequently, inflation is getting more serious at every moment, and the shortages – not only of food, but also of transportation, communication, fuel etc. – are creating havoc in our daily lives. So, we have to overcome the capitalist's sabotage. We cannot stop at the control of industry by workers. (Tokuda 1945, 7 November)

Even so, the JCP was not present in the Yomiuri struggle, because there was still not a consensus about the production control in the JCP at that time. It was only after the Yomiuri dispute that the JCP's hegemony in the production control was established. As a matter of fact, various groups refined the struggle by mutual arguments during the process of the dispute (Taisuke, 1993: 41).

In Yomiuri the management executives publicized anti-communist propaganda against the struggle. They warned that if the struggle continued, the communists would seize the rights of management, and subsequently, the rights of property. The communists would begin to control industry and plan a "violent revolution". President Syoriki saw the production control as the theft of his property. Meanwhile, the 12 December editorial stated: "We hereby declare that the Yomiuri newspaper has become a true friend and organ of the people" (Taisuke, 1976: 129).

In another article entitled, "The appearance of the Japanese Communist Party", the Yomiuri newspaper gave its full support to JCP policies and general principles, except for abolition of the imperial system, believing that most Japanese people would not accept it. It was the first time that a commercial Japanese newspaper had published an article favorable to the JCP, and the article also called for the development of the Popular Front. At this time, the role of the JCP was still restricted. It was only after the Yomiuri struggle that its influence increased drastically. At Yomiuri it was the people who had been oppressed during the war – mainly the marxists, anarchists, liberals and social democrats – who led the dispute. They had had to disguise and camouflage their political views for a long time, which had the effect of creating solidarity across ideological lines. The end of war, the collapse of the militarist-fascist system, and the repeated riots by the Chinese and Koreans drove them to action that seemed like the floods after the collapse of a dam.

General conditions of production control

As a struggle tactic the production control emerged in Japanese labor disputes during the year immediately following the end of World War II. The Japanese bourgeoisie consciously and systematically sabotaged production as a tool of political and economic calculation. It also used inflation and provoked shortages to sell hoarded material and commodities at an exorbitant profit. In such a situation the usual strikes and sabotage could not build up pressure on capital, but instead would benefit the bourgeoisie. Moreover, the recovery of production was socially necessary. The national economy had collapsed immediately after the war. The lack of supplies was severe. The recovery meant also rebuilding the national economy and saving lives. In Japanese working–class consciousness it was the mission of the working class to restart production as fast as possible for the good of the people.

Though the percentage of production control cases compared to all labor disputes was low (148 of 1568 cases, or 9 percent), the decisive element was their quality. After mine and traffic industries, the third focus of production control was manufacturing. The struggle for production control emerged in 27 percent of labor disputes in the machine industry, in 12 disputes in the metal industry, in 10 percent of disputes in the chemical industry, gas and water services, in 2 percent of disputes in food industries, and 0.8 percent of disputes in textile industries. All in all, 121,929 workers out of the 1,396,817 involved in all disputes, participated in production control struggles (Central Labor School, 1947: 14–15).

The most common origin of labor conflicts in immediate postwar Japan was the demand for increasing wages, which was a paramount necessity in light of the rising prices and food shortages. But their demands were not limited to wages. Demands for collective bargaining, participation in management, rejection of supervisors and others increased gradually. That meant the transformation of economic demands to political ones. Trade unions and workers moved increasingly towards autonomous regulation. In particular, the communists insisted that the production control movement was merely response to the capitalists' sabotage, and that the capitalists were the ones who wanted to stop production in their factories. The unions created a chief struggle committee (also called supreme leading authority) for labor disputes and emergencies. The committee was usually composed of elected union chairpersons.

Regarding management, workers often continued working under the conventional company organizational structures, but in an important number of cases they founded a production control committee in charge of management decisions. In the Nippon Seiki Adachi electronic equipment factory, for instance, the orders of the plant manager and the section managers were rejected. The functions of plant manager were taken over by the council system. In the Yokohama electric wire factory of Furukawa Electric, the workers replaced the plant manager with the chairman of the production committee, while the other managers kept their posts. In contrast to these cases, in the Nippon Kokan Tsurumi Mill, the union did not utilize the company organizational structures, but instead set up a committee for the production control and appointed a person in charge for each section.

To set up a successful production control system the union needed the cooperation of engineers and office workers. Technical instructions by engineers or expertise of office workers on finances, the acquisition of raw material and marketing the products were essential. Fortunately, white-collar and blue-collar workers cooperated with each other. This was also because trade unions organized engineers, factory and office workers into one union (except in the coal mines). Concerns about subsistence and food shortages affected everyone. The new unions started to organize directly in the workplaces, based on face-to-face contact. Though the jobs were different, there was a fundamental feeling of solidarity shared among people who worked in the same place or nearby.

Consolidation of workers' control

Keisei Electric Railway: from a struggle for free transport to the production control

On 9 December 1945, Keisei Electric Railway's workers decided to transport passengers free of charge as a form of struggle. For the railway companies and workers this was equivalent to the production control. When the new Trade Union Act to come into effect on 22 December 1945, was announced allowing new unions to be constituted, the company anticipated that antagonistic unions would be formed by the workers and they made a pre-emptive move by forming a company-controlled union. The company selected the union leaders in advance and lied to the workers, telling them the initiative was taken on behalf of an umbrella union organization. But the preparation committee for the union saw through the plot and recommended the election of their own executive committee members and the workers built their own union. The Keisei Electric Railway union was built by connecting the committees organized spontaneously by workers in most of the workplaces belonging to the company.

On 5 December the new trade union presented some demands to the company, but the company's answer was far from satisfactory. Though the union exercised collective bargaining, the company demanded negotiations with only 14 members of the committee on 9 December. The demand incited workers' anger and they started chanting "Rise up, *workers!*" and "Temporary train service now!" (Teruaki, 1946: 88) The angry crowd of workers sought the executive managers and found them hiding in the storeroom. They pulled them out and brought them up to the roof, pressing them for an answer to their demands. However, the managers insisted that they had not decided anything and offered longer talks. The Keisei workers were ready for a full-scale dispute. One worker in the crowd shouted, "Strike! Stop the trains!" Another worker responded that stopping trains was bad for the public and proposed instead giving free rides. The proposal was widely accepted, especially as the workers recognized the need for popular support (Teruaki, 1946: 88).

The workers decided to take all dangerous train cars out of service. Accidents and injuries or blockages were frequent because of the war damage. For 3 days the service was reduced to a third while the damaged cars were repaired. The workers defied the company's order and stopped conventional work entirely, while all the union members restored the damaged train cars. Those absent without permission were seen as traitors. Carpenters fitted boards in broken train windows, and the repair crews repaired what they could, while engineers worked throughout the night to restore the motors. In this period repairs grew by 300 percent. The workers felt empowered and were proud of their own work. Even the GHQ stated: "The free ride struggle is a rare tactic in the United States. We would not spare help for your fair work". After ending free rides on 13 December, the union started production control the next day. The highest decision-making body concerning production control was the executive committee in the union (Keisei Electric Railway Union, 1962: 103).

Efficiency improved drastically and the absenteeism fell to zero. Young workers changed beyond recognition. The Keisei workers demonstrated their ability to run the company harmoniously and assign human resources appropriately. The workers' production control exposed the sabotage committed by the capitalists to the light of day. The workers perfectly understood the problematic state of the company management and accounts and recognized the weak points and faults of capitalist management. In the case of the railway, the income from passenger fare was steady every day and the profit on investments was thus foreseeable and direct. That made it easier to carry out production control. The company owners opposed the workers' decisions and demanded:

> Stop the free ride actions taken by the union immediately. The money obtained by the union so far belongs to the company. Deposit the income in the company bank account, otherwise, your actions are illegal. (Keisei Electric Railway Union, 1962)

The union completely ignored this demand and deposited the money in a bank account in the name of the union chairman. (Keisei Electric Railway Union, 1962).

The company offered to recognize collective bargaining, pay a temporary allowance for base salary and a family allowance four times higher (the workers were demanding base salary multiplied by five). It also offered to disclose and distribute the account ledger but it absolutely denied having made any alterations or having destroyed evidence n these accounts. The workers were dissatisfied with the company's answer because it really only recognized collective bargaining. Although the union policy was not to suspend train services, some union members had already sabotaged trains as a means of struggle. Worker morale was very high. Therefore, during a rally on 22 December the union presented new demands 13 days after the dispute began, as follows: (i) a management conference was to be established (ii) the executive management was to resign and (iii) working hours were to be reduced (Chiba Prefecture Labor Union, 1967: 111).

At the rally the workers' slogans were intense: "Expel those who complain!" "Comrades, unite! Unity is the union's weapon, the key to victory!" "The fight is decided in the last five minutes! Those who complain are the tools of the villain or the betrayer!" "Unite, unite!" "The villains and gangs of capitalists are going to destroy our unity. Don't be caught in the trap of the enemy! If you have been caught, inform us immediately!" "Let's communicate kindly with passengers and achieve business gains for ourselves!" "Defend our workplace!" (Chiba Prefecture Labor Union 194: 111).

The public and media were generally on the side of the workers. Public opinion was overwhelming in their support. The workers continuously talked about "the beloved dispute", which was the question of the duties of management, including the democratization of personnel management, and the establishment and increase of the voice of the workers. Therefore the possibility for worker control was always present, in which the production control was exercised as a tactic and not the purpose itself. The demand for a management conference to be set up also expressed the workers' desire for a democratic workplace and bottom-up control.

The struggle of the Keisei workers continued for 20 days. On 26 December the union settled with the company. Most of the workers' demands were accepted and the dispute ended. The company agreed to pay a minimum wage based on cost of living, automatic wage increases linked to inflation, and changes to the wage system. Dismissals required union approval, full-time union officers were introduced and many more workers' demands were met. As for the conference, "100 people above the subsection chief class cannot participate in the union, and 2,100 union members diverged into three branches according to their workplaces – train, automobile, and head office" (Chiba Prefecture Labor Union, 1967: 112).

The beloved struggle: Nippon Kokan Tsurumi Mill Union

On 24 December 1945 a trade union was constituted at the Nippon Kokan Tsurumi Mill. The union adopted production control tactics and won the dispute. The steel mill is situated in the Keihin industrial area, stretching between Tokyo and Yokohama. The branch of the sailors' union in the industrial area had already been formed on 5 October. On 26 October the workers of the Tsurumi shipyard began a struggle for the reinstatement of four dismissed workers. Supported by the United Metal Organization Promotion Committee, under the leadership of Syoichi Kasuga of the JCP and the Tsurumi branch of the Trade Union Preparation Congress, the struggle was successful.

At the beginning of November 144 Korean workers of the Tsurumi Mill, who had been forced to work in Japan during World War II, demanded an allowance to return home and the improvement of working conditions. Their actions inspired Japanese workers. As a union document recalled, "the struggle of Korean workers and Chinese prisoners reinforced the Japanese workers' liberation struggle. Their struggles encouraged Japanese workers who had been slow in taking up action" (NKK Tsurumi Union, 1956: 49–50).

Takeo Hayashi, cost clerk, and worker Seiichi Ishijima decided to build a union for all Tsurumi Mill workers. Hayashi was a JCP member, though he did not practice cell activities during working hours, but he participated in the JCP cell meetings at night. Hayashi had been with the company for only a year and did not know many people there. Therefore, Hayashi and Ishijima visited each other's dormitory after work and together they investigated the state of young workers by listening to their stories. They understood their dissatisfaction and anxiety. They gathered together more than 10 people who were influential in the workplace or were able to inform young workers of their plans, and together they formed a union and set up demands. The main demands were the recognition of the union and collective bargaining, a significant wage increase and the rescinding of announced dismissals. The union spread fast throughout the mill, organizing workers and employees. Hayashi became first chairman of the union. Nevertheless, he did not intend to fill the executive positions with party members. He said: "I hope that the party members work as hard as the other people in each workplace".

The company unwillingly recognized the union but rejected any wage increase or the cancellation of dismissals. As a consequence, the union started production control on 10 January 1946. The foremen were immediately excluded from the production process. The company's director and the department managers were quietly confined in the director's room and a locker room. The union's production control had to struggle with several obstacles. They had to sell their steel to a wholesale merchant. But the wholesale market was dominated by Nippon Kokan Steel, which exercised an oligopolistic control over the steel sector. Therefore, there was a risk that the wholesale merchant would not buy steel from the union. Steel was also rationed and was allocated through ration tickets distributed by the wholesale merchant. The products the workers could bring to market were thus limited to galvanized iron plates or drums and a few machine parts. The union therefore negotiated to replace monetary payment with the product the wholesale merchant wanted. Salable products were sold for cash as quickly as possible to encourage workers' morale.

The company claimed that the production control movement was illegal, and accused the workers of behaving as if they were under orders of the occupation forces and of having a bad influence on some of the workers. (NKK Tsurumi, 1956: 61). Hayashi and other union members visited Anthony Constantino, GHQ civil information and education section manager. Constantino had experiences with activities in a trade union affiliated with the CIO and he understood the labor movement. "The GHQ does not intervene in the labor movement. We are prepared to support trade unions against unfair pressures by capitalists" he commented favorably (NKK Tsurumi, 1956: 61).

The negotiation between the union and the company did not advance. To break the impasse, the workers decided on surprise attacks on every executive's house. They named this form of action *uchiiri*, after the targeted attacks on houses practiced by the samurai in feudal Japan. They chose one person to be in charge of a group and went to the executives' houses in groups, with the intention of negotiating directly. In the atmosphere of impatience and stagnation, this attempt was effective in raising morale.

On the other hand, in order to bring the dispute to an end in one swoop, they surrounded the board of directors with a demonstration. By targeting the board, they hoped to get a reply from company president Asano. The workers, formed picket lines around the headquarters' building with flags, placards and drums. They searched all the rooms in the building, intending to lock all the executives up in one room. They ran up the steps in great numbers and filled the corridor. They found the white-faced president and the other executives and shouted out "They're here!" The crowd answered "Great!" and cornered the executives on the roof. Hayashi courteously pressured the president for a reply. Finally he urged: "Yes or No? We do not want to hear any excuses. Just say it". President Asano agreed to all the demands (NKK Tsurumi Union 1956: 61).

Nevertheless, behind the scenes the company maneuvered with the Japanese government. On 1 February 1946, four ministers told the press that the union's action amounted to assault, threats and infringement of propriety rights, and that the union must be strictly punished for their illegal acts:

> The Japanese government hopes for the positive development of the trade union movement, therefore we think that it is very regrettable that assaults, threats, infringement of propriety rights and so on are on the rise recently. Responsible workers who wish to help rebuilding Japan should not engage in such conduct. The Japanese government cannot overlook this and can only judge strictly. So we earnestly advise you, as

responsible workers, to be careful not to make such mistakes or violations. (Ministry of Labor, 1946: 131)

The union promptly organized a demonstration and went to the Ministry of the Interior. The negotiation committees condemned the deputy minister who came out to talk with them, and demanded to know why the Japanese government had issued this one-sided statement without hearing the opinion of the union. He was at a loss to answer. The four ministers who had released the statements were at the prime minister's official residence and the demonstrators next went there, but police blocked the crowd from entering, granting access only to the negotiation committees. The ministers refused to withdraw the statement and the dispute ended without a result.

The union publicly protested against the ministers' statement, accusing them of being apathetic towards inequality and of deceiving the nation by adopting President Asano's point of view without questioning and inquiring into to the truth regarding the threats, assaults and breach of promises committed by the company itself. In the end, the Tsurumi Union won; the company gave in to all the union demands and the workers were not put on trial. But it became evident that the Japanese government had abandoned the idea of representing the nation and was allied with the capitalists.

The people's court: the struggle of Mitsubishi Bibai Coal Mine Union

At the Mitsubishi Bibai Coal Mine in Hokkaido, there were about 4000 Japanese workers, 5000 Koreans and 264 Chinese. As before mentioned, the Chinese and Korean workers in the coal mines had risen in revolt immediately after the war. They had been mistreated by forced labor and violence throughout the war. They not only attacked distribution stations and shopping areas and looted food and clothes but also searched for the foremen who had treated them so cruelly, so that those who had maltreated them had to hide to avoid their vengeance. The Japanese police could do nothing to stop the riots. During the war, the Bibai Coal Mine produced 7000 tons of coal a day. After the war production dropped sharply to 350 tons a day. The food situation continued to worsen. The whole coal mine was in a state of chaos. Japanese coal mine labor took place under almost-slave conditions.

In these circumstances, a group of workers began holding secret meetings to prepare for the establishment of a labor union. One of the organizers was JCP member Takashi Mizutani. The group grew to 40 workers from all residential districts and villages and they decided to put their plans into action on 31 October. In each of their villages the activists approached the workers to invite them to join the union. Recruitment was not as easy as the activists had expected. Some workers were afraid because of the union oppression they had seen, or they were simply ignorant about work matters. However, some villages welcomed the effort and spread the manifesto of "The Preparation of Mitsubishi Bibai Coal Mine Union Foundation Committee" urging the workers to action:

> 5000 brothers in the whole coal mine!
>
> Brothers, you continue wearing split-toe socks with holes and straw sandals. You have tried hard! Brothers, you continue working with the substitute food of mugwort dango [a round cereal]! Brothers, with just one word to win, you continued working without complaining! Your patience is reaching the limit! We get only leftovers! We live in a mouse nest instead of a human house, with ragged tatami mats and a naked light bulb. Why aren't our lives improving, in spite of Japan's conversion to democracy?
>
> Break down the distribution station, search for hoarded goods!
>
> Smash the heads of those who have deceived us!
>
> It is natural for us to be furious. But, please, wait a bit, brothers! If we take action immediately, this coal mine will be a river of blood and fire. GHQ considers our action illegal,

even though we are in a hopeless situation. Brothers! Haste makes waste. If we make legal demand in solidarity with all the coal mine workers, we will find a way.

Let's organize our union to defend our interests by ourselves. A bundle of arrows cannot easily be broken. Choose one representative for each 15 people in your workplace! Send them to the foundation meeting! Join our union, one and all! Progress under the flag of victory! (Mitsubishi Bibai Coal Mine Union, 1960: 134–6)

The company tried to build a company-dominated union, Kyowakai, a subsidiary of the Industrial Patriotic Society during the war. But it failed to elect representatives and died a natural death. The Chinese workers encouraged the Japanese workers. Zhāng Lián Róng, the chief secretary of the Chinese dormitory and second lieutenant of Bā Lù Jūn (the Chinese Communist Party), approved the foundation of the union and sent a large sum of money to the committee. "After returning to our home country we, too, are going to struggle for the liberation of workers", the Chinese said (Mitsubishi Bobai Coal Mine Union, 1960: 136–7).

On 4 November 1945, workers filled the huge meeting place, in spite of bitterly cold weather, and founded the Mitsubishi Bibai Coal Mine Union. The Japanese government provided large financing and subsidies for coal mines as a key industry, intending to increase production after the war. A new wage standard was announced: 18 yen per day for labor in the pit and 10 yen for labor outside the pit. Instead of adopting this standard, the company announced it would pay 5 yen for pit labor and 3 yen outside, and even worse, instead of cash, workers would be partly paid with a kind of sardine. The coal mine workers were enraged. The workers cried out in desperation, accusations against the executives were raised and rumors spread: "Are they trying to get back the fish we ate? What did they do during the war? They hid sugar in the air-raid shelters we built". "Investigate the executive is filling his pockets with!" "Crush the warehouse!" "Set fire to the club!"

"While they made us eat potatoes and pumpkins, they ate polished rice and drank liquor in the club every day". "There are 30 bags of rice in the director's house!" "There are piles of butter in the vice director's house!" (Nishimura, 1946: 149).

The *Red Flag* wrote:

> The company is planning to dismiss many more workers and they are going to employ only a few workers at an even lower wage. After gaining some subsidies, they are waiting for a rise in the coal price, inflating the price additionally by stocking production. So, we must build up the workers' control of monopoly capital. (*Red Flag,* 20 October 1945)

The new union demanded that the company reintroduce the extra payments it had cancelled, double wages and introduce an 8-hour day. The demands were rejected by the company. The union therefore decided to take over the mine and start production control on 4 February 1946. Union commands were announced and immediately obeyed by the workers. Worker control was very different from the conventional bureaucratic administration that required a large quantity of documents at every step of the process. The warehouses were opened. Materials and resources were piled up and carried steadily into the mouth of the pit. Moreover, sugar and Japanese socks were also distributed to the workers; something the company did not do before and the food warehouse was even left open.

In the beginning many office workers refused to cooperate because office workers often felt superior to miners and did not want to get mixed up with them. As time passed more office workers gained class consciousness and joined the miner's labor union, and the employer-friendly office workers' union gradually disappeared. The company executives issued more and more administrative orders, but the workers completely ignored them.

Notwithstanding the difficult conditions, coal production rose rapidly. Disruptive workers had to face workers' courts and were pushed to cooperate. Women were mobilized for snow removal on the roads to expedite transport. The production secretariat paid daily allowances and distributed food, gloves and shoes to the workers. The snow was removed rapidly and broken roofs and bent rails were restored. All the work was done without pay. The Bibai Coal Mine Union asked the railroad union to cooperate. The railroad workers readily agreed to transport 2000 tons of coal a day to customers. The union uncovered several documents proving the management's abuse of authority during the war. Someone wrote: "the people's court" in big letters on the wall. The police turned up at the mine, pushed by public pressure engineered by the entrepreneurs, but were unable to do anything (Mitsubishi Bibai Coal Mine Union, 1960: 145).

Since the company still did not accept the workers' demands, the union decided to exert control not only of production but also of management. On 12 February 1946, a number of production control workers passed over to control management. The control secretariat announced that anyone who would not cooperate with this control, including the directors, would be suspended. When the workers looked the director, vice director and other executives, they found them drinking liquor at the company club. The union committee asked to have a negotiation meeting in front of the crowd. The executives repeated, "We may negotiate with you sincerely". The crowd of workers present felt insulted because the executives had never been sincere. So they became infuriated. One worker hurled himself at them and other workers began to hit them with placards. It was not possible for the committee members to stop the crowd.

When the situation calmed down, negotiations with the crowd went on for a while without result. The management insisted on the impossibility of raising wages, the workers accused the directors of lying: "You deceive us all the time!" and insisted on a positive answer. The executives denied the accusations. The workers accused them of eating expensive food and consuming alcohol paid for from company funds. The workers decided they would not let the executives go until they responded to the workers' demands (Mitsubishi Bibai Coal Mine Union, 1960: 155). The director told the workers they could repeat these actions as many times as they wanted, it would not change anything. The workers were boiling with rage and shouted angrily at the director, who was suddenly overcome with illness and had to retire from his seat. The union told the vice director now in charge: "Even if it means your life, you should accept the demands of these 5000 workers. When your responsibility to do so is questioned, we will help you. Save these starving people!" And the vice director accepted the demands (Mitsubishi Bibai Coal Mine Union 1960, 156).

The limits and possibilities of production control: communists, labor union and worker control

Difficulties of production control

Production control had to face six main difficulties:

1. Financial problems. Huge capital-intensive industries need a high cash flow to operate. In the post-war situation this was a problem. The risk of financial problems is considerably smaller in labor-intensive industries like coal mines, transportation, communication, the media and so on. Workers in those days demanded the nationalization of banks in order to provide the capital needed to restart industrial production. The Japanese government solved the problem partly by providing funds to staple industries, but only after the October Offensive in 1946.
2. Raw material supply. In cases of production control in huge factories usually belonging to corporations and with resource-intense production, the company headquarters would immediately issue an order to all subsidiaries to stop supplying the factories in question.
3. Sales to customers. Huge production sites had serious problems finding customers to buy large quantities of their production.

For instance, in the case of production control in the Tsurumi Steel Mill, the union had to change their main products to be able to sustain production financially. Tsurumi under production control acquired cash mainly through sales of secondary products, such as buckets, pans, pots, kettles and so on, because they could be sold easily.

4. Paying wages. Industries with a slow turnover of capital (especially shipyards, factories producing machines, rotary presses and trains) faced considerable difficulties in paying wages. Moreover bourgeois law approved only the payment of the same wages during a strike as before, profits legally still belonged to the company, and if the union paid higher wages during production control it would be considered embezzlement.

5. Cooperation with engineers. The participation of engineers in production control was crucial, especially in factories with high technology.

6. Interference of capital and government. Factory owners constantly threatened and interfered with production control using bourgeois law to accuse workers of illegal occupation of houses, embezzlement, breach of trust, infringement of mine rights and so on (Hiroshi, 1946: 196–7).

Building unity to overcome difficulties and transform the labor struggle into a political struggle

In the early stage, production control was accomplished in single companies by workplace unions. With the extension of production control, different unions started to cooperate or associate with each other, as in the case of the Mitsubishi Bibai Coal Mine Union and the railroad union. This cooperation helped to overcome difficulties of funds and resources. As production control struggles intensified, counter-attacks by capital also stepped up and workers were exposed to illegal company dissolutions and threats and attacks by criminal gangs (*yakuza*). At the same time, the Japanese government attacked production control with political, legal and economic measures.

Five months after production control began, the need for a national industrial union became evident to the activists. Single unions in one workplace run huge risks opposing the capitalist class and had little chance to win. The working class had to build a unified coalition and transform its economic struggle into a political one, thus solving various problems at once. In February 1946 the preparatory meeting of the All Japan Congress of Industrial Organization (*Zen Nippon Sangyo-betsu Rodo Kumiai Kaigi*, in Japanese known as Sanbetsu, in English, CIO) was organized through the joint efforts of various district councils. The initial demands of the unions building the new CIO were recognition of unions and the right to bargain collectively. After these rights were granted in the Labor Union Law in December 1945, the demands of the struggles turned to establishing general collective agreements and participation in management.

Production control as a form of workers' struggle had spread to all industries. The struggles often developed cooperation between companies with production control in the same or allied branches. Most production control struggles were led by Japanese CIO unions. The structure of the national organization was a consultation body of unions. While the official founding date was August 1946, the CIO had existed and showed its capacity to mobilize prior to that date. The Japanese post-war labor movement now had a leading organization.

The CIO was close to the JCP; in fact many key CIO leaders were JCP members. After the threatening declaration by the four ministers on 1 February 1946, the JCP had warned: "This statement is the starting signal for a new wave of oppression against workers. We are determined to advance the struggle". The Socialist Party hesitated at first, but the radicalization of the workers' struggles against oppression of production control led the socialists to join the struggles.

Struggles were not limited to production sites and neither were the goals. On 7 April the anti-government demonstration "Overthrow Reactionary Shidehara Cabinet People's Rally" took place. The JCP and the Socialist Party sought a united popular front and formed the Democratic People's League together with workers' movement organizations and organizations from other popular movements. About two million people participated in the League's May Day marches throughout the country; 500,000 in Tokyo alone. The sphere of consumption also became a field of conflict. After May Day 1946, the Food May Day or People's Rice Acquisition Rally was held on 19 May. People demanded rice, a "crisis breakthrough fund", and a huge wage increase, among other things. The expanding labor and people's front pushed back the capitalist camp.

The Allied Occupation Force was shocked by the rapid pro-liferation and radicalization of struggles and GHQ declared: "We will not permit these mob demonstrations". Emperor Hirohito was urged to talk to the people of Japan about the food crisis on the radio. The authority of the emperor was intended to prevent the radicalization of the revolutionary mass movement. The labor offensive continued explosively until early June. The Japanese government was determined to rebuild industrial capitalism at the cost of sacrificing the working class. It was a priority to confine limits of production control in the Labor Union Law. The GHQ, on the other hand, had planned to transform the radicalized revolutionary movement into a moderate and corporatist trade unionism.

On 22 May 1946, pro-Western Shigeru Yoshida became prime minister of Japan. Yoshida was close to the USA and Britain. On 12 June his Cabinet promulgated the Imperial Ordinance 311 (1946) on the Punishment of Acts Prejudicial to the Occupation Objectives. One day later the government released a statement about social order, declaring:

> It is difficult to consider production control a legal means of dispute. If this situation continues, company organizations will be destroyed and the national economy will be adversely affected. Besides, if violent assault and threat is carried out, it will be a menace to society. (Central Labor School, 1947: 319)

The GHQ had gradually changed its policies against production control. This situation encouraged the Japanese government and the Japanese bourgeoisie to strengthen their counter-attack. The Japanese government established the Economic Stabilization Board to reorganize and rebuild Japanese industry, at the sacrifice of the working class. Capitalists took the opportunity to organize a managers' association and began to plan massive layoffs.

The denial of production control, as a form of struggle, with the argument it would negatively affect the economy, was unacceptable to the Japanese working class and could not be forgiven. When the Japanese CIO was formally founded on 1 August 1946 it had 1.5 million members and immediately started to prepare an offensive called The CIO October Struggle. It mobilized all member organizations and intended a decisive counter-attack against capital through a general strike. The economic struggle had definitely turned into a political struggle. The JCP launched a political general strike for the October Offensive.

The October Offensive was a strike organized by 12 industrial unions. It started with a strike of newspaper and broadcast unions. In the next stage, the Electric Industry Union Council began wave-like strikes named "5-minute blackout or power cut strikes", which demonstrated their tremendous power. The energy sector was a stronghold of the strike movement along with the coal mines and the electrical equipment industries. The key demands of the strike movement were: the establishment of a legal minimum wage based on the cost of living, higher wages, improved retirement schemes and the democratization of the energy industry. During the strike the CIO unions declared their goal was to topple the government if their demands were not met. The strike caused violent tremors in Japanese companies and the government. As a result, Electric Industry Union achieved a wage system based on the cost of living. Triggered by this union victory, the wage system continued to spread widely in Japan during the October Offensive. The Alliance of Toshiba Trade Union continued its October Offensive strike for 50 days. In conclusion, the October Offensive yielded a rich harvest, as most of their demands were met and the experience a huge gain for the Japanese labor movement.

The Japanese government, the national bourgeoisie and the GHQ agreed on the need to defeat the movement. The counter-attack began in November 1946, with a foundation rally of the right-wing Japanese Confederation of Labor Unions. The new confederation was organized by prewar corporative union leaders. A second general strike planned by the CIO to start on 1 February 1947 was called off by order of the occupation forces. Repression followed. Production control was over. It was the first decisive defeat of the post-World War II Japanese labor movement.

The role of the JCP

Without a doubt, the JCP played a central role in the strong post-war workers' movement and its members were a driving force in establishing the production control. However, opinions on the production control were not very clear within the party. It was only during the fourth party convention in December 1945 that JCP adopted the workers' control of important industries as a principle of action. JCP Chief Secretary Kyuichi Tokuda thought that the production control could extend well beyond mere dispute tactics. They could become "factory soviets". The JCP had already decided the so-called "1932 thesis" before the war: "organization and freedom of activity for working-class labor unions" and that "when the revolutionary situation, especially, when the moment comes to overthrow the Japanese imperial system, we will establish worker-farmer-soldier soviets in the entire country". Then, "all banks will be combined into a single bank under the control of the revolutionary situation" and "the worker-farmer-soldier soviet will control production in large capitalist corporations and banks". But not even 3 months later, at the fifth party convention, the JCP declared it would pursue "industry management by the institution of joint management councils in which workers participate" (Katzuo, 1960: 37; Kiyoshi, 1977: 112–13).

This was not a minor question of organization. In the former case, the workers have the right to decide on all aspects of company management. This means a de facto negation of the private ownership of the means of production. It implied that revolution was necessary and that the working class would hold state power. In the latter case, workers would participate within the capitalistic economic system. The policy of joint management councils did not contain the element of revolution. Tokuda and a minority of JCP members followed the 1932 thesis and supported immediate revolution in Japan. The majority in JCP supported the two-step revolution theory. First, a democratic revolution was needed: the Japanese imperial system had to be overthrown by a democratic revolution while the socialist revolution would be only the second step. The theory was based on the assumption that a relatively stable capitalism would be established in the long term. The 1932 thesis, on the contrary, saw an existing "tendency for the forcible transformation" of Japan through a socialist revolution and understood factory soviets to be the basic units of the revolution (Kiyoshi, 1977: 112).

The strategy adopted by the JCP at the fifth party convention saw production control as a mere instrument of labor struggle. The goal, according to the JCP, was to establish a joint management council within the company with production control, and as a next step, to reinforce a union of industries (Kiyoshi, 1977; 112–13; Profintern, 1981: 111–19; Wakao, 1973: 41–50) The one-step-revolution strategy was abandoned since it was considered almost impossible to carry out a socialist revolution under occupation by the USA. Previously, the JCP had identified the US Forces as a liberation army, an interpretation that the JCP held for a time, and which had the lingering effect of dividing the party.

The production control movement

The struggles between 1945 and 1947 are often presented as red trade unionism guided by the JCP. This is incorrect. Even if many union militants were members of the JCP and the JCP actively supported production control and building a new leftist union confederation, production control was developed and deepened by mass radicalism beyond legal tactics and party guidance. Triggered by the release of political prisoners in 1945, labor unions sprung up everywhere like bamboo shoots after rain. Marxists were not uncommon among office workers. Many of them had a history of running labor campaigns before the war and often they took the lead in the formation of new unions. But most of the JCP members active in workers' struggles did not act in the name of the JCP or follow JCP directives, but organized on the principles of working-class autonomy. Factory workers and office staff formed the unions together. They were built upon human relationships in the work-places and based on face-to-face contacts with some key leaders. This modality expanded from some factories to all companies in Japan and it became a distinct feature of unions in Japan.

Moreover, a characteristic of the production control struggle was its close link with tough street fighting with the police and with direct action: it was a joint struggle with other companies and factories. Demonstrations, public gatherings and sympathetic strikes also occurred very frequently. This was the political and cultural foundation that served as the backbone for the production control struggle.

Since over 90 percent of factories and business sites in Japan were supplying military goods, the economy collapsed once Japan surrendered and the war ended. Living conditions forced Japanese workers to struggle for improvement. At the same time, the classical repertoire of union struggles was not applicable, it would have ruined the workers and probably raised little sympathy for their struggles. In the production control, the workers found a way to struggle for their rights and at the same time restart production; something the Japanese bourgeoisie was not interested in, because the difficult economic situation promised them higher profits.

Workers used production control as a means to force manage-ment to accept their requests – from the recognition of unions, the banning of layoffs and granting wage increases and structural changes. The overall objective of production control was the participation of workers in management. Therefore, even if production control was not itself a goal, the experience showed workers that they held the key to production and could proactively develop their power. But because, even after achieving participation in management, the workers were not able to attain any authority over matters of personnel, and this facilitated capital's counterattack. The dismissals of activists, especially during the Red Purge (1950), when GHQ urged that he JCP should be declared illegal and its members were dismissed from their workplaces. Massive dismissals of all identified communists took place in the fields of the media, government institutions and private industry. This triggered even more existing divisions inside the JCP and weakened the union movement considerably. A wave of anti-communist and nationalist propaganda during the Korea War and the founding of communist China swept through Japan and capitalist restoration was finally consolidated.

Notes

1. The authorities of the allied occupation force in Japan following World War II (1945–1952).
2. Throughout the entire war and especially in the post-war period, struggles of Koreans and Chinese played an important role in Japan. The JCP was the only Japanese political party that opposed the colonization of the Korean peninsula. Since the Comintern's policy was "One country, one Communist Party", most Korean communists had to be members of the JCP. They engaged in JCP activities and were vigorous and aggressive at the front of the struggle, as they had the clear objective of gaining the independence of Korea from Japanese imperialist oppression and plunder.
3. The communist international trade unions' organization, with a union directed by the communist party in every country. Its policy was called red trade unionism.
4. The labor-peasant group supported a one-step revolution. Since Japan was a highly developed capitalist society, the socialist revolution had to be take place without a prior democratic revolution.

5. The lecture group was communist and many of its members had been JCP members before the JCP was made illegal in 1930. They insisted on a two-step revolution. According to them, Japan was a backward, half-feudal and half-capitalist, country. Therefore, the first step has to be a bourgeois democratic revolution. The socialist revolution would follow afterwards.

References

Central Labor School (1947) *Japan Labor Annual*. Tokyo: Central Labor School.

Chiba Prefecture Labor Union (1967[1974]) The history of Chiba Prefecture labor movement. In Jokyo (ed.) *Documents of the "Postwar Revolution", in Japan*. Tokyo: Jokyo, 107–12.

Hiroshi, K. (1946[1974]) The limit of workers' control. *Democratic Review*, 2–3. March.

Imperial Ordinance 311 (1946) *Official Gazette English Edition*. 58, 12 June: 153–54. Available at http://jalii.law.nagoya-u.ac.jp/official_gazette/hom_pdf/19460612d_ea.00058.010.000_0010.0010.0_b.006600.00660100.pdf (accessed 23 November 2014).

Katzuo, T. (1960) *History of the Japanese Communist Party*. Tokyo: Gendaishichosya.

Katzuo, T. (1971) *History of the Japanese Revolutionary Movements*. Tokyo: Gendaishichosya.

Keisei Electric Railway Union (ed.) (1962[1974]) History of our struggle and construction. Chiba. In Jokyo (ed.) *Documents of the "Postwar Revolution", in Japan*. Tokyo: Jokyo: 103.

Kiyoshi, Y. (1977) *Labor Movement in Crisis after War*. Tokyo: Ochanomizu Syobo.

Ministry of Labor (1946[1974]) *History of the Labor Movement 1945–1946*. Tokyo: Labor Administration Research Center. In Jokyo (ed.) *Documents of the "Postwar Revolution", in Japan*. Tokyo: Jokyo: 131.

Mitsubishi Bibai Coal Mine Union (1960) *Life in a Coal Mine*. Tokyo: Iwanami Syoten.

Nishimura, T. (1946[1974]) The revelations of the People's Court. In Jokyo (ed.) *Documents of the "Postwar Revolution", in Japan*. Tokyo: Jokyo: 149.

NKK Tsurumi Union (ed.) (1956) *History of Labor Movement at Tsurutesu*. Tokyo: Sundaisya.

Profintern (1981) *Profintern Programme of Action*, trans. Junzo Nomura and Akira Mizutani. Tokyo: Tsuge Syobo.

Round Table Conference of Labor and Agriculture (ed.) (1947[1974]) The real labor movement. In Jokyo (ed.) *Documents of the "Postwar Revolution" in Japan*. Tokyo: Jokyo. 38.

Taisuke, M. (1976) *Yomiuri Dispute 1945–1946*. Tokyo: Aki Syobo.

Taisuke, M. (1978) *Japanese CIO October Struggle*. Tokyo: Gogatsusya.

Taisuke, M. (1993) *An Inspection: The Labor Movement during the Occupation of Japan*. Tokyo: Renga Syobo Shinsya.

Teruaki, H. (1946[1974]) A true record: the diary of the Keisei Electric Railway dispute. In Jokyo (ed.) *Documents of the "Postwar Revolution" in Japan*. Tokyo: Jokyo, 88.

Wakao, F. (1973) *Labor Dispute Act*. Tokyo: Tokyo University Press.

SEVEN

The Factory Commissions in Brazil and the 1964 Coup d'État

Henrique T. Novaes and Maurício S. de Faria

Introduction

This article discusses the formation of the factory commissions in Brazil in a context of the rise of the workers' struggles in the years 1950–1968. The factory commissions were formed as embryos in the self-management struggles in Brazil, which were rapidly strangled by the hardening of the military dictatorship in 1968 and subsequently by the restructuring of production.

The factory commissions in the period 1960–1970 cannot be understood as isolated from the struggles of the 1950s and 1960s. For this reason, in the first part of the article we narrate the numerous struggles that occurred at that time, emphasizing the role of the critical new architecture and new cinema, the students' movement and the campaigns in defense of public education, and the struggles for agrarian reform. We close this part with the analysis of the basic reforms in João Goulart's government and the historic rupture initiated with the 1964 coup d'état. According to Ribeiro (1997: 295) at that historic moment the "1960s experimental scientific and cultural flourishing was drastically weakened" by the oppression of the civilian-military dictatorship of 1964–1985.

The article's second part begins with a panorama of the formation of the Brazilian working class and the factory commissions until the end of the 1950s. Subsequently, we approach the cycle of the factory commissions from 1968 (hardening of the civilian-military dictatorship) to 1978 (the phase of the diminution of tensions and the gradual opening or liberalization of the regime). We close the article with some final considerations.

Rise of the workers' and intellectuals' struggles

The Revolution of 1930, led by Getúlio Vargas, strengthened Brazil's industrialization, built up a national industry, improved living conditions of the Brazilian population, established workers' rights, built the state companies, and taught literacy to some workers – in short, it finally constituted our republic. Let us remember that Brazil was, and still is, a country in which a land, income and power was brutally concentrated, with high rates of illiteracy and malnutrition, and very bad working conditions, housing and transportation. Nevertheless, Brazilian historians affirm that in the period 1930–1980 Brazil ceased to be – to a certain extent – a colony for extracting resources and became an economy with a project of national development. We must also remember that the abolition of slavery (1888) and the proclamation of the Republic (1889) did not bring fundamental changes to the Brazilian economy (Prado Jr., 1977).

In other words, even with a "Conservative Revolution" (Lima Filho and Macedo 2011: 307), or what the Gramscian theorists call "passive revolution", that is to say, an incomplete revolution that did not liquidate the power of the oligarchy and where the left-wing forces did not have the strength to achieve a complete revolution, there was a belief that Brazil was in a state of evolution and "could be successful" (Ribeiro 1997).[1]

During the years 1950–1960 Brazil experienced a moment of scientific and cultural flourishing. This process disrupted the oppression of the civilian-military dictatorship of 1964–1985. In the article "Arquitetura nova" (new architecture), written in 1967, Sérgio Ferro – an activist in this movement – expresses the impact of the 1964 coup on the hopes raised by modern architecture in the national developmental project. The New Architecture was born at the beginning of the 1960s, when primarily young people hoped for a more just society: "people believed with greater or lesser intensity and with leftist and rightist variations that Brazil had a chance to be successful" (Ferro 2006: 321; see Arantes, 2002 Koury, 2004 and Kapp *et al.,* 2008).

In this context of social effervescence, innovative ideas and proposals in the domains of painting and architecture appeared. The atelier of Sérgio Ferro, Flávio Império and Rodrigo Lefèvre was a sort of political nucleus in which artistic production and criticism occurred simultaneously. Ferro reminds us that the "office was frequently visited by people from the domains of philosophy, theater, music, literature. It was a melting pot in a sort of project for the creation of a national consciousness, of a culture of our own, which was not imported. It was a period of extraordinary fertility" (Ferro 2001, cited in Arantes 2002: 52).

In the same way Glauber Rocha (2004), one of the representatives of the New Cinema, criticized the national reality that was marked by hunger and poverty. According to him:

[T]he *new cinema* narrated, described, poetized, discoursed, analyzed, developed the subject matters of hunger: characters eating soil, characters eating roots, characters stealing to eat, characters killing to eat, characters fleeing to eat, dirty, ugly, skinny characters, living in dirty, ugly, dark houses. . . . This *miserabilismo* of the *new cinema* contrasts with the tendency of the digest published by the major critic of Guanabara, Carlos Lacerda: films of rich people in beautiful houses, driving luxurious cars; cheerful, funny, rapid films, without messages and with purely industrial objectives. . . . The *new cinema* is a project, which is carried out in the policy of hunger and thus suffers all the consequent weaknesses of its existence. (Glauber Rocha, cited in Koury 2004: 97–8)

According to Koury (2004), the political and cultural manifestations of the 1960s reflected the importance of the artist's role in formulating a critique of the national reality, mainly the models of development and patterns of behavior, and the commitment to the elaboration of alternative projects. The antinomies of that time – participation and alienation; oppression and freedom – signaled the debate polarizations between the right wing and the left wing, and their perspectives for the transformation of society.

In this context, the ideas and the proposals of Sérgio Ferro, Flavio Império and Rodrigo, expressed in the process of their collective creation, artistic practices and written texts, were at the same time a critique of the nation's problems and a response to them. Their works, from a material point of view, were adapted to the economic restrictions of underdevelopment and to the lack of resources, but from a cultural point of view represented the challenge of the new values, thus rendering an audacious project of transformation viable (Koury, 2004: 27).

The Arena Theater was a low-cost playhouse that brought subject matters to help conscienticize the Brazilian people. The directors and playwrights José Renato Pécora, Augusto Boal and Gianfrancesco Guarnieri are outstanding in these domains.[2]

In the 1950s, 50 percent of the Brazilian population was illiterate. This is the context in which Paulo Freire developed his proposals. The formation of a public education system was part of the struggle of the workers, intellectuals, students, educators, trade unionists, parts of the left-wing Catholic Church and even of some industrial sectors.

At the beginning of the 1960s, the National Students' Union (UNE) presented a comprehensive set of demands which covered items such as university and education reform, inflation, foreign capital, imperialism, independent foreign policy, support for Cuba, solidarity with strikers, literacy campaigns, agrarian reform and technical assistance to the rural trade unionism movement.

In 1961 the UNE became an integral part of the national-reformist block and eventually an important component of the People's Mobilization Front, which united all the political and cultural organizations and institutions of the left-wing workers' movement (Dreifuss, 1980). These developments coincided with the growth of People's Action (AP) in the student movement, after the election of Aldo Arantes, a student from the State of Goiás and the leader of AP, as president of the UNE in 1961. The AP represented Catholic left-wing students and went on to win the UNE presidency in 1962 and 1963.

The Declaration of Bahia, a politico-ideological conclusion of the I National Seminar of University Reform, held in Salvador in 1960, represented an important landmark in the political development of the student movement. The declaration described Brazil as "a developing capitalist nation" with "an agrarian infrastructure under the control of powerful foreign groups" and an "oligarchic state" studded with contradictions that "indicated the collapse of the liberal bourgeois structure". The solution the document proposed was the "nationalization of the fundamental sectors of the economy", an end to the alienation of the proletariat, an "effective participation of the workers in government organs" and the "creation by the government of conditions for the complete development of the proletariat's organizations". These items constituted the strategic targets of the student movement. Nevertheless, they recognized they lacked the tactics to help them achieve their objectives, therefore the II National Seminar of University Reform was convened in Curitiba in 1962.

The Paraná Charter declared in Curitiba is a compilation of all the political and ideological decisions of the meeting (Dreifuss 1980). It became one of the most important documents of the student movement. The students' organizations were intended to create an "alliance of workers, peasants, progressive intellectuals, the democratic military and other sectors of national life" to unite and strengthen their claims. They made agrarian reform the cornerstone of the students' struggles.

On the other hand, they hoped that transformations in the educational system would become integral to the workers' and peasants' objective and subjective aspirations. The UNE sought to synthesize these demands in its program of university struggle as the need to "expand the Student-Worker-Peasant Alliance" (Dreifuss, 1980: 300). Although the UNE students promoted university reforms, they understood the limits of the "situation of the university" and of the possibilities university reform offered. They understood that the specific social and political relationships within the space of the university were also manifestations of broader political and social relationships in national society, thus establishing real links between university reform and the general transformation of society.

Brasilia, Brazil's capital, was inaugurated in 1960. The creation of the University of Brasilia (UnB) brought some innovations to Brazilian higher education. According to Darcy Ribeiro, what was involved was the creation of "a university of a new type, articulated in a different way, as the university of the capital of the republic should be" (Ribeiro 1997: 236). Ribeiro believes that the UnB project fascinated Brazilian intellectuals, mainly the scientific community, so that our chief scientists accepted posts as coordinators of the departments of the University.

According to Ribeiro:

> [T]his university was intended to give Brazil the dominance, at a doctoral level, of all the sciences and of the main technologies. These were the fundamental objectives of the UnB, the task of which it was to diagnose Brazilian problems judiciously and seek concrete solutions for them. (Ribeiro 1997: 238)

Ribeiro believed that the major importance of the UnB project was not in its existence per se, but in the effects it brought about. According to him, throughout Brazil there was a real campaign in favor of university reform, in the course of which all became conscious of the serious problems of the Brazilian university, which could not be overcome if one kept on the same path. (Ribeiro 1997: 248)

Ribeiro's dream was that at UnB no one could be persecuted because of their ideology. Nevertheless, this did not last long since

> The military dictatorship that was installed in Brazil, put . . . an end to all cultural life, persecuting, torturing, exiling, killing. The life of all of Brazil's intelligentsia was impoverished drastically by this bloodshed. But a more disastrous effect, on the academic level, was to prevent banned professors from practicing their function of cultural multipliers, which consisted of conducting preparatory programs for new scientists' bodies in Brazil. Thus we lost, in addition to them, hundreds of other specialists equally capable, whose training they would have guided and who were indispensable. (Ribeiro 1997: 260)

Non-university sectors already considered the UnB a focal point for "left-wing" thought, a vision which was only strengthened by the actions of the military. University students and professors were labeled "subversive" and "communists". The campus was invaded and surrounded by the military police and by the Army several times during that year. On 18 October 1965, after the dismissal of 15 professors accused of subversion, 209 professors and instructors signed a document with their collective resignation to protest against the repression they had suffered at the university. In one go the institution lost 79 percent of its teaching staff. Brazil suffered a scientific and cultural brain drain equivalent to that in Franco's Spain, and which debilitated the creativity of the Spanish spirit for decades (Ribeiro, 1997).

Rural struggles

In a country that had never had agrarian reform, the struggle for land was always a vital question. Let us give two examples. It took the state more than 30 years to crush the Quilombo of Palmares[3] and the Canudos rebellions or War of Canudos (1893–1897): a conflict between the Brazilian state and a settler community in the state of Bahia. In the 1950s and 1960s the subject was back on the national agenda. The Ligas Camponesas or peasant leagues (Novaes, 2009), and many progressive rural trade unions were established, the Brazilian Communist Party actively supported non-violent and armed struggles in Brazil. Numerous regional and national congresses of the ULTAB, the Agricultural Union of Cultivators and Workers, took place under the motto "Agrarian reform through the law or through force".

Josué de Castro, a federal deputy and later president of the UN, asked the executive to take action "for basic reform, to change the national economic infrastructure". He specifically fought against the appropriation of federal public funds by the oligarchies of the north-east that used the capitalist state to maintain their domination in that region.

The ruling classes, especially in the Brazilian north-east, were alarmed:

> [Just a]s important for the Brazilian revolution as denouncing the *latifúndio*[4] was the analysis of the capacity for revolt of the inhabitants of the hinterland, that is, the possibility of finding the way towards transformation for themselves. (Dória, 2007: 425)

This appeared in the films of the *cinema novo*[5] as well as in the writings of the intellectuals of that time and in the analyses and actions of the ruling classes (Dória, 2007).

Reforms, coup and repression

The 1950–1960 social struggles became stronger with President Jânio Quadros's resignation. According to Darcy Ribeiro – who was one of the founders of the UnB and President João Goulart's Minister of Civil Affairs – Goulart wanted to proceed with the structural reforms.[6] During his government (1961–1964) the reforms needed to start overcoming Brazil's structural problems[7] entered the political agenda: the need for agrarian reform, reform in education (Mélo, 2009) reform in housing (Maricato, 1987), health reform and the control of foreign capital.

The USA, the conservative wing of the Catholic Church, the *latifundiários* (big landholders) and the national bourgeoisie planned the coup d'état, which had profound consequences for the workers' struggles. The civilian-military dictatorship (1964–1985) recomposed the hegemony of capital in Brazil and inaugurated a counter-revolution that acquired world features (Ianni, 1965, 1970; Fernandes, 2006; Schwarz, 2007).[8] As Aarão Reis (1980) observes, the left-wing forces were not sufficiently organized to resist and had overlooked the possibility that a coup d'état would take place in 1964.

There is clearly a historical rupture in Brazil, which destroyed the construction of the hegemony of the Brazilian left. The seat of the UNE was destroyed by the civilian-military dictatorship in 1964 on the day of the coup d'état. A large number of militants were assassinated or compelled to leave the country. Glauber Rocha, one of the most ingenious film producers, moved to Cuba. Paulo Freire went to Chile. Darcy Ribeiro went to Uruguay. Sérgio Ferro went into exile in Grenoble, France, Florestan Fernandes to Canada, Luís Carlos Prestes, the main representative of the Communist Party, went to Russia.

The coup broke the historical rise of workers' struggles and the flourishing of intellectual theory and action in Brazil. Francisco de Oliveira describes the repercussions of the coup d'état in Pernambuco, an important state in the Brazilian north-east:

> The 1964 coup affected Pernambuco with special fury. They decimated the left, the workers' movement, the Catholic politico-intellectual movement [and] the students' movement;

exiled an important section of the leaders, the climate of debate and the innovating initiatives disappeared, as well as the Popular Culture Movement and Paulo Freire, the transformative reform of the Sudene [Superintendency for the development of the north-east]. The only thing left was Bishop Hélder Câmara's solitary voice, who, by the way, was installed in the archdiocese [of Olinda-Recife] in the first post-coup days, where he made a speech, the courage and dignity of which would lead to its incorporation in an anthology of the great Brazilian civic-political speeches. There the Resistance Church came into being; with Bishop Hélder Câmara and Bishop Paulo Evaristo Arns it had its highest moment and expression. (Oliveira 2008: 85)

The formation of the Brazilian working class and the factory commissions

Workers' organization in the workplaces, as a form of resistance and struggle against the conditions of exploitation of the workforce, expressing the collective capacity of control of the work process, became present, in Brazil, in the field of ideas – in the heart of militant, intellectual groups and left-wing organizations – as well as through concrete experiences of factory commissions or councils, worker control and worker management or self-management of productive units by the workers themselves.

It was a long way from the first references to mutualist tradition and resistance societies (Simão, 1966) in Brazil in the initial period of the constitution of its working class, with a predominantly anarchist or anarcho-syndicalist influence, to the outbreak of the factory commissions in the decades 1960, 1970 and 1980. Factory commissions, namely, worker-based organizations that clashed with employers, with the state and sometimes with the very trade union apparatus itself, surfaced continuously as the form of organization and struggle of the Brazilian workers.

The following account on the formation of the Brazilian working class by Rolando Fratti, ex-trade union militant and politician, a prominent figure from 1930 to 1970, explains the first steps of the working class in Brazil, its organizations and political guidelines:

> The working class in Brazil came into being in the year 50 of the past century [1850] . . . . Why did the working class appear then, what causes determined this? In the first place, the proclamation of the country as a colony of Portugal until 1822 [Brazil's Independence] and, before this, also the opening of Brazil's ports to all the countries of the world, the work of King João VI, who fled from Portugal pursued by Napoleon and was installed in Brazil. Another factor was the prohibition of the African slave trade in 1850, on behalf of the then queen of the seas, England, which was no longer interested in maintaining slavery in Latin America. What interested her was the development of capitalism, which would finally result in an advantage for her, that is, in the domination of Latin America. Another factor was the beginning of the cycle of coffee production.
>
> Together, all these factors determined that the bourgeoisie needed a free workforce (free in quotation marks, of course). The African slave no longer served its purpose. And so the working class came into being in Brazil. In 1865 the stream of migration began: Poles, Italians, Portuguese, Japanese, Hungarians and Spaniards, among people from other countries, moved to Brazil. With them anarcho-syndicalism, which was the politico-ideological current that led the workers' movement at that moment in Europe, came to Brazil. . . .
>
> The merit of this ideological current was to organize the small proletarian group for the first struggles. The associations in the small factories; from the associations to the leagues, which connected these associations; the mutuals.[9]

In this period of the formation of the working class in Brazil, with the abolition of slavery at the end of the 19th century, the immigration of European peasants and workers and the beginning of industrialization, we find the first associative forms which the workers use to help each other mutually as well as to resist the tough working conditions in the productive units. The initial parameters of these forms of organization were chiefly provided by the experience the European immigrants brought in their luggage. Thus the mutual aid societies appear in the first associative forms created by the workers in this moment of social struggles in Brazil.

The appearance of the mutuals in São Paulo was due

> on the one hand, to the economic-social effects of the incipient urbanization and, on the other hand to the resuming of associative models already elaborated in the European industrialization process. (Simão 1966:160)

The mutual aid societies possessed as propaganda the achievement of assistance programs, such as access to physicians and pharmacists, support in sickness, unemployment, payment in case of the inability to work, funerals, and so on. At least one short-lived attempt of a mutual aid societies' federation in 1899 is known. The workers' leagues appear later, and are closer to the trade union model, assuming the role of resistance societies and constituted by their function. Simão mentions the possibility that, since the mutuals and leagues existed side-by-side, a "significant process of structural and functional hybridization" had occurred, with the mutuals assuming some professional functions of defense and the leagues some functions of assistance (Simão 1966: 162).

He quotes the newspaper *A Plebe*, which describes the functioning of these first workers' associative forms:

> The first workers' organizations in Brazil were the workers' leagues that included almost always without differentiation

workers of different functions and industries and the objective of which was, except for one or another benevolent goal, the defense of the immediate and common interests of all classes, that is, the improvement of wages and the diminution of [working] hours, and they achieved very little because they lacked the necessary strength due to the amorphousness that characterized them. Later, there appeared the resistance societies, that were more homogenous nuclei emerging from the first centers or leagues. They are unions of functions which, by developing, founded branches or subsidiaries in the entire country that were dependent on the central organization established in the big city. Next to these existed autonomous, more or less benevolent unions, now supporting strikes, now organizing political manifestations. (Simão 1966: 160)

Nevertheless, ideological distinctions were already present at the heart of the Brazilian working class, and multiple tendencies appeared that followed, to a greater or lesser extent, the divergencies in the international movement. Simão (1966) points out that four great currents existed in this period: the anarchists, the socialists, the communists and the chambers of labor or the labor stock market.

As far as the communists were concerned, Fratti expressed the following critique, in retort to a similar analysis dedicated to the anarchists:

The great socialist October Revolution in Russia, which had an enormous repercussion all over the world, has created as a consequence the Communist Party [CP] in 1922, which is gradually exerting an influence in the workers' movement left empty by anarcho-syndicalism. One replaced the other. Nevertheless the CP also came into being and it brought to Brazil a political line, which did not correspond to the needs of the Brazilian population and to those of the proletariat in the first place. This is the line traced by the Communist International in its second Congress in 1920, which did not permit class alliances of the proletariat. It was the so-called class against class line; and at that time people believed that development would lead to such growth of the working class that it would be the predominant force in Brazil and would lead the country to socialism without the need to form a front, an alliance with other forces. That line was quite wrong, since it was mainly a dependent country.

In the following decade, along with the workers' federations, a new theme arose of the organization in the workplaces through factory committees or trade union representations in the companies. According to Rago (1985), the appearance of this subject in the workers' press between 1918 and 1922 reflects the process of factory occupation in the "hot October" of Turin, in Italy (Di Paola, 2011) and confronted the Brazilian workers with the need to organize and to struggle for control of the labor process, including the occupation of the factories and the reorganization of the productive process.

Continuing from the creation of the factory committees, a new form of production organization can be imagined and experimented with; every committee sending a representative to the industry council that in turn engenders an executive committee in the city or region, with district committees functioning in the city districts. In general, it is an anticipation of what would be used on a grand scale in the republican Spain of 1936–1939.

On the organizational level, all the representatives would have to respect collective decisions and their positions, responsibility and authority could be revoked at any moment. Rago cites the Italian movement, but the 1905 and 1917 experience of the soviets in Russia might have influenced this model, due to the intense contacts and relationships between the main Brazilian labor leaders and the socialist or Communist International movement.

From then on, the factory committees or commissions constituted

an associative practice of struggle and organization historically repeated by the Brazilian workers, in the course of the constant industrial conflicts that marked their own formation as a class. (Pedreira Filho 1997: 39)

Pedreira Filho's research traces the history of the Brazilian experience of factory commissions or groups to 1907, although he states that only in the 1919 strike movement did the initiatives taken by the factory commissions gain importance and significance.

Even in this period, the organizing struggles of the factory commissions or committees were constituent, in a certain way, of the deployment of the workers' associative forms carried out in the workers' districts and of social and cultural centers, associations, trade union sections, clandestine groups of companies and so on. On the outbreak of the 1919 strike, for example, coinciding with an anti-capitalist wave of the immediate post-war period in Europe, the movement was coordinated by a "committee", initially created among the trade-unionist organizations for the 1 May mobilization. With the generalization of the conflict, a General Council of Workers was formed of a leading member from each existing factory or workshop commission. The strike was defeated by the repression of the movement and dozens of imprisonments.

The strikes of 1919 and the results of the III Congress of Brazilian Workers, held in Rio de Janeiro in 1920, were a pretext for extending repressive measures at the beginning of the decade of 1920, beginning with the Adolfo Gordo Law, which made it possible to expel foreign workers involved in unrest from the country. Amid these repressive measures and the strain of increasing social conflict, and following the October Revolution, the weight of the communist tendency grew within the workers' movement, which was until then guided mainly by the anarcho-syndicalist tendency, leading to the creation of the Communist Party of Brazil in 1922.

The creation of the Peasants' and Workers' Block (BOC) in 1927 at the beginning of Washington Luíz's government was of communist inspiration.[10]

The 1930s were marked by the creation of labor legislation, particularly the trade-unionist corporative structure, with the creation of the Ministry of Labor, Labor Justice and the Consolidation of the Labor Law of the Vargas era, aimed at "harmonizing" the relationship between capital and labor in view of the industrialization of the country. With the *Estado Novo* dictatorship (1937–1945), a new repressive wave hit the Brazilian workers' movement and its organizations, at that time already under strong communist influence.

Starting in 1946–1947 and throughout the 1950s the creation of factory commissions spread significantly. The beginning of the decade was marked by a rising workers' movement. In 1953 the "Strike of the 300 thousand" paralyzed São Paolo's industries for almost one month, accompanied by imprisonments, conflicts with the police and threats of all kinds. During the struggle strike commissions emerged as supra-union structures. They outstripped the unions over the conduct of actions and mobilizations based on the practice of mass assemblies and the creation of the "Inter-union Strike Commission formed by various independent strike commissions from each category" (Couto 2003: 105). Besides the economic benefits gained (including a 70 percent wage increase), the result of the strike was the experience of a class organization that coordinated confrontations with the employers and the state, imposing in practice the need for a supra-union organization antagonistic to the spirit of the existing union legislation.

In the 1960s new actors entered the political scene to discuss the workers' question, such as the National Labor Front, the Catholic Workers Youth, Catholic Workers Action and dissident tendencies of the Brazilian Communist Party. It is from this field that the leaders of the factory commission of the Cobrasma railway car factory in Osasco (an important city in greater São Paulo) arose; and the clandestine action of the commission from the beginning of the 1960s resulted in the 1968 strike. The workers occupied the company protesting about the squeeze on wages as well as the military regime. The regime responded with police intervention in both the company and the Metallurgists' Trade Union of Osasco (Couto, 2003; Ibrahim, 1986).

While the working class in Brazil and in a great part of Latin America entered the leaden years, in Europe the movement of autonomous struggles grew during the 1960s and the first half of the 1970s. The "wild" and "spontaneous" general strikes shook regimes and the capitalist system, with millions of lost workdays through multiple forms of struggle and resistance in the workplaces, resulting in hundreds of occupied companies being controlled for long periods by the workers. João Bernardo reminds us that, in this period, the field of the anti-capitalist struggles was on the verge of being won:

> In the course of these 30 years (1950–1980), strikes and other protest movements emerged; increasingly organized outside the trade union apparatus and alien to the official institutions of negotiation. By showing themselves to be capable of maintaining the control of the struggles, without alienating their condition from the trade union leaders, the workers began more and more often to occupy companies and to have them function under their authority, thus progressively remodeling their own work relationships and questioning production criteria. In these struggles, the workers did not limit themselves to merely claiming control, but actually applied it in practice. It was not a simple aspiration, but an effective action modality. (Bernardo, 1997: 2)

The factory commissions (1968–1978) during the military-civilian dictatorship

The world revolution had repercussions in Brazil at the end of the 1960s. The flourishing of struggles worldwide led to the hardening of the civilian-military dictatorship in 1968. After the repression suffered by the Cobrasma workers in Osasco, as well as by workers of the Braseixos car and motor parts factory in Contagem in the state of Minas Gerais, and facing the growing repression of the military regime, the workers' reorganization happened in a molecular way, from people's dwellings to the re-articulation of the factory groups in the 1970s, regrouping their forces until the moment in which they could agitate again. Factory commissions emerged again massively, with the explosion of workers' strikes initiated in 1978, from São Paulo and its outskirts, which include the towns of Santo André, São Bernardo and São Caetano.[11] Based upon long and patient organizational work by groups under the influence of communist dissidents and the Catholic Church, clandestine groups were forged in companies, committing acts of sabotage that signaled a possible resumption of workers' strikes and struggles. From the point of view of the ruling classes, the end of the 1970s were already a process of "democratic opening", which was slow, gradual, controlled and without ruptures (Fernandes, 1986).

The idea of autonomous workers' organization in the workplaces as a necessary condition for the efficiency of the struggles and the creation of a new trade union structure, inspired by the experiences of the workers of Cobrasma and Braseixos in 1968, was propagated by the trade-unionist opposition movement in São Paulo, mainly in the metallurgic and chemical sectors. But it was in the region of greater São Paulo in May 1978 that the movement gained ground and unleashed a cycle of workers' struggles that marked the beginning of the "re-democratization" of Brazil. At the end of the 1970s and the beginning of the 1980s, numerous struggles broke out that culminated in the creation of the Movimento dos Trabalhadores Rurais Sem-Terra (Landless Workers' Movement), the Movement of People Affected by Dams, and the Workers' Party and also in struggles for popular housing, public universities and so on.

On 12 May 1978 Scania bus factory workers paralyzed production and remained in the factory, mainly demanding wage adjustments. From then on, factory stoppages became generalized in greater São Paulo, home of the big auto assembly plants in Brazil, as a consequence of which they moved to other sectors and regions of the country (Antunes, 1992; Sader, 1988). The commissions formed the dynamic and stimulating element of the strike movement: they organized general assemblies within the production units to decide what steps should be followed and involved the trade union for the conclusion of the negotiation processes.

Employers began to focus their interventions and repression on the members of the factory commissions, since they believed that many commissions had become the voice of the workers. So the new trade-unionism, which emerged from the greater São Paulo area, stopped endorsing the creation of factory commissions, arguing that they ended up exposing shop-floor leaders to employers' repression. Instead the new unionism defended the trade union commissions formed by the union leaders who operated at the workplaces and enjoyed the legal status conferred on trade union leaders. Some also accused the commissions of trade-union parallelism.

In terms of the extent of the activities of the factory commissions and their meaning for the Brazilian workers' movement, we find in Maurício Tragtenberg's work the key to understanding the commissions as manifestations of workers' autonomy. Tragtenberg refers to heterodox Marxists, such as Pannekoek, Gramsci and Gorter (Tragtenberg, 1981). Comparing the practice of the commissions to that of corporate trade union structures, Tragtenberg understands the deep pedagogical meaning of the experiences of struggle through the factory commission insofar as

> through participation in the factory commission the worker learns that in the factory there is a division of labor which he must obey, outside the factory he learns that *politics* has to be practiced in the parties, *economic demands* in the trade unions, *knowledge* is confined to schools, and TV and radio define what does or does not have cultural value. His own life is divided in impervious fragments. It is the practice of his struggle through

the commissions, which gives him the elements for taking a stand regarding political, economic and cultural questions. He learns through the school of struggle. It teaches him that, by struggling for wages (economy), he is confronted with the factory hierarchy (power), he has recourse to self-organization and develops his politico-social and cultural conscience. They are *parts* of a whole. (Tragtenberg 2011: 23–4)

In this process of self-organization, the workers create their own horizontal organizations, forming a "struggling community" that controls the very process of the development of the struggles as well as their objectives. Thus, one prevents the domination and oppressive relationships experienced outside the workplaces from being transferred to organizations that intend to "represent" the workers in vertical processes that reorganize the division between the "directors" and the "directed".

Tragtenberg made an enormous effort to propagate, through articles in newspapers, books and journals, the experiences of the factory commissions in Brazil that emerged during the strike cycle initiated in 1978, such as the commissions created in companies like Ford, Máquinas Piratininga, Asama, Massey Ferguson, Aliperti, Barbará, and so on. Tragtenberg (2011), like the International Workers' Association earlier, affirms: "workers' liberation must be the work of the workers themselves". This liberation cannot be delegated to the "vanguards" on duty, since it depends on the initiative and participation of all the people involved. Ford's factory commission, for example, used the slogan: "worker, if nobody works in your place, nobody will decide in your place". It is a question of an authentic commission that is neither tied to the entrepreneurs nor to the trade union because the commission does not have an owner; it belongs to the drudging workers who labor there.

While commenting on the experience of the factory commission at Asama, Tragtenberg (2011) points out that it was different from the others because it was created to correct the injustices meted out to the workers, demanding that the employers grant them better working and living conditions. The major organ of the commission was the general assembly, and the trade union according to the statutes was a "consultative organ". The terms of its representatives are revocable at any time. In synthesis, the importance Tragtenberg attributes to the factory commissions and to the workers' autonomous struggles is due to the understanding that

> [t]he workers' self-organization at their workplace and the democratization of labor relationships constitute the basic pillars of any democracy on the level of global society because the existence of factory despotism together with formal democracy, outside the walls of the factory, is a profound contradiction. (Tragtenberg, 2008: 87)

Final considerations

The factory commissions represent more advanced associative practices of workers' struggles inside production units recurrent during almost the entire 20th century. In the process of these struggles, the workers solved their problems by occupying the production facilities and, at an even more advanced stage, they reinitiated production autonomously. But occupation and resuming production was considered an option by the workers' movement only in the 1990s, when the economic and labor crisis provoke the emergence of recuperated factories in Brazil and in other countries (Faria and Novaes, 2011).

Factory commissions or committees always suffered from the implacable attack by employers, and very often they were badly misunderstood and boycotted by trade union leaders. They are worker-based organisms going back to the workers' former associative traditions, inspired by a feeling of common destiny, of a community of practice which cooperates and resists within the process of capital and the production of commodities. In some cases the commissions emerged from the activities of clandestine groups within big companies, or were articulated in the spaces of trade union associations. They are institutionalized during the conflicts as organs of the workers' representation in the companies, maintaining relationships sometimes complementary and sometimes in conflict with the trade union representatives.

The historical reason for these autonomous practices of workers' struggles within capitalism, as João Bernardo explains, is that

> [t]he factory commissions [in] giving importance to the workers' combative solidarity in their workplaces constitute the main expression of the workers' capacity for self-organization. The proletariat considers itself here as a real historical subject. It is no more a mere matter of academic reflection, or the moral bond which the zigzags of the party guidelines refer to in order to become the acting subject of their own story. The stages of the workers' movement, its transformations and ruptures, after all, consist in the trajectory of the internal forms of organization adopted by the proletariat in the confrontation with capitalism. The clash between the institutions created during the struggle and the institutions of the ruling order have dictated the evolution of the forms of contestation and at the same time the profile assumed by the society in which we live. (Bernardo, 1997: 15)

The immense experience that the Brazilian workers went through in the sphere of organization in the workplaces, particularly through the creation of factory committees or commissions, besides having contributed decisively to the acceleration of a Brazilian democratic transition, obliged the employers and the state to adopt new strategies for managing the workforce and to regulating the class relationships in the heart of Brazilian society. The mechanisms applied in Brazil, as in other countries, included Toyotist "participation", workers' involvement, wearing the colors, making suggestions, working in teams, being proactive and volunteering – subject matter that is well-known in the sociology of labor literature.

With social struggles in retreat in the 1990s and with trade unions focused on institutional relationships to negotiate working conditions, the commissions saw themselves in the crossfire, being attacked by the employers and disputed by pragmatic trade union leaderships interested in their pension funds. At the end of the 1980s the process of the assimilation of the factory commissions was already at an advanced stage within Brazil's major companies integrated as representation organisms inside the companies, in the spirit of German co-participation (Bruno, 1992).

Inspired by the experiences of the Russian, Italian and Hungarian factory councils, as a tendency of self-administration socialism the factory commissions in Brazil were completely transformed and were integrated into the system of the production of goods as spaces for labor–capital dialogue and as an arena for the resolution of conflicts.

Certainly the existence of factory committees or councils represents some progress towards more democratic forms of management in spaces marked by despotism and authoritarianism. But, under the present conditions, the factory commissions cannot point to a perspective beyond capital.

Notes

1. To illustrate the importance of the theme of revolution it is sufficient to remember that the title of the book by Caio Prado Júnior, an important Marxist intellectual was *A Revolução Brasileira* (The Brazilian Revolution) and the one by Nelson Werneck Sodré was *Introdução à Revolução Brasileira* (Introduction to the Brazilian Revolution). Many intellectuals even say that it is from 1950 to 1968 that we experienced the flourishing of Brazilian intellectual critique, particularly the understanding of the particularities of our capitalism and of our revolution. At the same time, it is at this time that we will find intellectuals immersed in the struggles of their time.

2. From 1900 to 1950 workers carried out vast projects in the cultural field, with the creation of numerous workers' newspapers, and also considerable production in the literary field, besides theater, music and the cinema. According to Foot Hardman (2002), the process of rupture such as in the initial period of workers' autonomy, which led to the bureaucratization

of trade unionist life under Getúlio Vargas' government as a result of State control, cannot be dissociated from the cultural question. It proposed the existence of a "simultaneity (and probable correspondence) between the bureaucratization of Brazilian trade unionism, the emergence of the authoritarian state and the increasing 'popular culture' transformation into 'mass culture,' accompanying the progress of the cultural industry and the monopoly of cultural mass media" (Foot Hardman, 2002). See also Lima and Vargas (1986).

3. Quilombos are settlements of fugitive slaves, the largest of which was established in Palmares.

4. Huge estates often owned by absentee landowners and traditionally worked by poor peasants.

5. See, for example, "*Deus e o Diabo na Terra do Sol*" (English title: Black God, White Devil) by Glauber Rocha (1964).

6. For further information on this historical context, see also Dreifuss (1980), Gennari (1999), Moniz Bandeira (2001), Campos (2009) and Schwarz (2007).

7. The rise of struggles in Brazil cannot be disconnected from the rise of workers' struggles in other Latin American countries. Latin America as a whole experienced a period of social effervescence. The Brazilian civilian-military dictatorship played also a central role in the coups that took place in other Latin American countries, as numerous documents on Operation Condor have shown.

8. Darcy Ribeiro, among other historians, observes that Getúlio Vargas' suicide in 1954 deferred the military intervention in Brazil to 1964. In his words: "The news of the suicide hit me like a bomb. Above all his Testament Letter, the highest document ever produced in Brazil. The most touching, the most significant one, Since I have read it, it has been to me the political letter which has guided me. And this it is [true] for the more lucid Brazilians. But it is not for a minority that has made this country unhappy ever since by governing in a corrupt, oppressive and petty way. I perceived instantaneously, after all, just as all Brazilians perceived, that the campaign of the "sea of mud" was a dirty trick by the press supported by big foreign companies in order to overthrow the president who was creating Petrobras and who announced the creation of Eletrobras, thus being opposed to the very powerful foreign groups: those involved in petroleum and in electricity" (Ribeiro, 1997: 228). Petrobras and Eletrobras are state-owned oil and electricity companies.

9. Speech held at the International Meeting of the Trade Union Opposition in Exile, Brussels, 1979. The meeting, held on the 30 and 31 March and on 1 April 1979, counted on the presence of representatives of trade union

organizations from 14 countries, the GAOS (Support Group for the Trade Union Opposition in Exile) among them Fratti, exiled in Italy and of leaders of Brazil's Trade Union Opposition. All speeches were recorded (part of them has been transcribed), and are part of a study carried out by Claudio Nascimento on this subject, with which one of the authors collaborated in the initial phase of the organization of the material of the meeting.

10. Washington Luíz is known in Brazilian history for having expressed in a sentence what Brazil's dominant class thinks of the people: "A social question is a question for the police".

11. For more information about these struggles, see the films *Braços Cruzados Máquinas Paradas* (Folded Arms, Idle Machines) and *ABC da Greve* (ABC of the strike), both with subtitles in English (Gervitz and Toledo, 1978; Hirszman, 1979).

References

Aarão Reis, D.A. (1980) *A revolução faltou ao encontro: os comunistas no Brasil*. São Paulo: Brasiliense.

Antunes, R. (1992) *A rebeldia do trabalho: o confronto operário no ABC paulista: as greves de 1978/80*. Campinas, SP: Editora da Unicamp.

Arantes, P.F. (2002) *Arquitetura Nova – Sérgio Ferro, Flávio Império e Rodrigo Lefèvre, de Artigas aos Mutirões*. São Paulo: Editora 34.

Bernardo, J. (1997) Apresentação. In Pedreira Filho, V. *Comissões de Fábrica – um claro enigma*. São Paulo: Editora Entrelinhas.

Bruno, L. (1992) *O que é autonomia operária?* São Paulo: Brasiliense.

Campos, F. (2009) A arte da conquista: o capital internacional no desenvolvimento capitalista brasileiro (1951–1992). PhD thesis. Instituto de Economia, Unicamp.

Couto, A.M.M. (2003) Greve na Cobrasma: uma história de luta e resistência. São Paulo: Annablume.

Di Paola, P. (2011) Factory Councils in Turin, 1919–1920: the sole and authentic social representatives of the proletarian class. In Ness, I. and Azzellini, D. (eds) *Ours to Master and to Own: Workers' Councils from the Commune to the Present*. Chicago: Haymarket

Dória, F.O. (2007) Nordeste: 'problema nacional' para a esquerda. In Quartim de Moraes, J. and Del Roio, M. (eds) *História do Marxismo no Brasil – Visões do Brasil*. Vol. VII. Campinas: Unicamp.

Dreifuss, R. (1980) State, class and the organic elite: the formation of the entrepreneurial order in Brazil, 1961–1965. PhD thesis. University of Glasgow.

Faria, M.S. and Novaes, H.T. (2011) Brazilian recovered factories: the constraints of workers' control. In Ness, I. and Azzellini, D. (eds) *Ours to Master and to Own: Workers' Councils from the Commune to the Present*. Chicago: Haymarket.

Fernandes, F. (1986) *Nova república?* Rio de Janeiro: Zahar.

Fernandes, F. (2006) *A Revolução Burguesa no Brasil: Ensaio de Interpretação Sociológica*. São Paulo: Global.

Ferro, S. (2006) *Arquitetura e Trabalho Livre*. São Paulo: Cosacnaify.

Foot Hardman, F. (2002) *Nem Pátria nem Patrão! Memória Operária, Cultura e Literatura no Brasil*. 3rd edn. São Paulo: Editora da UNESP.

Gennari, A.M. (1999) *Réquiem ao Capitalismo Nacional: Lei de Remessas de Lucros no Governo Goulart*. São Paulo: Cultura Acadêmica Editora.

Ianni, O. (1965) *Estado e Capitalismo, Estrutura Social e Industrialização no Brasil*. Rio de Janeiro: Civilização Brasileira.

Ianni, O. (1970) *Crisis in Brazil*. Columbia University Press.

Ibrahim, J. (1986) *O que todo Cidadão Precisa Saber Sobre Comissões de Fábrica*. São Paulo: Global.

Kapp, S., Baltazar, A.P. and Morado, D. (2008) Architecture as critical exercise: little pointers towards alternative practices. Available at http://www.field-journal.org/uploads/file/2008%20Volume%202%20/Architecture%20as%20Critical%20Exercise_MOM.pdf (accessed 24 November 2014).

Koury, A.P. (2004) *Grupo Arquitetura Nova: Flávio Império, Rodrigo Lefèvre, Sérgio Ferro*. São Paulo: Edusp.

Lima, M.A. and Vargas, M.T. (1986) Teatro operário em São Paulo. In Prado, A. (ed.) *Libertários no Brasil: Memória, Lutas, Cultura*. São Paulo: Brasiliense.

Lima Filho, P.A. and Macedo, R.A. (2011) Poeira dos mitos: revolução e contrarrevolução nos capitalismos da miséria. In Benini, E., Faria, M. S., Novaes, H.T. and Dagnino, R. (eds) *Gestão Pública e Sociedade: fundamentos e políticas públicas de economia solidária*. São Paulo: Outras Expressões.

Maricato, E. (1987) *A Política Habitacional durante o Regime Militar*. Petrópolis: Vozes.

Mélo, C. (2009) Estado e educação pela imprensa: o debate de Florestan Fernandes ante a lei de Diretrizes e Bases da Educação Nacional (1959–1961). 2009. M.A. thesis, Universidade Estadual de Maringá.

Moniz Bandeira, L.A. (2001) *O Governo João Goulart: as Lutas Sociais no Brasil, 1961–1964.* 7th edn. Rio de Janeiro: Revan; Brasília: Ed. UnB, 2001.

Novaes, H.T. (2009) Peasant leagues. In Ness, I. *International Encyclopedia of Revolution and Protest* – 1500 to the Present. Oxford: Wiley.

Oliveira, F. (2008) *Noiva da Revolução – Elegia para uma re(li)gião.* São Paulo: Boitempo.

Pedreira Filho, V. (1997) *Comissões de Fábrica – um Claro Enigma.* São Paulo: Editora Entrelinhas.

Prado, C. Jr (1977) *A Revolução Brasileira.* São Paulo: Brasiliense.

Rago, L.M. (1985) O controle da fábrica: os anarquistas e a autogestão. In Rago, L.M. *Do Cabaré ao Lar: a Utopia da Cidade Disciplinar: Brasil 1890–1930.* Rio de Janeiro: Paz e Terra.

Ribeiro, D. (1997) *Confissões.* São Paulo: Companhia das Letras.

Rocha, G. (2004) *Revolução do cinema novo.* São Paulo: Cosac Naify.

Schwarz, R. (2007) *Cultura e Política – 1964–1969.* Rio de Janeiro: Paz e Terra.

Sader, E. (1988) *Quando Novos Personagens Entram em Cena: Experiências, Falas e Lutas dos Trabalhadores da Grande São Paulo (1970–1980).* Rio de Janeiro: Paz e Terra.

Simão, A. (1966) *Sindicato e Estado: suas Relações na Formação do Proletariado de São Paulo.* São Paulo: Dominus Editora.

Tragtenberg, M. (1981) *Marxismo Heterodoxo.* São Paulo: Brasiliense.

Tragtenberg, M. (2008) *Reflexões sobre Socialismo.* São Paulo: Editora da UNESP.

Tragtenberg, M. (2011) *Autonomia Operária.* São Paulo: Editora da UNESP.

Films

Gervitz, R. and Toledo, S. (1978) *Braços Cruzados Máquinas Paradas.*

Hirszman, L. (1979) *ABC da Greve.*

Rocha, G. (1964) *Deus e o Diabo na Terra do Sol.* Rio de Janeiro: Embra Films.

Rocha, G. (1967) *Terra em Transe.* Rio de Janeiro: Embra Films.

EIGHT

Self-management, Workers' Control and Resistance against Crisis and Neoliberal Counter-reforms in Mexico

Patrick Cuninghame

The focus of this chapter is on Mexico, where, with the exception of the Zapatista movement, the left in general is much weaker than in South America. The workers' movement has always been a junior partner of the more numerous but more conservative peasants' movements and of course it has been the prime objective of co-optation and corporatism during almost a century of Party of the Institutionalized Revolution (PRI) repression, coercion and corruption. Nevertheless, there have been important struggles in the recent past over issues of self-management and workers control, which deserve to be remembered and highlighted as an important part of the Latin American experience.

Self-management has been a controversial aspect of the international workers' movement since the early 19th century, when Robert Owen and Charles Fourier first gave shape to the cooperative movements in Scotland and France. Soon Marx and Engels were to criticize cooperativism and its practice of workers' self-management as part of "utopian socialism", which, according to them, aimed to coexist peacefully with capitalism and only break with it gradually, rather than accepting the challenge and urgency of violent revolutionary change and the necessity, above all, for the political destruction of capitalism, as they made clear in *The Communist Manifesto* of 1848. These criticisms continue today, when in most parts of the world the cooperative movements have long since been recuperated by and re-integrated into capitalism, forming an often leading role in the post-Fordist neoliberal paradigm shift, as in the case of the Third Italy[1] (Bagnasco, 1977). The argument that self-management was little more than a form of self-exploitation, of workers by workers, seemed to have won the day, until the rise of the occupied, self-managed social centers related to the autonomist movements in Italy, Germany and Spain in the 1980s and 1990s demonstrated that it still had a clearly anti-capitalist connotation, at least under certain circumstances. In reality, many of the social centers were to be either repressed or shut down or, in a few cases, develop into successful commercial enterprises such as the Leoncavallo social center in Milan (Katsiaficas, 1997).

What has perhaps given greater credibility to the renewal of these practices have been more recent events in Latin America, particularly the rebellion of the EZLN (Zapatista National Liberation Army) in Chiapas, Mexico, on 1 January 1994 against both the implementation of North American Free Trade Agreement, one of the pillars of global neoliberalism and the death knell for Mexican sovereignty and living standards, and the corrupt, authoritarian neoliberal regime both in Mexico and throughout the world. Since then the Zapatistas (or neo-Zapatistas, since the first Zapatista movement was part of the Mexican Revolution over a century ago and was led by a radical but devout peasant leader, Emiliano Zapata) have advanced, despite perpetual repression and counter-insurrection from the Mexican state and its US and EU backers, to the point where they not only self-manage rural and manufacturing cooperatives as the mainstay of their anti-capitalist economic model, but above all they self-govern themselves in a directly democratic manner through the good government juntas, set up in 2003 after the Mexican government had reneged on the 1996 San Andrés Accords on indigenous autonomy. All this tends to confirm the thesis of those who criticize purely economic self-management as more being useful to capitalism than to anti-capitalism (Stahler-Sholk, 2011; Wright, 2002).

The second Latin American initiative has been the recuperated factory movement in Argentina since the social revolution of December 2001 when, together with the mass demonstrations of those who rejected the neoliberal policies that had brought their country to a state of economic and political collapse, as president after president fell from power and company after company shut down and sacked its workers, the dismissed industrial and service sector workers refused to be sent home penniless. Instead, they occupied their workplaces, demanding that the employers reopen them for business. Once it became clear that the capitalists had no intention of reopening, the workers were faced with two options: go home to unemployment and poverty or stay and self-manage their workplaces as cooperatives and so attempt to defend their income and productive activity, even if as part of a still very much capitalist economy, with all the exploitation and alienation that that implies. Often these recuperated workplaces were at the center of community initiatives which demanded that the workers kept them open to prevent the impoverishment and collapse of those working-class communities. Today, over a decade later, more than 300 such recuperated (occupied and self-managed) workplaces, many of which are factories, remain open and functioning as worker-controlled cooperatives. Moreover, Argentina, having been a bastion of neoliberalism under Menem, still has under Fernandez an at least rhetorically post-neoliberal government. Internationally and regionally Argentina supports more radical governments in Venezuela and Ecuador. In the latter countries self-managed cooperatives are very much at the center of the attempts, above all from the grassroots and often against so-called progressive governments, to make another world possible and to construct a successful post-neoliberal economy, even in the midst of the worst global economic crisis since the Depression of the 1930s.

Mexico 2012–2014: neoliberal counter-reforms and social resistance

Having looked briefly at some of the discussions on the merits or otherwise of self-management as a form of workers control, I want now to present an updated overview of the status of social resistance against the anti-working-class neoliberal offensive of the first year in office of President Enrique Peña Nieto of the PRI. Nieto's reform programme has been supported by the two other main political parties in the coalition, known until recently as the Pact for Mexico. The Pact ended when the nominally center-left Party of the Democratic Revolution (PRD) withdrew in protest against the energy reform designed to partially privatize Pemex, the notoriously corrupt state oil company nationalized in 1938 and one of the last vestiges of the Mexican Revolution of 1910–1938.

This neoliberal offensive to date has included two anti-labor reforms. The first was strictly a reform of the Federal Labor Law in late 2012, the first act of the PRI/Pact for Mexico government, which focused, among several other initiatives, in formalizing out-sourcing and subcontracting. This was an attempt to formalize (for fiscal reasons) the now larger informal sector, given that the richest sectors pay few taxes and have avoided punishment for any tax evasion by investing in the informal sector of the economy. Thus, it has exceeded the formal sector both in size and in its ability to generate revenue and new jobs.

The second neoliberal counter-reform of labor was disguised as the "education reform law" of September 2013. It directly attacked the largest employment sector in Mexico, more than a million basic education teachers, among the lowest paid in the country, which in effect reduces them to second-class workers with even less rights than those still protected under the reformed 2012 Federal Labor Law. Now teachers will be forced to endure continuous control and monitoring by the state's new educational supervisory agency, the National Educational Institute. The youngest teachers now face the constant threat of summary dismissal and the more experienced teachers of being reduced to bureaucrats and losing their rights attached to the number of years of service they have accrued as teachers. This has all been done all in the name of "improving" basic education (that is, preparing for privatization, uncritically copying the disaster in the USA which led to the closure of over 50 state schools in Chicago last year), and under constant international criticism and pressure from the Organization for Economic Cooperation and Development and the World Bank.

Nevertheless, this privatization-precarization attack on the largest number of teachers in a union in Latin America has caused one of the most important movements of labor resistance in recent history, organized by the dissident National Coordinator of Education Workers (CNTE), an independent tendency in the National Union of Educational Workers (SNTE) since 1979. The CNTE has organized a general strike that has affected almost all 32 states of the Republic, including some in which the CNTE has been historically weak, such as the State of Mexico, the most populated state that has always been governed by the PRI. In Mexico teachers from the pro-boss SNTE union have broken with their leaders' class collaboration and corruption. They now support the CNTE's initiatives against the education reform of 2013. Their actions include the occupation of two of the most important squares in Mexico City for more than 6 months and the daily organization of marches, sit-ins and picketing of federal government ministries. In this they are supported by college, university and high school students and by the 16,000 Sindicato Mexicano de Electricistas (Mexican Electricians Union) electricians summarily dismissed in 2009 by former President Calderon, and their actions have frequently paralyzed economic activity and movement in the city center. However, after over 6 months of relentless struggle by tens of thousands of teachers, especially women teachers who form the majority, it seems that this fight is also approaching its end. The goal of the abrogation of the educational reform law has not been achieved, especially as the CNTE has been abandoned by the so-called independent trade unions, which in reality are close to the PRD and are now working in close collaboration with the ultra-rightist PRI and National Action Party (PAN) parties.

The CNTE's direct action-based struggle has been easily the most substantial response against these neoliberal reforms, although there have been several other major strikes against the harmful effects of the new Federal Labor Law. Taking an important stand have been workers in the Honda transnational corporation car manufacturer, an industry which is growing increasingly important in the formal economy. These workers want to form their own independent union and not have to remain part of the *charro* (pro-employer) Congress of Mexican Workers (CTM), the corporatist union branch of the PRI. It is clear that the various neoliberal reforms of 2013 represent an attempt by the Mexican oligarchy to pass the bill for the global economic crisis that began in 2007 on to the most vulnerable sectors of the working class and peasantry in the name of an ill-defined "competitiveness". Footing the bill will be Mexican workers who are even cheaper to hire than they were previously, if possible, and increasingly those whose work is more skilled and qualified, many of whom are university graduates with masters degrees, in order to make the economy more attractive to capitalist investors and speculators from both within but above all outside Mexico.

This brief update focuses on the precarious situation of the Mexican workers' movement and of both the institutional and extra-institutional political left in Mexico. It leaves out the Zapatista movement, which continues to make important progress, such as the recent Escuelita (Little School) initiative. In Escuelita thousands of Mexican and foreign activists have been able to renew their knowledge of and support for the various autonomous communities and good government juntas on a one-to-one basis with a *votan* (tutor, under the traditional Mayan educational system), although this has been confined to the most marginalized areas of the state of Chiapas and is constantly vulnerable to government and paramilitary attack.

I now turn to the attempts by the social movements of the urban and rural working classes to protect their productive activity and income from summary dismissal or their reconversion from formal to informal and precarious jobs, as part of the present worldwide trend. Thus, Mexico has an important place in the history of the Latin American recovered factories movement, particularly in the cases of the Pascual Boing light refreshment drinks and bottling company in the 1980s and of the Euzkadi tire production company in the 2000s. In the latter the Democratic Workers of the West (TRADOC) Cooperative initiated one of the most important struggles for the defense of workplaces in Mexico, but also, and above all, for the advancement of workers' counter-power against and autonomy from the power of capital.

Euzkadi-TRADOC: 1100 days of resistance to recuperate a factory

The TRADOC cooperative in the state of Jalisco in western Mexico constitutes an important struggle for labor rights and the advancement of workers' power. Its workers struggled for over 1100 days between 2001 and 2005 before they could regain control of their firm, Euzkadi, from the former owner, the German-based transnational corporation Continental Tyres, and so convert it into a cooperative, with all the attendant and previously discussed problems of self-exploitation and competition in capitalist markets.

In 1931 Euzkadi, meaning "Basque homeland" was established in El Salto, in the western state of Jalisco, by a Basque business-man. As a company of foreign origin, it became very attractive to Carlos Slim, a Mexican tycoon and, according to *Forbes* magazine, the world's richest man, who wanted to get into the world's largest tire market across the border. Finally he bought the Euzkadi Rubber Company along with the General Tire Company in San Luis Potosi, which gave him an almost 40 percent share of the whole national tire production (*Enlace Socialista,* 2007).[2] In 1998 the German consortium Continental Tyres, globally the fourth largest producer of tires and very interested in penetrating the

North American market, the main consumer of tires worldwide, acquired 82 percent of its shares of Euzkadi.

A year later, working conditions changed drastically to the extent that 16 workers considered to be union leaders were summarily dismissed. In 2001 Continental tried to reform the collective labor contract against the interests of the workers, including lengthening the working day from 8 to 12 hours, in breach of Federal Labor Law. Continental had made it clear that failure to reach an agreement would result in sanctions and layoffs. At that time several tire companies, such as Goodyear and Michelin, were forced to shut down their factories and eliminate hundreds of jobs. Two days after the plant in Jalisco was closed on 16 December 2001 due to lack of progress in negotiations, the Sindicato Nacional Revolucionario de Trabajadores de la Compañía Hulera Euzkadi (National Revolutionary Workers Union of the Euzkadi Rubber Company) called a general meeting where it was decided unanimously to fight the closure. The cost of the conflict that lasted more than 3 years, was high: and, as well as five comrades who died, at least four others were denied proper medical care and their accumulated benefits were no longer paid out by the PAN government under Vicente Fox (former head of Coca-Cola in Mexico), which denied them any kind of social security.

Due to the workers' opposition to any changes in their collective contract, on 17 December 2001, Euskadi opted to lay off some 1114 workers. The conflict included death threats and attempts to corrupt the leaders of the strike and factory occupation, as well as financial and marital problems for the strikers. Union leader and now Chairman of the Board of Directors of the TRADOC, now a limited liability cooperative society, in which the board is made up of the workers themselves, who are also owners of the majority of the capital shares of the company, Jesus Torres Nuño relates:

> As we all know, in Mexico union struggles always end with gunfire or money for the union leader, because in legal issues, the general secretary has unlimited power, and your signature

can decide what will happen to hundreds or thousands of the
workers you represent. . . . in this case, Continental offered
me a million dollars to sell out the conflict, but I didn't
accept it, because we still have the principles which we were
brought up with. But also, this did not happen because of
the way we are organized as a union. Ours is a democratic
union and decision-making always came from the bottom
upwards from the general assembly, which was the highest
authority in the union. . . . it's a battle that should inspire
workers everywhere. . . . Yes, even those in Europe. (*Enlace
Socialista*, 2007)

It was not until the remaining 624 workers (941 began the strike
in 2001) were able to internationalize their struggle, following the
successful example of the 1997 Liverpool Dockers strike (Munck,
2006) that they were able to put real pressure on Continental to
force them to return to the negotiating table. They decided to take
the struggle to Continental's headquarters in Hanover, Germany
and speak out at the shareholders' annual general meeting (AGM).
With badges given to them by critical shareholders who gave up
their places at the AGM, the workers' delegation presented themselves before the company's executives and other shareholders to
denounce the violation of their labor rights in Mexico. An encour-
aging development on 18 February 2004 occurred when the strike
and occupation were recognized by the Mexican courts. This decision gave not the Euzkadi workers greater certainty but became a
precedent for other union movements. Negotiations became less
strident and gradually an agreement was hammered out in which
the workers won half their back pay, allowing them to reopen the
Euzkadi business as a worker-controlled cooperative.

On 17 January 2005 the tire plant was reopened and began
work with the participation of the company's main investor Llanti
Systems. Thus, TRADOC became a co-owner. In 2007 the cooperative was producing 6000 tires a day and exporting 10 percent
of its production to Colombia, Honduras and Guatemala, even if

they are virtually unknown, compared with their main competitors such as Michelin, Continental and Firestone, as they cannot afford to pay for advertising campaigns. Euzkadi was a leading brand in Mexico, at least in the early 1980s, when there was still a protected market and no free trade agreements to undermine its solidity and strength. Torres' weekly wage in 2007 did not exceed 2200 pesos (about US $200 at the time):

> I have to say with great pride that our union has nothing to do with traditional corporate unions that just look to dominate and subdue the workers. Ours was always a union with a huge democratic tradition, independent, very classist and a support-ive organization. This paid off in the end by our survival as workers because when the conflict broke out, we received a lot of solidarity. . . . The union decided to reject the package of amendments that Continental had offered under the sole argument that we were not globally competitive. I mean, we do not accept the view which is pushed by large transnational corporations that it is cheaper and more profitable in Asia than in Mexico where there is a regulatory framework, that is, the Federal Labor Law, which protects the rights of workers and employees. (*Enlace Socialista*, 2007)

The strikers also had to face the power and wrath of the federal and state governments, who pressurized them to give in to Continental, with the disinformation that, thanks to the union, one of the most important companies in Mexico had closed not only in El Salto, but also its plant in San Luis Potosi, neither of which in the end happened:

> We received a lot of criticism at the time, but we knew we were defending not only our rights . . . but also the rights of all workers, because of the issue of the right to strike, we were fighting for almost 3 years because our movement was not legally recognized by the government during that time, despite

the law stipulating that it has to be recognized within 24 hours from the start of a strike (*Enlace Socialista*, 2007)

The Euzkadi strikers were supported by many unions, especially other cooperatives, like Pascual Boing:

> Thanks to the great solidarity of many organizations, a lot of people and mainly our wives and families, we could resist for 1141 days without receiving any wages, which of course was not pleasant, but today we have a great reward: we own the factory. And it's a decent job, because we are now co-owners, we are managing our factory, we are dealing with the means of production, and so we are showing that the workers are not only meant to handle some machines, but we are also made to manage the means of production and distribution. Why not the whole of society too? (*Enlace Socialista*, 2007)

In 2005 there were 624 workers, including technical, administrative and production staff:

> Restarting work was very complicated. We practically had to start "from less than zero". Just think how we found the plant after 3 years of idleness, with absolutely no maintenance. . . . The workers themselves are now converted into owners, we're back to operate these machines, which was really urgent and immediate. Today, these comrades have wages and employment, we have a prospect of growth and we are still making the same tires, because naturally we did not invent anything, but we now have the prospect of significant growth, we believe that the template will increase and of course, also production levels. Right now we're doing 6000 tires per day. A far cry from the 12 or 14,000 tires that we made a day before closing. I can proudly say that we are already exporting to places like Honduras and Guatemala, Colombia and very shortly we are going to sell in the USA. This huge

market is experiencing a phenomenon that we already saw coming from the time of the plant closings. Continental workers called countries with higher wages "First world", because they are treated equally, but the TNCs have no fixed interest [in any particular factory] and will gradually close these factories. (*Enlace Socialista*, 2007)

A group of Germans came to see the facilities and find out how this group of workers had beaten a powerhouse in their own country. They included Mechthild Dortmund, and Jürgen Dietrich Höper Scharna of Intersoli/Volkswagen in Wolfsburg, a historian and some other workers:

"The visit by these people who came from Germany was one of many", says Jesus Torres:

> In reality, we must recognize that in the more than 3 years (of the strike) we received a lot of solidarity from organizations and individuals in Europe. This is impressive for a union like ours, which was on strike without resources and in a precarious economic situation. . . . We walked into the bowels of the company, in Hanover, Germany, and we faced down the president, Manfred Wennemer, whom I am sure, it hurt a lot to have to admit defeat in Mexico, not because of the money, but for what it meant for all its workers all over the world, in over 20 production plants. (*Enlace Socialista*, 2007)

This was also achieved thanks to the solidarity of many organizations and the critical shareholders who gave the strikers their cards so that they could enter and use their own voice. They became shareholders for a day, once a year, during the 3 years of their struggle:

> All this gave the German and Austrian workers, and many people who were watching our scheme, an example to follow and they invited us to many places. Last year [2006], our organization

received first prize in the Alternative Social Economic Forum in Davos in Switzerland. Usually they point out the negatives, such as violations of the rights of the employees of companies like Coca-Cola or companies that violate environmental standards. In this case, the first international award was for us and that is a source of great pride. (*Enlace Socialista*, 2007)

Today the struggle of the TRADOC cooperative is seen as a successful example of a struggle for labor rights. Since 2001 TRADOC has nearly doubled its membership, from 587 during the resistance movement to about 1000 today. TRADOC is currently in partnership with the North American company Cooper Tires, and according to figures from 2011, about 13 million tires are manufactured annually, of which 70 percent are exported to the US market. Their struggle to protect their jobs and labor rights constitutes an internationally recognized symbol for many labor movements, although obviously it is a reformist one that does not threaten capitalist labor relations or challenge the highly polluting car industry, as rubber tires are particularly toxic and hazardous to dispose of.

Pascual Boing: "Kill them, break this up"

Pascual Boing is a soft drinks producer, whose most well-known products are the Pascual, Boing! and Lulu brands. It began in 1940 and successfully held its own in the Mexican market despite foreign competitors. However, various labor disputes led to a strike in 1982, which ended in 1985 with the workers obtaining the right to take over the company and run it as a cooperative. Since then, it has remained a profitable business, although it its market share in Mexico has been reduced due to competition from Coca-Cola and Pepsi. This has led the company to protest against the unfair practices that exclude it from retail venues as well as looking abroad for new markets, especially in the USA (Sociedad Cooperativa Trabajadores de Pascual, 2007).

The company, originally a private enterprise, was established in 1940 by Rafael Victor Jiménez Zamudio. In the 1960s Jiménez began using tetra paks and acquired its northern plant from Canada Dry, along with a franchise to produce and market these products. From its beginnings to the early 1980s, the company enjoyed significant growth in the face of competition from multinational corporations. Two plants were opened in the 1960s. In 1980, the company was fourth in the Mexican soft drinks market. However, the working conditions at the plants were highly exploitative, with workers forced to work overtime without extra pay. There had been several attempts to organize workers at the plant due to these abuses, but management had fired the organizers. In March 1982, the Mexican federal government decreed that all workers, including those in private companies, must receive 30 percent wage increases because of the devaluation of the peso. However, Jiménez refused to implement the increase, claiming that he could not afford it. Several political activists organized the workers in protest and when 150 workers were dismissed for participating, all the workers went on strike on 18 May 1982, shutting down operations. On 31 May Jiménez and an official CTM trade union "shock group"[3] confronted the striking workers at the plant in Colonia Tránsito. Violence broke out and two strikers were killed, with 17 wounded. Jiménez was formally accused of murder but was not prosecuted.

The work stoppage went on for 3 years. The workers took over the federal arbitration offices in protest, and a formal committee to represent them was formed, so gaining legal recognition and public support for their cause. In 1983 the courts found in favor of the workers in their litigation against the company and in 1984 the workers met President Miguel de la Madrid. Jiménez declared the company bankrupt and tried to sell the facilities. However, the workers and federal authorities worked out an arrangement so that the workers would take over the whole company, including the facilities and the brands. A cooperative called the Sociedad Cooperativa Trabajadores de Pascual S.C.L. was formed on 27 May 1985.

After years of inactivity, the new worker-owners needed 1.5 million dollars to restart operations. During the strike, hundreds of artists and intellectuals supported the workers by donating artworks for auction. The money raised was not sufficient, so Sindicato de los Trabajadores de la Universidad Nacional Autonoma de Mexico/ National Autonomous University of Mexico Workers Union (STUNAM), the main union of the largest and most important university, the Universidad Nacional Autónoma de México, provided the funds needed to obtain permits and service the machinery (Maranón-Pimentel, 2013).

The cooperative has experienced several struggles and conflicts since it was established. To begin with, there were internal struggles among the workers as to how to organize and operate. However, operations as a cooperative began on 27 November 1985 with the workers receiving their first share of profits in May 1986. The former owner lost the legal right to use the name Pascual Boing but nonetheless was doing so from a plant in Aguascalientes until the cooperative negotiated a deal. Another problem was that the land on which the original factories were located belonged, not to the original company but to the owner's wife, Victoria Valdez. She was allowed to sue the cooperative in 1989 and won the case in 2003, with the court ordering Pascual off the land. The then Mexico City mayor Andrés Manuel López Obrador expropriated the land from Valdez to return it to Pascual. However in 2005, the Supreme Court decreed the expropriation illegal, as it did not benefit the public but a private company that produced a non-essential product, even if Pascual Boing does not consider itself to be a private, for-profit company. Being worker-owned, they claim to perform a social function and as such expropriation in their favor is for the public benefit. Since their founding, they have received vocal and political support from the center-left PRD, intellectuals, writers such as Elena Poniatowska, college students and alterglobalistas (Poniatowska, 2010 online).

Despite its problems, the cooperative has grown, opening processing plants in San Juan del Río, Querétaro in 1992, in Tizayuca,

Hidalgo in 2003 and in Culiacán, Sinaloa in 2006. Despite its growth, the cooperative has had to deny claims that it is on the verge of bankruptcy, as was rumored in a 2007 chain email (Notimex, 2003 online). Today, Pascual Boing is the only remaining wholly Mexican-owned major soft drink bottler, employing over 5000 people and generating over 22,000 jobs indirectly. Part of its mission is to show that employee ownership as a cooperative can work. The organization of the cooperative consists of a general assembly of founders and other partners, which controls several boards including corporate investment, administration and the cultural foundation. Under these are four commissions called education, social outlook, arbitration and technical control. It also has a strong sense of social responsibility and has been recognized as a "clean industry" by the Secretaría del Trabajo (Ministry of Work) (Sociedad Cooperativa Trabajadores de Pascual, 2007).

However, it must be said that, as with the Euskadi-TRADOC struggle, the victory was only partial as the Mexican law on cooperatives does not allow for new recruits to join the cooperative. In effect, the original members of the cooperative have become a relatively privileged managerial-type elite compared to the rest of the workforce, who earn much less. There is further restriction on founding new worker-controlled cooperatives, as some were started with money from the payment of back wages after successful strike movements. However, under Mexican laws on work the possibility of exercising this option has become more limited. A clear example of this is Article 48 of the 2012 reformed Ley Federal de Trabajo, which now restricts the payment of back pay to 12 months and only 2 percent each year thereafter in wages.

Ruta 100: a self-managed public transport network repressed by corrupt neoliberalism

The Urban Passenger Motor Carrier Route 100, also known as Ruta 100 (R-100) or Metropolitan Transportation System 100, was a partially worker-controlled, decentralized body with a legal personality and its own capital under the overall control of the then Department of the Federal District[4] (DDF), renamed the Government of the Federal District (DF) in 1997, which served passengers in both Mexico City and neighboring municipalities in the State of Mexico from 1981 to 1995, when it was declared bankrupt by the government as part of the privatization of public transport and subsequently disappeared, with grave consequences for the quality of the public transport network in the greater Mexico City and Valley of Mexico area. It is perhaps the most tragic example in Mexico of how a combination of globally imposed neoliberalization and locally imposed corruption and political skulduggery destroyed a well-functioning worker-controlled enterprise to the detriment of one of the world's largest cities.

In the opinion of public transport experts like Jorge Legorreta, R-100 "became the most important and efficient state-owned bus service that Mexico City has ever had", and existed in a "golden age of public transport, based on a social policy of fully justified subsidies" (Legorreta, 2004 online). The disappearance of R-100, enacted by the Regente (literally Regent)[5] Óscar Espinosa Villarreal, accelerated the process of the privatization of public transport in the capital city, initiated by his predecessor, Manuel Camacho Solís, now a leading figure in the PRD.

The history of R-100 began in 1942, when the first-class service Lomas de Chapultepec bus line was offered on Paseo de la Reforma, Mexico City's main central avenue. In 1958 the DDF took over the line, whose owners were facing insolvency, so it was placed under the administration of the capital. The new state line was characterized by its efficiency and good service. Meanwhile, the Mexico Trucking Alliance had captured most of the routes running through Mexico City, offering an efficient service: engines in good condition, well-trained operators, increasingly affordable tariffs and a fair distribution of routes and itineraries. This alliance, known as the Octopus Hat, was mainly in the hands of Isidoro Rodriguez and Rubén Figueroa, two powerful urban leaders.

In January 1981 the then Regent Carlos Hank Gonzalez announced the revocation of unfair concessions granted to individuals for the provision of urban transport passenger buses. A liquidation committee proceeded to draw up compensation under the law. Given the situation, the DDF and the Mexico Trucking Alliance signed an agreement to improve the quality of transport. The beneficiaries agreed to renew units, rationalize routes and provide traveller insurance. However, after 7 months, the signed agreements had not yet been enacted, so then President López Portillo issued a decree creating a decentralized organization with legal personality and assets, called Urban Passenger Transport R-100, with the aim of providing services in the city and wider conurbation.

After López Portillo's decree Hank González announced that all the assets of the 86 private transport companies operating at the time in Mexico City would became part of the DDF through R-100. The goal was to create a model urban transportation system both in administrative and operational terms. By 1985 there were 1000 kilometres in service and it was generally recognized as the best planned urban transport system with the lowest fares in Mexico.

On 3 May 1989 the SUTAUR-100 (the R-100's independent trade union which was the only one to actively and openly support the EZLN rebellion in 1994) began a strike to demand wage increases. Immediately an emergency bus plan was activated by the DDF in which the Army participated using their official vehicles. The union demanded a wage increase of 100 percent, while the government offered first 12 percent and then 14 percent, but the union decided to go on strike "fully confident of its strategic importance and resilience". A labor court outlawed the strike while the army and police provided the bus service, disabling the workers' ability to put pressure on the government. On 6 May the immediate and total occupation of the rights and property of the body was decreed. On 9 May the union accepted the offer of a pay increase of 14 percent and the service was restored. Meanwhile, the DDF, then headed by Camacho Solis, allowed the urban transportation routes taken away from R-100 to be operated by the privately owned pesero minibuses, which had begun operating in 1987.

After this period of both administrative and labor crisis, a modernization programme was introduced, which involved the purchase of new buses and the rehabilitation of the rest of the fleet. Despite this new momentum, the days of R-100 were numbered. On 8 April 1995, the DDF, now headed by Espinoza Villarreal, declared R-100 bankrupt due, according to the capital's authorities, to its economic insolvency and indequate service. The reason for the financial deterioration of the entity, as Jesús Salazar Toledano, then Secretary General of the Government of DDF said, lay in its "co-administration" between SUTAUR-100 and official bodies (*Reforma*, 1995). At 1.30 am that Saturday police armed with shields and batons took control of 27 operating modules of the parastatal company and at 3 am prevented the entry of those who had arrived at their workplaces ready to start their shift. Also on that day and subsequently Ricardo Barco and 11 other SUTAUR-100 leaders, were arrested and accused of diverting 9 million pesos from the workers' savings fund.

The DDF put a system of emergency transport into operation, giving free service on 45 routes for 10 days, but they were they did not function well − or at all, in some cases. R-100 had been daily carrying 2.8 million users on 207 routes and employed 12,098 unionized workers and 1694 "trusted employees".[6] The bankruptcy proceedings began in 1989, after the strike. Six years after the first bankruptcy court a judge in the DF gave permission to begin the break-up of the parastatal, whose responsibility fell to the Banobras bank. The city authorities offered the R-100 employees more than the compensation law provided for, but most of them opted for mass mobilization to demand the return of their employment. After the bankruptcy was filed, a series of mysterious events occurred which have yet to be clarified: the suicide of the then Secretary of Transportation for the DF Luis Miguel Moreno on 10 April, the machine gunning on 18 June of Humberto Priego, the prosecutor assigned to the case against the SUTAUR -100 leaders, and the execution (disguised as suicide after a lovers' tiff), the next day, of the judge in charge of the case, Abraham Polo Uscanga, who had already publically denounced pressures from the then Chief Justice of the DF, Saturnino Aguero, to renew arrest warrants against the union representatives.

Five years after the disintegration of R-100, and after repeated attempts to sell off the organism, now divided into 10 companies, the former parastatal workers were declared bankrupt as part of the negotiations to defuse the conflict. That same year the then PRD head of the DF, Rosario Robles Berlanga,[7] issued decrees that the decentralized public body, the Urban Passenger Motor Carrier R-100, had been wound up and its assets were declared to be part of the property of the DF. The Passenger Transport Network (RTP) of the DF was then created with the objective of providing radial public transport for passengers, giving preference to the peripheral areas with scarce resources in the DF.

Of the 10 companies into which the R-100 was divided only eight are still operational, despite the DF government having created corridors for road transport and Metrobus projects. Although by 1997 the political situation had radically changed when the first Head of the DF Government election was won by the PRD, the R-100 and the public transport situation remained the same. Even today it provides the population with many benefits especially those that are supposed to benefit the neediest residents, but these are all paid for with taxes that are meant to be used to improve the quality of public services. The goal of the RTP to serve low-income areas has not permitted the overall improvement of the quality of transport. The bankruptcy of R-100 caused irreparable damage to the connectivity of the metropolitan area, which could take decades to restore to the former quality of the service provided by the worker-controlled R-100. Moreover, many areas of the State of Mexico still experience unsatisfactory public transport because its buses do not have a scheme that can ensure safety and faster travel, coupled with the breakdown of power and the failure by both the DF and the State of Mexico governments to put together a comprehensive transportation plan, which has left the city with a set-back of 35 to 40 years in this area.

Self-managed cooperativism in the Zapatista autonomous municipalities in Chiapas

In Chiapas, the EZLN and its support bases have organized autonomous municipalities based on the old indigenous custom of self-government. In these municipalities an assembly of local representatives forms the juntas de buen gobierno, or councils of good government (JBGs). These are not recognized by the federal or state governments but they oversee local community programs on food, health and education, as well as taxation for both Zapatistas and non-Zapistas and even anti-Zapatistas, such as PRI and some PRD supporters. Thus, they are a clear example of both political and economic collective self-management by an important sector of the rural working class.

During 2004 Subcomandante Marcos, the spokesperson of the EZLN, sent a series of communiqués around the globe in order to report on the setting up of the JBGs. The term "councils of good government" is meant to be in direct opposition to the "bad" government of the official party-political system that these councils are designed to counteract. There are a series of them across Chiapas, each one acting according to Zapatista guidelines but carrying out their own independent decisions. The councils do not only accommodate Zapatistas, but also their non-Zapatista supporters and allies, especially those in the Other Campaign which is now known as the Sixth, both nationally and internationally, since the renewal of the EZLN communiqués in 2013 after a long period of silence (Brenner, 2014).

The JBGs use a rotation method for those who serve on the council. Each citizen within the jurisdiction of the JBG is required to serve on the council for 2 weeks, and then a new council is put into power. It is set up this way in order to ensure that no political figures become corrupt or fall under the influence of outside forces. It also accommodates the needs, interests and concerns of each member within the area that the JBG covers. The federal government ignores them, not only because they are few and located in remote parts of the state but also as part of its routine counter-insurrectionary policy. Some outside non-governmental organizations (NGOs) that do interact with them find it difficult to do so, claiming their composition changes too quickly to have any clear knowledge of what is going on. The councils have created their own laws and enforce them, applying punishment when deemed necessary, under a community-based system. The JBGs have taken a firm stance against the trafficking of drugs and people.

The JBGs appear to be succeeding in implementing the Zapatista ideology in their limited areas of influence. Ten years after they were established in 2004 the results are remarkable. They now have 600 health promoters, trained in anatomy, physiology, symptomatology, diagnosis and treatment, especially in preventive medicine, personal and collective hygiene and holding vaccination workshops, and who are also knowledgeable of parasitic and respiratory diseases. There are 500 community health houses equipped with essential medicines and a herbal pharmacy, together with a hospital with a surgical and dental clinics, clinical and herbal laboratories, ophthalmology and gynecology wards, a pharmacy and general wards. There are eight municipal clinics, including one with a dental clinic, a clinical laboratory (where blood counts, urine tests and other basic tests, and blood exams against malaria and tuberculosis in the area can be carried out) and an ambulance. Four municipal clinics offer free consultations and, when it is available, free medicine, together with a herbal laboratory and home-canned food. There are also 300 women herbalists, bone healers and trained midwives who promote agroecology and veterinary science. Similar advances have been made in education and specifically Zapatista autonomous schools have been established to which non-Zapatistas are also encouraged to send their children (Brenner, 2014).

As for the self-management of economic logistics, three supply warehouses serve hundreds of community convenience stores, both

Zapatista and non-Zapatista; there are autonomous cooperatives producing organic coffee, embroidered goods, handicrafts, footwear and technology workshops; the New Dawn Trade Center, auditoriums, an internet café, a publishing house, Autonomous Editions in Rebellion, with their own publications, an autonomous media communication system, regional radio stations (which involve a broadcaster from the Zapatista support base) and a workshop for video processing.

Apart from petroleum, coffee is the second most traded raw material in the world. Worldwide, 6.7 million metric tons of coffee beans were produced annually in 1998–2000, and the forecast at that time was for an increase to 7 million metric tons annually by 2010. Around 25 million small producers worldwide work in its direct cultivation and if their families and all related workers (harvesting, processing, and trading) are included, then possibly hundreds of millions of people depend on this crop. Mexico is a significant coffee producer (the seventh in the world). Specifically, the climatic and geomorphological conditions in Chiapas make this state the biggest coffee producer in the country, producing 25 percent of the national total. Only a small part of the profit goes to the producers, as most of the retail cost of a bag of coffee goes to the intermediaries trading and processing the coffee, mainly big corporations. In the last 20 years this tendency has been rapidly increasing. In 1989 the protective regulations of the International Coffee Agreement were suspended. In the same period, the World Bank and the International Monetary Fund gave generous loans for the development of coffee cultivation in countries that until then were not producing it (like Vietnam). As a result, there was an oversupply. The prices in the international market collapsed and, despite temporary rises, still remain low. The average price of Arabica coffee in the New York stock market was, for the period 1976–1989, $3.30 per kilo. For the period 1990–2005 it fell to 2.20 dollars per kilo. Counting in the loss of value of the dollar due to inflation, the producers saw the return from their product fall more than a half.

That was the so-called coffee crisis. During the same period, the big coffee corporations experienced a remarkable rise in their profits. The benefits of the reduced price of the raw material was not passed on to the consumers but to their shareholders. On the other hand, the small producers had to face difficulties, especially in Central America. Their income was no longer enough to cover the cost of production, so hundreds of thousands abandoned their lands and emigrated to nearby cities or the USA. Thousands disappeared trying to cross the border between the USA and Mexico and since Calderón's war against drugs some 25,000 have disappeared within Mexico itself, victims of the collusion between the Zetas cartel and the authorities in Chiapas. Moreover, the fall in the price impacted on the broader local economy of the region, which was significantly supported through the exports of the product. The indigenous population of Chiapas was even worse hit by the crisis. They were cut off from the rest of the economic activity of Mexico, while the cultivation of coffee was their only real income. In this region, intermediaries in 1993 were paying 8 pesos (€0.6 cents) for one kilo of coffee, while its resale price in Europe was more than €10. A lot of people claim that the collapse of the coffee price was the last straw for indigenous people in Chiapas. Those who did not abandon their plantations and their families and emigrate to the USA joined the Zapatista army during their 1 January 1994 revolt.

After the revolt, the demands of the indigenous people for the recognition of their culture and of their collective, economic and political rights were not satisfied. Their struggle moved to the reconstruction of their autonomy from the Mexican state. This struggle was joined by thousands of indigenous coffee producers experienced in productive cooperatives, who were not only concerned to find an economic solution for their members. As a result of their experience and the new relations that the EZLN created with the international solidarity movements, an idea was developed; to establish the first Zapatista coffee cooperative. The goal of the producers was to develop an alternative way to supply and export coffee, which would allow them to end their total dependence on intermediaries and the unpredictable global market. Their call for the creation of "another" coffee market, with more dignified conditions for the producers, drew a quick response from the small coffee shops in the USA with existing cooperative structures and a progressive political orientation, but also from solidarity collectives and people with no previous trading experience.

As for the structure of these cooperatives, the general assembly of the producers is their supreme body, and is convened at least once a year and elects a new administrative council every 3 years. There are around 2500 producers in total, while hundreds of tonnes of coffee go to the solidarity networks, depending on the specific conditions of production every year. The cooperatives are an integral part of the Zapatista movement and therefore they cooperate with the political structures of the movement, especially the JBGs. They respect their decisions, which aim at the wider interests of the autonomous structures and communities.

The Zapatista coffee cooperatives may be the best example of the development of alternative and autonomous economic structures in Chiapas. The producers do not depend either on the local or the global coffee markets for their economic survival, because, through their collective organization and their cooperation with solidarity networks, they receive one price for their product that covers the cost of production while also bringing in a respectable income, which has increased over the years despite the global economic crisis. Moreover, they have gained access to common structures and technical support. But it is not only the producers that benefit. For as long as the cooperatives develop and improve their functions, they contribute some of their income to the autonomous programs of education and health, and to other social structures. Furthermore, the initiatives and the organizations that participate in the solidarity distribution networks return a proportion of their income to the Zapatista communities themselves. In this way, the coffee cooperatives operate as a driving force of the Zapatista movement.

Nevertheless, the cooperatives have faced, and continue to face, remarkable difficulties. The building of an effective organizational structure that will respect the horizontal and directly democratic political orientation of the Zapatista movement was their first, biggest difficulty. They specifically refused any kind of help from the Mexican state and dealt with the technical and bureaucratic processes of coffee production, distribution and sales with the support of independent solidarity organizations in Mexico. At the same time, they have tried to develop infrastructural projects, such as warehouses for the storage and preprocessing of the coffee. The main obstacle, currently, is the Mexican authorities, such as the fine they unfairly imposed on the Mut Vitz cooperative in 2007, for supposed tax irregularities.

Nowadays, Zapatista coffee is distributed to at least 12 European countries from a variety of initiatives. All these local initiatives are connected through a horizontal network RedProZapa (the Distribution Network of Zapatista Products), which holds central assemblies twice a year in a European city. The common characteristic that unites them is their political solidarity with the Zapatista struggle. The sale of coffee provides economic support to the productive structures in Chiapas.

Conclusion: the limitations of cooperativism and economic self-management in Mexico

The TRADOC cooperative is also a member of the G-50 cooperative network that organizes and expresses itself through the Coperacha website (2012). The two recuperated firms, Euskadi and Pascual Boing, have converted themselves into cooperatives and have become two of the main examples of workers control in Mexico, albeit with many problems and limitations. In fact, even the social democratic neoliberal Mexico City local government, under the control of the PRD, continues to promote the training and establishment of small-scale cooperatives in the name of the solidarity economy, even if under the neoliberal small and medium enterprise model, that have been converted into market-integrated, for-profit capitalist firms that do not really function as cooperatives or do so only partially at best:

> These experiences have created an oasis by enjoying their own processes, but sometimes they are faced with very major limits. Even if they do not really break with business dynamics on a general scale, these spaces are still very rich, because although they fail really to be a general alternative, they are partial alternatives for the community, and the social is also a challenge that requires higher levels of confrontation in order to build the strength to break with the existing order. (*La Coperacha.* 2014)

Another, more controversial perspective from an orthodox Marxist point of view on cooperatives, comes from Laura Collín (2014):

> Cooperatives are integral to capitalism, they work with the logic of the expanded reproduction of capital, as well as production for the market, which is why I argue that they are at the core of capitalism, rather than the private ownership of the means of production, as Marxism claims.

So today, worker-controlled cooperatives can be an alternative model for survival against the prolonged crisis of neoliberalism but they do not necessarily provide a model for anti-capitalist resistance. Obviously, every job rescued from outsourcing and precarity, not to say unemployment, is a kind of victory, though a profoundly bitter one because the advance of capitalist abstract labor or work is increasingly based on the alienated self-exploitation of human living labor (Holloway, 2011).

In Mexico the example of the neo-Zapatistas of the EZLN and the Sixth is the most emblematic of the extensive use of cooperatives and self-management among objectively anti-capitalist political strategies for autonomy from the state and the political party system, but it is not the only example, either in rural areas or among indigenous peoples. To ensure that anti-capitalist economic self-management thrives it must be combined with political autonomy or self-government.

Another important example of self-management in Mexico has been the struggle of the Popular Front for the Defense of the Land (FPDT) in Atenco in defense of the common, collective ownership of land and against the construction of a new international airport on what remains of Lake Texcoco, near Mexico City, which was halted by mass mobilizations and other types of direct action in 2002 and which would have been totally destructive of the already gravely damaged environment of the Valley of Mexico. The FPDT was a major supporter of the EZLN's Other Campaign in 2006–2007, but suffered terrible repression from the Mexican state, after which it took several years to recover and re-emerged a political force only in 2011, now in alliance with the more moderate #Yo Soy 132 (I am 132) students movement to form the short-lived National Convention. It continues to oppose the PRI government's plans to revive the project of a new international airport near Atenco and continues to practice the communal self-management of the land.

In general, the situation in Mexico is even more precarious than in the rest of Latin America in terms of building an autonomous anti-capitalist urban–rural movement which could be genuinely independent of political parties, trade unions, NGOs and other forms of state-controlled political mediation and co-optation, whether or not they are called independent. It has still not been possible to go on the offensive, as in Venezuela, Argentina or Bolivia, and organize the recuperation of enclosed workplaces and commons, which in Mexico have also been informalized by a global capitalism in deep crisis and in the middle of a new phase of primitive accumulation, according to Harvey (2010) and others. However, the example of the both determined but highly intelligent and innovative struggle of the CNTE has set the pace for the next stage of anti-capitalist resistance. While the current scenario is dominated by a set of self-managed cooperatives and small-scale experiments, essentially integrated into neoliberalism or at least unable to break with it, in the recent past other sectors of the Mexican population have demonstrated a capacity for self-management and remarkable antagonism towards capital.

Notes

1. One of the primary examples of specialized post-Fordist production, often in the form of cooperatives linked to the Italian Communist Party, took place in a region known as the Third Italy. The First Italy included the areas of large-scale mass production, such as Turin, Milan and Genoa, and the Second Italy was the undeveloped South. The Third Italy, however, was where clusters of small firms and workshops developed in the 1970s and 1980s in the central and north-east regions of the country. Each region specialized in a range of loosely related products and each workshop usually had five to 50 workers, often less than 10. The range of products in each region reflected the post-Fordist shift to economies of scope (Kumar, 1995).

2. All translations are by the author.

3. "Grupo de choque" in Spanish. Paramilitarily trained and armed gangs of PRI-CTM workers or party members who specialized in violently attacks on striking workers, marching students and teachers and any social group or movement challenging the PRI regime. They were similar in many ways to the fascist *squadroni d'azione* in Italy or the storm troopers of Nazi Germany.

4. The official name for most of Mexico City, which also includes parts of the surrounding State of Mexico, historically and currently a fiefdom of the PRI, of which President Peña Nieto was governor from 2006 to 2010.

5. Until 1997 the DF Mexico City did not have a locally elected mayor, but a government-appointed ruler, being the only city or state directly ruled by the Federal Government which suspected, rightly as events have turned out, that there was a built-in center-left majority in the megalopolis with a total of over 20 million inhabitants.

6. This term is used in Mexico to describe high echelon workers who, in return for agreeing not to join a union, receive better pay and more secure employment conditions than the rest.

7. Robles' potentially dubious role in this affair is highlighted by her later political disgrace in 2004 on being named, as part of the Video Scandal, as the lover of corrupt businessman and PRD GDF government associate Carlos Ahumada, leading to her resignation from the PRD and later recruitment by the PRI, for whom she has been a government minister since 2012.

References

Bagnasco, A. (1977) *Tre Italie: la Problematica Territoriale dello Sviluppo Italiano*. Bologna: Il Molino.

Brenner, J. (2014) The Zapatistas at 20: building autonomous community. Melissa Forbis interviewed by Johanna Brenner. 23 March. Available at http://www.solidarity-us.org/site/node/4135 (accessed 23 March 2014).

Collín, L. (2014) La economía solidaria es un modelo en construcción. *La Coperacha*. 4 February. Available at http://www.lacoperacha.org. mx/economia-solidaria-laura-collin.php (accessed 18 February 2014).

Enlace Socialista (2007) Una historia que va sobre ruedas; de obreros en Euzkadi a llanteros. Available at http://www.enlacesocialista.org.mx/ articulo/una-historia-que-va-sobre-ruedas-de-obreros-en-euzkadi-a-llanteros (accessed 23 March 2014).

Harvey, D. (2010) Organización para la transición anti-capitalista, *Argumentos (Méx.), 23* (63) 35–58.

Holloway, J. (2011) 1968 and the crisis of abstract labour. Available at http://www.johnholloway.com.mx/2011/07/30/1968-and-the-crisis-of-abstract-labour/(accessed 23 March 2014).

Katsiaficas, G. (1997) *The Subversion of Politics: European Autonomous Social Movements and the Decolonization of Everyday Life*. Amherst, NJ: Humanity Books.

Kumar, K. (1995) *From Post-Industrial to Post-Modern Society: New Theories of the Contemporary World*. London: Blackwell.

La Coperacha (2014) La economía solidaria genera experiencias ejemplares pero no cuestionan el orden capitalista: Massimo Modonesi, *La Coperacha*. 18 February. Available at http://www.lacoperacha.org.mx/ vision-marxista-de-la-economia-solidaria.php (accessed 18 February 2014).

Legorreta, J. (2004) De cocodrilos al pulpo verde, el transporte dominante de la urbe. *La Jornada*, 23 September. Available at http://www. jornada.unam.mx/2004/09/23/02an1cul.php?origen=cultura. php&fly=1 (accessed 23 March 2014).

Maranón-Pimentel, B. (2013) La cooperativa agroindustrial Pascual en México: presente y futuro de la economía popular y solidaria. In Maranón-Pimentel, B. (ed.) *La Economía Solidaria en México*. Mexico City:

UNAM, pp. 59-82. Available at http://ru.iiec.unam.mx/2378/1/EconomiaSolidariaTexto.pdf (accessed 2 December 2014).

Munck, R. (2006) *Globalization and Contestation: The New Great Counter-Movement.* London: Routledge Chapman & Hall.

Notimex (2003) La Cooperativa Pascual no está en quiebra ni se vende. Torres Cisneros. *La Jornada.* 14 April. Available at http://www.jornada.unam.mx/2003/04/14/026n2eco.php (accessed 23 March 2014).

Poniatowska, E. (2010) Cooperativa Pascual: 25 años. *La Jornada.* 15 June. Available at http://www.jornada.unam.mx/2010/06/15/opinion/a13a1cul (accessed 23 March 2014).

Reforma (1995) Quiebra R-100 por ineficiencia. 9 April.

Stahler-Sholk, R. (2011) Autonomía y economía política de resistencia en las Cañadas de Ocosingo. In Baronnet, B., Mora Bayo, M. and Stahler-Sholk, R. (eds) *Luchas "Muy Otras" Zapatismo y Autonomía en las Comunidades Indígenas de Chiapas.* Mexico City: Universidad Autónoma Metropolitana.

World Population Review (2014) Mexico City population 2014. Available at http://worldpopulationreview.com/world-cities/mexico-city-population/ (accessed 1 December 2014).

Wright, S. (2002) *Storming Heaven: Class Composition and Struggle in Italian Autonomist Marxism.* London: Pluto Press.

NINE

Collective Self-management and Social Classes: The Case of Enterprises Recovered by Their Workers in Uruguay

Anabel Rieiro

> Human beings aren't born forever
> the day their mothers bring them to the world
> but forced by life
> to be born out of themselves
> time and again
>
> (Gabriel García Márquez)

Introduction

> What other resource bases for survival and what new types of socio-economic relationships will there be for these workers who are cast aside or made redundant? (Quijano, 1973: 180)

This article investigates this question through an analysis of the recovered enterprises in Uruguay, which stand as specific examples of self-management. In 2002 between 35 and 40 percent of all Uruguayan companies closed during the socioeconomic crisis that swept across the region. This crisis would soon give way to another: a crisis of the model of accumulation based on neoliberal principles[1] that had ruled economic policy in Latin America for more than three decades. As the crisis set in, the Uruguayan working class faced both the highest rate of unemployment and the largest decrease in real wages in the history of the nation.[2]

Amid the unsteadiness and the disintegration that comes from mass unemployment emerged a space of political opportunity (Tarrow, 1997) for initiatives to defend and recover employment. It was evident to unemployed workers how difficult, if not impossible, it was to find a new job. Yet society had also begun to legitimize certain collective endeavors and reactivate its mechanisms of resistance, opening up the possibility of other forms of employment to take root.

The ensuing phenomenon resulted in the recuperation of more than 20 different businesses employing approximately 1500 workers, mainly engaged in industrial work. These recovered companies include tanneries, pasta factories, potteries, laundries, providers of printing services and grain mills, as well as factories producing transformers, tires, glasses, pork products, polyester staple fiber, hospital uniforms, plastics, locks, hinges and cylinders.

Most of these recovered companies chose to organize and incorporate themselves as cooperatives: businesses that are legally owned and controlled by the workers, who make decisions democratically. Only three of these recovered companies – Urutransfor, Funsa and Envidrio – did not form worker-owned cooperatives. In these three exceptions, Urutransfor became a public limited company in which 100 percent of the investors are workers; Funsa became a public limited company owned by an investor, who holds most of the company's stock, and a workers' cooperative; Envidrio became a public limited company in which 100 percent of the shares are held by an association of former workers.

In most of these cases, the recovery of these companies arose from "a situation of ideological and organizational anomy"

(Carretero, 2010 3). This means that the workers did not choose to take hold of the means of production as an ideological-political project. Rather, their collective actions were a response to the threat of exclusion posed by the closure of their workplaces amid the generalized crisis.

However, the fact that these collective actions were inspired by defensive than offensive reasons did not stop them from becoming intense experiences that led to deep subjective transformations for the workers involved.[3] When workers take over a company, they redefine their conceptions of work and their status as laborers. The new collective decision-making mechanisms also shift the way in which peers relate to each other (Huertas *et al.*, 2011). In most cases, this transformation occurs because the collective members learn previously unknown facts about assembly practices and models of decision-making.

In a country like Uruguay, which is historically reformist and state-centered, with muted social conflict, the workers' recovery of businesses and production was a form of direct action that resulted in the emergence of a new set of tools and tactics. The broader importance of studying and understanding this topic does not depend on the number of businesses and workers who were actually involved in these experiences of industrial self-management. Rather, the core significance is in the symbolic impact of worker self-management as a possibility. It is through such moments of cultural breakdown that *latent contradictions* (McAdam *et al.*, 1999) emerge, inspiring new debates that make political renovations possible. Today, during the second progressive presidency of the Frente Amplio (the Broad Front) and 10 years after the socio-economic crisis hit Uruguay, workers are once again recovering their companies. The aim of this article is to better understand the organization of collective subjects[4] within such processes of recovery, analyzing both their collective conformation and the way they stand in relation to trade union networks and the rest of the social framework.

Profile of workers and characteristics of recovery processes

The recovery phenomenon is highly heterogeneous. Once an enterprise has been recovered, the workers organize themselves through dynamic processes that change based on the number of people who are involved, the type of business, the way the group is organized, the previous history of the enterprise, and so on. Most recovered companies are industrial enterprises that are at least 40 years old and most date back to the time in which the Uruguayan development model was that of import substitution, before the application of neoliberal measures.

About 70 percent of workers in recovered enterprises are between 40 and 60 years old, with an average age of 48. The majority (56 percent) of workers do not have a college degree. On average, 18 workers at an enterprise had previous experience at the company, and about 60 percent were part of their respective trade union when the company shut down.[5] Although many workers come from strong union trades, none have ever managed a company. Most of the collective actions and initiatives undertaken by the trade unions are aimed at defending the workers' wages and their workplace conditions, rather than aiming at teaching workers how to become owners.

We can characterize the pre-recuperated companies as being highly hierarchical. Workers are cogs in a machine. They agree to be part of the system exchange for their wages, yet they do not know about – or have an impact on – the way the global unit is organized.[6] Work is regarded as something one has to adapt to, and the attitude of workers towards their activity is a contemplative one.

Setting aside the question of how much interest and commitment workers have towards the recuperation, through the process they begin developing a collective subjectivity that allows them to operate collectively. A timid change can be perceived. This new manner of operation, which aims to effect a change in the environment, modifies the former contemplative position. A psychical and existentialist change is at play, in which workers stop being mere onlookers of what is happening around them. Instead, they become a constitutive and active part of the operation. Individual trajectories are neither automatic nor homogeneous. The process of adapting the productive and political project of recuperation includes discussions, disagreements and internal struggles that can be arduous. However, this process ends up generating an intersubjective stance in which all the workers begin to see themselves as a part of the collective "us".

A central debate that often arises is how to open a business when there is no available capital. As a result of the tensions between the economic and socio-political factors, workers arrive at one of two different solutions: self-management or co-management.

In Uraguay are three cases where workers tried to co-manage their businesses with investors: Funsa, Urutransfor and Alur. In all three cases the workers defended this position by arguing that high seed investment was necessary for opening the enterprises. They also argued that co-management would let them face the market with more advantages, since it was easier to procure working capital.[7] However, these three case studies show that workers always lost control when they had to negotiate with investors. None of these worker collectives was able to retain more than 50 percent of its company's shares. At the time of writing this article, Funsa is the only co-managed business still in operation. A public limited company, Funsa is manufactures tires and gloves and is co-managed by both an investor and a workers' cooperative. As for the other two enterprises, Alur has shut down, and Urutransfor has become a public limited company owned entirely by the workers. The investor, who owned 51 percent of the company's shares, has left the company.

Workers who chose self-management contend that, although co-management might give an enterprise a certain degree of market freedom at first, it curtails a business' internal decision-making structures over the long term. These workers further argue that, although self-management requires a longer development process and is originally tied to outside capital and *façoneros*,[8] it is indeed possible to implement strategies that move the business towards self-management. If these strategies succeed, the enterprise can meet its own production quota with a greater degree of autonomy.[9] Case studies of businesses like Molino Santa Rosa, which began as a *façón* and is now entirely worker-owned, show that some worker collectives have indeed succeeded. Others did not.

The pursuit of worker autonomy provokes tension in the socio-economic realities, and some untenable contradictions invariably arise. An example of these contradictions is the indirect expropriation that results from the model of *façón* production mentioned above. In this system, an entrepreneur provides the self-managed workers with the raw materials and working capital necessary for production. The capitalist then sells the product on the market. In a certain sense, the self-managed workers' production in this situation is a mere outsourced service that benefits the capitalist more than the workers. Capitalists no longer have to worry about managing the equipment or the production: they simply have to worry about maximizing their profit when selling the product.

Of course, this critique is not to downplay the importance of diluting the power relationship between owners and non-owners of the means of production. Nor does this critique seek to infuse private property with the ghostly attributes of exploitation and domination – dynamics that are only exerted between human beings. However, it is important to note that the logic that rules private property not only applies to the means of production; it also applies to social property as well.

In many of the collectives, government support allowed the workers to acquire the means of production more quickly than they could otherwise have done. However, this does not mean that, in the majority of cases, the workers were not denied a portion of their earnings or that their relationships were not dependent on capitalistic logic.

The relationship between capitalists and self-managed workers does not follow the script of workers being directly exploited by forced labor or exploitative contracts. That is not to say, however, that these workers were marginalized from the global productive sphere. Rather, capitalism is able to find novel regulation mechanisms in order to assimilate these forms of production into its prevailing logic.

When the division between owners and non-owners disappears in a business, one of two phenomena is likely to occur. The first is that the some workers assume authoritarian roles, thereby reproducing hierarchical class relationships. The second is that the workers question not only the exploitation relationships inherent in the division between workers and owners, but also the very code that permits, re-enacts and justifies this exploitation through a culture of naturalized submission. The workers who are capable of understanding and defining themselves as part of a collective endeavor that does not need either bosses or capitalistic relationships achieve the type of autonomy that challenges the very tenets on which capitalism is based, and as such, its very hegemony.

Although recovered businesses have been (and still are) under suspicion because the workers have become owners, that does not mean that the new self-managed workers have simply become small business owners or entrepreneurs. This phenomenon must be understood historically and within a specific class structure. The appropriation of the means of production is not an end in itself; the recuperations are action undertaken to fight back against underemployment or unemployment.

Once an enterprise has been recovered, the process usually follows two directions. The acquisition of the means of production could propel some workers to move from one socioeconomic class into another if they reproduce the former hierarchical culture and exploit other workers. The second course is that all the workers move collectively into a new class struggle. Case studies show that the latter direction is more prevalent. In most recovered businesses, the new owner-workers choose not to hire any wage-earning workers at all. Some chose to hire fewer than 20 percent of the total number of workers in the business. Half of recovered businesses chose to distribute income equally, with everyone receiving the same hourly rate. The other half chose more hierarchical systems, paying different workers different amounts based on their qualifications and or responsibilities. Yet all recovered businesses chose to distribute profits evenly among all workers.

What is most important, and what will be analyzed in greater detail later in this essay, is how this process inspires a collective awareness in workers. This awareness can manifest itself in the issuing of public demands, the creation of social alliances, the reproduction of forms of dependence and, ultimately, the creation of new social struggles led by the working class.

Collective self-management: class struggle versus social mobility

The aim of this section is to contrast two core paradigms, class struggle versus social mobility, and to analyze how recovered, self-managed business can revitalize the larger struggle of social classes. This discussion is relevant in understanding the tensions between self-managed ventures and trade union movements.

While some claim that analyzing class struggle is meaningless in a globalized world (for example, Touraine, 2005), I contend that the logic of capital and the power of the market arise from the coalitions of specific interests and the worsening of the logic of the class in question. Even though the world of work and the wage ratio have experienced irreversible changes as a result of globalization, the exploitation and domination of capitalism has found new states of marginalization that exceed all wage categories but that continue to function within its exclusive logic. This essay follows a class analysis based on Marx (1985) and Holloway (2004: 20), who regard class as a relationship of struggle.

It is still possible to understand society from a dialectical point of view and to study it as the struggle between exclusive and contradictory forces. However, that is no reason to attempt to import and impose categories such as social classes from other historical and regional contexts.[10]

As many authors have illustrated (Mignolo, 2007; Quijano, 2007), South America must establish an epistemological break that will allow us to build categories and analyses based on our own realities. This approach to social classes can be appreciated much better when we understand the differences between the industrialization processes that were unleashed in Europe and the substitutive industrialization attempts in Latin America.[11]

In industrial societies, the transition from craft markets to manufacturing industries coincided with urbanization, a context that was competitive and favorable to an entrepreneurial mindset. In Latin America, the substitutive industrialization is backed by the government, taking the shape of a political project intended to decrease the need to import products. Monopolistic relationships often arise. In the first example, industrialization is linked to other factors and class struggles. But when it comes to societies like ours, an exogenous factor is at play, and its existence accentuates, rather than alleviates social tensions:

> In Latin America, not even the penetration of technical progress manages to substantially ease social conflicts. And the masses accumulated in big cities aren't necessarily structured in classes that give them a clear understanding of their interests, either. The direct transposition of these ideological diagrams is what created the mental inflexibility that made understanding the Latin American historical process so difficult. And that also hindered the formation of a political way of thinking capable of playing a role comparable to the one played by liberal and socialist ideologies in perfecting the political institutions of modern industrial societies. (Furtado, 1966: 23)

As a result, in our societies there is no absorption of the surplus labor created by the dismantling of the previous socioeconomic reality. Unemployment, therefore, is more of a structural condition than a collateral effect.

When seen in this light, class struggles and the role of unionized workers in our region become essential in understanding the position of the underemployed and the unemployed. In a class analysis, the struggle for the redistribution of work cannot be separated from the struggles to be included in this new economic order.

The primary question, then, is why can we not we find a common struggle between these two sectors?

One of the reasons for the lack of a unified movement is the ideological shift towards social mobility. As society has become more and more mobile, there has arisen the corresponding belief that individuals are equally mobile. Gaulejac (2001) analyzes how the concept of mobility has become a social norm, particularly in the world of work. This requirement for mobility has dismantled the analysis of fixed classes.

From an ideological point of view, the transition from class struggle to positional struggle hides the polarization and exclusiveness inherent in a society stratified based on class. Instead, individuals are blamed for the positions they occupy in a stratified society.[12]

In this context, class antagonism is dissipated and another conflict arises: one between individuals and broader society. This phenomenon makes it impossible to understand tensions that are actually structural in nature, since what is established as a universal form of society is actually a mobile society that enables individuals to move in an ascending order.

In industrial societies, the conflicts between classes are more obvious. The fact of belonging to a class creates a social identity that is passed down from generation to generation. Work is not only necessary for survival; it is also a key aspect of social insertion. In these societies, the chances of being promoted are scant, giving social classes a more stable identification.[13]

Uruguayan society is now experiencing paradoxical trends. Ever since the leftist Frente Amplio won the presidential elections in 2005, the nation has experienced sustained economic growth – at least according to the gross domestic product data. And yet, even though the rate of unemployment and joblessness had decreased, the growth in GDP has not led to a growth in real wages, nor has it ameliorated the uneven distribution of wealth (Red de Economistas de Izquierda de Uruguay, 2010).

These social and economic tensions deeply modify class relationships in Uruguayan society. Social classes were always amply represented by the country's sole central trade union, the PIT-CNT (the Plenary Workers Trade Union Federation – Workers National Convention). But now, its importance is beginning to change. Although the number of members has been increasing in recent years, the sense of class belonging (which was once one of the largest indicators for defining social identity) is weaker than ever since most people now see themselves as "middle class" again,[14] which makes the identifying references of classes[15] crumble and fall apart.

Flexibility, mobility and adaptability are named as the necessary norms for the survival of enterprises, and this has led to the weakening of the social classes that were key to any industrial society:

> The development of capitalism means that individuals have become less and less of a form of capital that has to exploited. Now, self-realization is what is expected of individuals, in accordance with the "management" ideology. In order to exist, one has to be useful and productive. It is in this sense that we can speak of a struggle for positions. This is a solitary struggle – each individual fights in a generalized competition where they try to exist in the social scene and be recognized. This begets a permanent violence, a desire to "win" and become "the best". The illnesses that come with excellence are yet little known, even though the symptoms can be felt. (Gaujalac, 2001: 236–8)

And that is how a new culture is shaped – one in which the concept of autonomy is no longer associated with social class collectives, but with the realization of individuals. Each person is responsible for themselves, everyone cares about their own "career" and their own place in the world. Yet, as Bourdieu and Wacquant (2005) point out, this process of individualization also makes each person responsible for their own failure. And eventually, this leads to laying the blame for social problems (such as poverty and unemployment) on individuals themselves.

When systems that are complex in organization and that are based on a reproduction logic that is abstract and de-territorialised thrive, then the dominance of capital becomes less identified with a class of owners that dominate the means of production. But in such a society (in which people have to fight for their place), the "losers" bear a negative mark (they are often the unemployed, people who are assigned a negative identity because they occupy a place that nullifies them).

The struggle of workers in recovered enterprises comes from trying to maintain a place of social existence, a worker's status, a social recognition. This struggle is born not as the class fight of a collective that tries to destroy an exclusive force, but as the recollectivization of individuals who fight to be included and recognized within the economic-productive world. And that is why the workers who have recovered an enterprise decide to fight collectively to change the conditions of their existence. Aware of their "unemployability", they decide to fight together instead of becoming part of heterogeneous trajectories that live under different circumstances, trying to fight back instability on their own.

Collective action is an answer that floods the personal drama of unemployment, and which brings recognition from one's peers at the same time that it turns the social class that is being fought back inadmissible. This joint action operates a visible re-collectivization,[16] in which people find a shared space where they feel contained and where relationships of organizational solidarity are made possible. These stand as a mechanism for resisting the social injustice that would otherwise be faced by individuals on their own.

We all agree, then, that these processes in which enterprises are recovered through collective self-management make it possible for people who are unemployed not to lose their linkages. And, at the same time, they provide a new support of identity. Recollectivization processes manifest themselves as a way to recreate what the workers had before: paid employment that was characterized by a strongly vertical structure that (according to Foucault, 1989) tamed and disciplined their bodies.

What is the self-management logic used by these collectives? Can it encourage previously docile workers to rise up in rebellion? The processes that have been analyzed are highly heterogeneous and some of the devices of direct democracy used in assemblies generate new practices and subjectivities. In general, workers go from a productive system (their former enterprises) in which they felt highly extraneous, to a situation in which they perceive their degree of participation as medium or high. According to a poll administered to 494 workers in 2008 (Rieiro, 2011: 131) in 80 percent of self-management enterprises workers feel that their personal participation in the venture is between high and very high.

New and old practices coexist. Sometimes, certain mechanisms of reproduction start operating, and sometimes the daily experiences of workers are radically transformed through self-management. A good example of a radical change is that (even if the degree of real participation is heterogeneous) all the enterprises that take the shape of a cooperative assume a collective management, which means that all strategic decisions are taken in assemblies. There is a move from a managerial model that was monopolized and focused by the businessman and previous owner of the enterprise, into an assembly-style model.

On the other hand, it appears that the way in which work and specific tasks are organized is slower to change. When they open again, workers have a tendency to regroup under control systems that resemble the vertical organization that existed before. However, when they are halfway through the process, 50 percent of these industries start implementing new organization systems that are horizontal in nature. Figures such as coordinators appear – people whose role is more to coordinate, organize, consult and inform than to control.

The fact remains that in a society that is structured on the ideological bases of individual mobility, self-management processes stand as an alternative for not yielding to unemployment as solitary individuals and as a process in which social forces that try to find a new way to forge ahead are re-collectivized. Since the figure of the owner is no longer present, the management process is smoother. When the time comes to reopen, work is often organized like it was before, and then new forms of organization are found. The presence of coordinators is a good example of that.

As a conclusion, the collective self-management experiences in the processes that have been analyzed can be understood in the context of social classes and mobility as a collective resistance to processes of growing individualization. In that way, the recovery and self-management of an enterprise can revitalize class struggles and deter exclusionary processes.

"Toned down" collective actions and renovation of the social fabric

Compared with Argentina, recovery processes in Uruguay have been generally unknown. This can be explained by recognizing some of the details that are specific to the situation that each faced, and also some of the inherent characteristics of our national history.

Historically, social conflicts in Uruguay have been characterized by being channeled institutionally. Such a national characteristic can be attributed to a political formation derived from a weak and late colonial implantation (Real de Azúa, 1984), in which political democratization and institutionalization were symbolically blended, as they existed at the same time in the welfare state of the early 20th century (Panizza, 1990). As such, one of the characteristics of social tensions in Uruguay is that these have usually been solved by resorting to institutional channels that tone down what could otherwise be extreme conflict.

As far as recovered enterprises are concerned, direct actions (such as occupying them) were only taken in a couple of cases, after having exhausted all other channels of negotiation. And, unlike Argentina, there were never confrontations with the police force or evictions that would have make the struggle of the workers all the more visible.

In Argentina, the phenomenon of recovered enterprises appeared in a context where (i) there was a strong confrontation with classical trade unions; (ii) there was a rush of new collective subjects such as neighborhood assemblies, new picket unions, and so on, that employed new action resources, and (iii) there was a political-institutional breakdown, summed up by the slogan "They must all go". Conversely, in Uruguay there was a context in which (i) each endeavor was seen as a singular process, as becoming part of a union; (ii) the crisis was approached from the point of view of historically collective subjects within a social framework in which no large renovations in the conformation of social networks took place, and (iii) there was a socioeconomic crisis that did not spill into the political-institutional plane; that plane remained socially stable and legitimate.

Does this mean that such a context is one in which no collective subjects capable of carrying out socially significant actions could emerge? No. The toning down does not happen because there is no conflict; it happens because of the processes that are used to solve it. Our country's social and political unity has been known to find channels of political feedback and renovation.

In Argentina, there are clearly-defined forces that oppose classical union movements, and there are several networks that bring these endeavors together, such as the Movimiento Nacional de Empresas

Recuperadas (National Movement of Recovered Enterprises; a movement that was to eventually split), the Movimiento Nacional de Fábricas Recuperadas por los Trabajadores (National Movement of Factories Recovered by their Workers), la Central de Trabajadores Argentinos (Union of Argentinean Workers), and so on. Conversely, in Uruguay the repertoire of collective actions within such experiences was articulated by the Mesa de Coordinación de Empresas Recuperadas (Discussion Table for Recovered Enterprises) itself a part of the Industry Department of the PIT-CNT. It became an independent organization in 2007: the Asociación Nacional de Empresas Recuperadas por sus Trabajadores (ANERT, the National Association of Enterprises Recovered by their Workers).

Moreover, most of the enterprises that have been recovered and restructured as cooperatives are beginning to make ties with the Federación de Cooperativas del Uruguay (FCPU, Federation of Uruguayan Cooperatives) while keeping intact their union ties.[17] In 2010 the ANERT inaugurated the Mesa de Encuentro por la Autogestión y Construcción Colectiva (MEPACC, Discussion Table for Self-management and Collective Construction) in the context of the 40th anniversary of the Federación Uruguaya de Cooperativismo de Vivienda por Ayuda Mutua (Uruguayan Federation of Unions for Mutual Home Assistance), and invited all the organizations that were involved in self-management processes, and which wanted to use such a tool for social transformation. The discussion board was also integrated by the FCPU and the University of the Republic. The Red de Economía Social y Solidaria (Network of Social and Solidary Economy) also became involved.

The MEPACC started work in May 2010, and its collective actions were fueled by a series of proposals and demands that aimed to cause substantial changes from within self-management. Thus, a series of debates were hosted, focusing on self-management with a view to social transformation. Three national meetings took place, and grassroots organizations were involved in the debates. And then, a final meeting was held in the assembly hall of the University of the Republic, in which a summary of all the debates that were conducted was presented to the governmental authorities gathered there.

The organizations that were represented there took as their starting point the view that self-management could be applied not only to specific endeavors, but also to society as a whole. They said:

> We understand that the collaborative relationships which lie at the heart of a true self-management experience are the kind upon which the basis for building a fairer and more inclusive society could be set. (Author's notes, Assembly MEPACC)

Actions and discussions gravitated around the following three points: (i) building a platform for joint action, (ii) opening a public debate over self-management in which government representatives are involved, and (iii) creating solidarity networks and generating new social relationships through the direct participation inherent in self-management processes.

In thematic meetings held in 2011 discussions centered on three topics: (i) a school of self-management, (ii) the self-management that we want, and (iii) inter-cooperation. However, the participation of both the ANERT and the FCPU ceased in 2011.

Finally, as from April 2012 (and in the context of a new regulation by the Uruguayan presidency which aims to create a development fund[18] that would give self-managed endeavors access to substantial loans) a true self-management space has been formed in the PIT-CNT. In this space recovered enterprises, productive associative endeavors and second-degree organizations (federations, associations and unions) are actively involved. The creation of such a space within a plenary of the PIT-CNT is interesting. As suggested by Tarrow (1994: 56), the mobilization of pre-existing social networks can reduce the transactional social costs of calls for demonstrations. And it can also keep participants engaged once the initial enthusiasm of the confrontation has waned.

And as in some international self-management experiences – such as in France with the CFDT (Defaud, 2009), or the experience involving workers' councils and trade unions that Fiat had in Italy (Burnier, 1980) – the relationship between trade unions and self-management has also resulted in permanent tensions within the Uruguayan social-political field. Even when the self-management practices that have been analyzed in this article basically emerged as strategies in the fight against unemployment, they initially took root (in a marginal and controversial place) within the PIT-CNT. And before too long, an independent association was formed. The evolution of this phenomenon means that today alliances are being forged once more, and this history makes it possible for such experiences to occupy center stage in the trade union movement.

Although one can never know what the future holds, the fact remains that the workers involved in these processes have managed not just to recover the unity of their ventures and their jobs, but also to stick together in larger organizations, finding new alliances and networks that let them become a driving force capable of renewing both actions and discussions in the widest social field.

Final reflections

Ten years have elapsed since we had to face one of the biggest socioeconomic crises in the history of Uruguay. In that time, many agonic and heterogeneous recovery processes were undertaken. And now, the light at the end of the tunnel can finally be seen. Some workers have managed to strike a balance, and consolidate projects that are both economically and socially viable.

These actions are not born from a utopian dream of overcoming existing economic, legal and social barriers. And they are not born from an immanent class struggle, either. No, they are born from the workers' simple need to defend their jobs and their means of survival. Yet the recovery processes often make them face the economic, legal and social barriers that were just mentioned. In order to overcome them, workers have to make conceptual transitions and widen the way in which they conceive and objectify reality. This progression will be dictated by the collective process itself, according to the new social relationships and configurations that are created.

The collective actions that must be undertaken to recover an enterprise revitalize old trade union solidarities and create new social relationships between workers who were faced with the grim prospect of unemployment. Collective actions emerge in the context of individual resignation and despair, and they come to constitute subjectivities and emerging fights.

Sometimes, collective self-management processes take on new characteristics. At the beginning, self-management and co-management processes are seen by workers as the way in which to recover their jobs. But once the enterprise has been recovered two different courses of action can be taken.

1. On the one hand, collective actions can be reduced. The emerging collective subject might focus alone indoors, and become chiefly concerned over individual survival in the capitalist market. This process of entropy and bureaucratization could be characterized as the passage from a single-owner enterprise to one which has a corporative-collective owner.

2. On the other hand, collective actions can renew themselves. Once the venture has resumed its production, some workers may begin to see self-management not just as a way to recover the enterprise but also as a political tool for transitioning into a different type of society. From the recovery process and the struggle for the means of production, then, new political subjectivities arise that transcend the productive project.

Thus, it is neither the recovery of the enterprise nor the act of making it viable again that automatically generates political subjectivities partial to a certain transformation. No; it is the result of the specific self-management process that the collective subjects decide to follow while battling with the structural contradictions and relationships of oppression that previously existed.

In this new scenario, in which the utopian element that motivated the initial actions of the collective has fulfilled its role (that is, the recovery of people's jobs), then this element can become updated and amplified, making way for newer and larger social struggles (and renovating existing social relationships), and also disappear completely.

The re-appropriation of knowledge and workers' control can create new spaces in which the political undertones of work are revived, and where it can become a universal right. The workers who decide to recover an enterprise have to rebuild their social relationships, deliberate and take collective decisions and actions that allow them to recompose the different elements that are needed for reopening the enterprise. In a society where identities are more and more defined by consumption and characteristics of individual nature,[19] the subjectivities that emerge from the processes that have been analyzed are rooted in the reconstruction of an intersubjectivity from the work which is done.

From the vantage point of political sociology, this phase of the process can be interpreted as a widening of the public sphere. An alternative political space is generated. Individuals and groups interact with each other, they debate on the course of action they should take, and they build their own demands, revitalizing class struggles.

In such cases in which the workers create a space to deliberate and legitimize the decisions of the collective, there is an evolution in the demands that materialize. At first, money is demanded from their former business owners. But then the demands made by the workers become concrete proposals and they gravitate towards the spheres of the public and the state. A new socio-political field is configured as a result.

By way of conclusion, the collective and self-managed subjectivities that emerge when workers recover their enterprises are something that can renew the socio-political framework and traditional class struggles, since the phenomenon is articulated via trade unions and popular cooperativism.

What symbolic unity is arrived at is not the result of a totalizing homogenization (as derived from a simplistic and schematic class conception). Rather, it is composed of different collective identities with a certain spontaneity (which comes from heterogeneous demands on the social field) that allows them to be articulated horizontally. This identity process has an anti-hegemonic and classist sense of purpose, and it aims to renew society by virtue of all its multiplicity and diversity. It is the act of becoming keenly involved in such an identity process that could lead its participants to a true human and political renovation.

Notes

1. This research is qualitative in nature, although both qualitative and quantitative triangulation techniques were used. The information was collected by polling 494 workers in different endeavors. These polls were conducted in 2008, as part of the research for a Master's degree. Subsequently, 20 in-depth interviews were conducted with workers in the 19 ventures studied in 2009. Observation techniques were also used. Companies were visited, and meetings attended. These included meetings at the National Association of Companies Recovered by their Workers in 2009–2010. The author also participated in the MEPACC.

2. Unemployment has rocketed, reaching 19 percent. This means no less than 255,000 people who are without a job. At the same time, the percentage of people who put no conditions before taking on a job is growing as never before. In September 2002, unemployment reached 45 percent in Montevideo, and 58 percent in the rest of the country. Workers received no pay increases during most of 2002, devaluation was in the order of 70 percent and inflation in the order of 35 percent. (Olesker, 2002).

3. We use the concept of subjectivity proposed by Fernández (2005), who defines it as a social construction of each subject, since they are both a product and a producer of social, political and economic relationships in the social framework they find themselves in.

4. Collective subjects are groups of people who manage to build social relationships that have a specific sense of belonging, and that end up becoming a new social space that transcends the sum of interests and individual reasoning.

5. These figures are extracted from a survey conducted in 2008, which polled 500 workers from recovered enterprises.

6. The organic unit in the whole productive process (which is more than the sum of its parts) is turned by capitalist rationalization into a fragment of biased systems, and the individuals who can make it work become just another component.

7. When it comes to co-managed units, these are accepted (more than defended) by claiming that there are really no other self-management alternatives, owing to the power relationships that the workers find themselves locked into. The workers feel that trying to self-manage the enterprises would expose them to the domination of economic-capitalist relationships, and leave them more vulnerable than ever by making the enterprises part of larger merchant chains that (in many cases) force them to accept the precariousness of the work of their own workers (self-exploitation).

8. From the French "façonnier"; a word used in Uruguay and Argentina to refer to manufacturing processes that are ordered by a third party. This third party is the one that owns the supplies and/or the means of production in order to do the job.

9. The concept of autonomy we use is not the one that reduces everything to the individual or the enterprise, but the one set down by Honneth (2007), in which autonomy refers to a capacity that exists only within the context of the social relationships that sustain it. "The relationship one has with himself is not linked to a solitary ego, but the result of a progressive inter-subjective process in which one's attitude emerges and meets with other person's attitude towards one" (Honneth, 2007: 131).

10. For more than half a century, many authors from Latin America (such as Cardoso and Faletto, 1971; Furtado, 1966; Prebisch, 1967) have described how the creation of industrial companies and the development of their productive and transformative forces have become an imposing and "unavoidable" ideal of progress, and one that all underdeveloped countries should aspire to, the truth remains that these are associated with social structures and institutional frameworks which are very specific to the western world, and, as such, cannot be extrapolated to other situations. By looking at the phenomenon from a relational perspective (and keeping the focus on the different power relationships), these authors note that the development of some countries and the underdevelopment of others are two sides of the same coin. They therefore cannot be understood as different stages of the same process: part of the explanation of the one is found in the other.

11. As far back as 1966, Celso Furtado explained that in European industrial societies the tensions and struggles between trade unions and the capitalist class consolidates these social institutions, thus generating a dynamic balance in the economy. That happens because in these societies the pressure

exerted by workers who demand higher wages is outweighed by the technological progress of capitalists, so that the process of class antagonism becomes institutionalized. However, the economic development in Latin America is marked by completely different characteristics, since the results of these processes of industrialization and the search for diversification do not keep in step with a growing domestic consumption.

12. On the other hand, industrial societies are unevenly stratified, and they are formed by classes that play a central role both in the conflict, and in the integration between their different members. Nowadays, the new management ideology (the one that values adaptability, mobility, flexibility and individual advance) has radically transformed the way that companies are run. A new concept of autonomy has arisen: one that is no longer relational, but is focused on the body, on the individual, as it goes from place to place.

13. "The social contract was clear. The way in which margins and the sub-proletariat were integrated was through work. . . . The "sub" category refers to a position below the strata of a society conceived as stable and with a hierarchical order. . . . Consequently, social conflicts revolved around how wealth was distributed between the two classes that existed, and that issue fueled political debate" (Gaujalac, 2001: 227).

14. In the history of Uruguay exists a social imaginary that conceives of the country as "America's Switzerland", "The country of middle classes", "The country of fat cows". These are all phrases used by the people to refer to the years in which the country was at its financial height.

15. It is worth mentioning that most of the workers affiliated to the PIT-CNT come from the official public sector, and as typical workers-capitalists there is no polarization in it.

16. The expression "work re-collectivization" is introduced by way of contrast with the generalized social processes of de-collectivization in work and politics. "To us, the concept of re-collectivization encompasses a condition that is connected not just with the workers' needs to perceive an income, but also not to be removed from a social space that had been fundamental for the creation of professional and identifying trajectories" (Wyczykier, 2009: 2).

17. In total, 19 enterprises were analyzed in 2008–2009 (Rieiro, 2011: 142). All stated they were part of the ANERT; 10 were part of the Federation and eight were part of their respective grassroots unions.

18. The Development Fund was created by amending the Organic Charter of the Bank of the Republic (Section 40, Law Number 18.716). It is controlled by the Uraguayan President.

19. Castel (1997) speaks of a process in which collective frames disappear. This would be deemed to be a form of social de-institutionalization, a

detachment from the objective frameworks of subjective existence. When seen in this light – and as pointed out by Wyczykier (2009: 4) – unemployment and work precariousness have a particularly destructuring effect on the working class.

References

Bourdieu, P. and Wacquant, L. (2005) *Una Invitación a la Sociología Reflexiva* Buenos Aires: Siglo XXI.

Burnier, M. 1980 *Fiat: Conseils Ouvriers et Syndicat.* Paris: Les Éditions Ouvrières.

Cardoso, F.h. and Faletto, E. (1971) *Dependencia y Desarrollo en América Latina.* México: Siglo XXI.

Carretero M.J.L. (2010) *Las empresas recuperadas. Hacia una comprensión de la autogestión obrera real. Nómadas,* 25. Madrid: Universidad Computense de Madrid.

Castel, R. (1997) *La Metamorfosis de la Cuestión Social. Una Crónica del Salariado.* Buenos Aires: Paidos.

Defaud, N. (2009) *La CFDT (1968–1995). De 1 'Autogestion au Syndicalisme de Proposition.* Paris: Presses de Sciences Po.

Fernández, A. (2005) Notas para la constitución de un campo de problemas de la subjetividad. In Fernández, A. (ed.) *Instituciones Estalladas.* Buenos Aires: Eudeba.

Foucault, M. (1979[1989]) *Microfísica del Poder.* Madrid: La Piqueta.

Furtado, C. (1966) *Subdesarrollo y Estancamiento en América Latina.* Buenos Aires: Eudeba Editorial Universitaria.

Gaulejac, V. de (2001) De la lutte des classes a la lutte des places. In Abécassis, F. and Roche, P. (eds) *Précarisation du Travail et Lien Social – Des Hommes en Trop?* Montréal: L'Harmattan.

Holloway, J. (2004) *Clase = Lucha. Antagonismo Social y Marxismo Crítico.* Buenos Aires: de. Herramienta.

Honneth, A. (2007) *Reificación: un Estudio en la Teoría del Reconocimiento.* Buenos Aires: Katz.

Huertas, O.L., Guevara, R.D. and Castillo, D. (2011) Transformaciones en las subjetividades de los trabajadores: casos de empresas colombianas recuperadas. *Universitas Psychologica,* 10 (2) 581–94.

Lukács, G. (1969) *Historia y Conciencia de Clase – Estudios de Dialéctica Marxista.* México: Grijalbo.

McAdam, D., Mc Carthy, J. and Zald, M. (1999) *Movimientos Sociales: Perspectivas Comparadas*. Madrid: Istmo.

Marx, K. (1985) *Manuscritos: Economía y Filosofía* 1844. Madrid: Alianza Editorial.

Mignolo, W. (2007) *La Idea de América Latina: la Herida Colonial y la Opción Decolonial*. Barcelona: Gedisa.

Olesker, D. (2002) *Informe de coyuntura*. October. Montevideo: Instituto Cuesta Duarte.

Panizza, F. (1990) *Uruguay, Batllismo y después*. Montevideo: Banda Oriental.

Prebisch, R. (1967) *Hacia Una Dinámica Del Desarrollo latinoamericana*. Montevideo: Ediciones de la Banda Oriental.

Quijano, A. (1973) *Populismo, Marginalización y Dependencia. Ensayos de Interpretación Sociológica*. San José, Costa Rica: Universidad Centroamericana.

Quijano, A. (2007) Colonialidad del poder y clasificación social. In Gosfoguel, R. and Castro-Gómez, S. (eds) *El Giro Decolonial-Reflexiones para una Diversidad Epistémica más allá del Capitalismo Global*. Colombia: Siglo del Hombre Editories.

Real de Azúa, C. (1984) *Uruguay: una Sociedad Amortiguadora?* Montevideo: Ciesu.

Red de Economistas de Izquierda de Uruguay (2010) *La Torta y las Migajas*. Montevideo: Ediciones Trilce.

Rieiro, A. (2011) *Gestión Obrera y Acciones Colectivas en el Mundo del Trabajo: Empresas Recuperadas por sus Trabajadores en Uruguay*. Alemania: Editorial Académica Española.

Tarrow, S. (1994) *El Poder en Movimiento. Los Movimientos Sociales, la Acción Colectiva y la Política*. Madrid: Alianza Editorial.

Tarrow, S. (1997) *Los Movimientos Sociales*. Madrid: Alianza Editorial.

Touraine, A. (2005) La mondialisation. In Turaine, A. *Un Nouveau Paradigme: pour Comprendre le Monde Aujourd'Hui*. Paris: Fayard.

Wyczykier, G. (2009) Sobre procesos de autogestión y recolectivización laboral en la Argentina actual. *Polis*, 8 (24) 197–220.

TEN

Self-managing the Commons in Contemporary Greece

Alexandros Kioupkiolis and Theodoros Karyotis

The commons are a figure of collective ownership that communities have instituted to cater for the well-being of their members. Whether material, such as earth, water and air, or immaterial, such as tales, knowledge and skills, the commons have woven a connecting tissue, drawing all individuals together in a web of social cooperation and mutual dependence. Contrary to what Hardin contended in his famous tragedy of the commons, the commons have been administered by collective means of control and rationing that secure their preservation (Linebaugh, 2012: 117). Hence, the existence of the commons presupposes, but it also propels, self-institution within a community (Ostrom, 1990).

The history of the 20th century is the history of the push and pull between the market and the state, between private and public property, at the expense, usually, of cooperative and communal forms of social existence and production. Following the dismantling of the apparatuses of redistribution by the triumphant neoliberalism in the late 20th century, we are now witnessing an intensification of new and old processes of enclosure. In response, a new mode of politics has come to the fore, dismissing both state and private capitalism and placing a reinvented form of community at the center of political life. It builds on the experience of commons-based activities that persisted through the 20th century to craft living institutions that piece back together the fragments of collective life in order to pursue needs-based rather than profit-driven economic activity and to foster equity and cooperation through horizontal decision-making.

In this chapter, we set out from an outline of the particular histories of the commons in Greece and go on to trace out their reinvention in the present, in response to the brutal onslaught of neoliberal capitalism. We dwell on producers' cooperatives and the self-management of production in agriculture and industry as a key instrument of commoning. Our aim is to bring out the alternative economies that nurture solidarity, workers' autonomous self-direction and social needs but remain concealed and repressed by the hegemonic forces of state and capital. Tracking the obstacles, the resistances and the dangers that these common alternatives have encountered, we seek to shed light on the different paths they chart and the new prospects they open up for workers' control over production and distribution within an enlarged social economy of solidarity for our times.

The ensuing excursus in the history of farmers' cooperativism and workers' participation, as well as the snapshot of the actual social economy in the next section, bring into visibility a variety of partly non-capitalist processes of collective self-activity. These have operated alongside and intertwined with a state-dominated market economy involving a multitude of small business, an under-industrialized production and a large service sector (commerce, tourism, finance and so on) (Angelidis, 2007; Milios, 2013). Taking our cues from the constructive critique of capitalo-centrism put forward by Gibson-Graham (2006), we adumbrate here the historical contours of a heterogeneous economy which is not fully captured by any single logic, global force or sovereign structure. Impure mixtures of economic practices, conflicting politics of social cooperation and ethics of solidarity, singular, fragile initiatives of self-management disclose moments of tension, openness and diversity in a hegemonic state-capitalist configuration driven by other determinations. The thrust of this analysis is that, if we can begin to see alternative activities and dimensions as diffused, viable, and persistent over time, "we may be encouraged here and now to actively build on them to transform our local economies" (Gibson-Graham, 2006: xxiv) and "[F]uture possibilities become more viable by virtue of already being seen to exist, albeit only in the light of a differentiating imagination" (Gibson-Graham, 2006: xxxi).

Coops and producers' control: the story so far

Cooperativism

Agriculture and farmers' cooperatives lie at the heart of productive activity where social collaboration and producers' self-management expanded themselves in modern Greek history. Primal associations for the common rearing and marketing of sheep had existed for centuries, long before the establishment of the modern Greek state. Perhaps one of the world's first industrial-agricultural cooperative was founded at Ampelakia in central Greece in 1780, dealing with the production and export of purple cotton yarn (Nasioulas, 2012: 156; Young, 1984). The enactment of the first law on coops in 1915 marked the beginning of a large farm cooperative movement. In the first decade thereafter, the endeavors of the first agricultural and urban coops, bolstered by prominent champions of cooperativism at the time, resulted in the creation of 2500 primary agricultural coops, most of which provided credit to fight the plague of usury that ruined common farmers (Kamenidis, 1996:138; Kroustallaki-Beveratou, 1990: 125, 130–1).

The ups and downs experienced by agricultural cooperativism since then reflect the impact of historical upheavals, political interferences, inappropriate legal frameworks and the lack of internal cohesion and commitment among its members (Papageorgiou, 2010: 34). Yet the number of first-degree local associations has ranged between 5000–7000 throughout most of this period to date, involving on average 500,000 to 750,000 farmers (Kamenidis 1996: 138; Panhellenic Confederation of Unions of Agriculture

Cooperatives [PASEGES], 2013; Young, 1984). Rural coops have overshadowed all other types of cooperative activity in the social economy of modern Greece, representing nearly 90 percent of the total (Young, 1984). In the times of Metapolitefsi after the fall of the Colonels' junta in 1974, primary, regional and national unions have concentrated on the provision of agricultural inputs (machinery, fertilizer, feed grain and so on), the handling of agricultural products (such as cereals, olive oil, tobacco, fruit and vegetables) and services (training, transportation and advertising, among others) (Kolumvas, 1991: 96–8; Papageorgiou 2010: 37).

These types of producers' association have broadly adhered to the international principles of modern cooperativism: the democratic control of individual associations and their higher level confederations, production attuned to social needs, local and ecological conditions and mutual aid (Kroustallaki-Beveratou, 1990: 130, 141). A number of them have displayed major economic achievements and social solidarity, while throughout its history the movement has contributed considerably to rural development, the construction of vital infrastructures and the sustenance of small farmers (Klimis, 1991: 110–11; Kroustallaki-Beveratou 1990: 129; Papageorgiou, 2010: 38). But it remained largely under state tutelage and political patronage since its very beginnings, preventing the rise of a self-directed and self-conscious cooperativist movement (Kroustallaki-Beveratou, 1990: 130–3).

In the 1980s the election of a socialist government (the Panhellenic Socialist Movement, in 1981) intensified attempts at cooptation by the state, leading to the suffocation of major agricultural coops in the late 1980s and the early 1990s (Papageorgiou, 2010: 39). The ruling party sought to use them as vehicles for the socialist transformation of society through the creation of agro-industrial complexes. It also employed them as instruments of its own policies in domains where it lacked expertise or capacity. As a result, farmers' coops became overstaffed, they got in debt, they paid producers above market prices and they made investments with dubious prospects. Party-political interventions, mainly by the socialists and the communist left, and clientelism on the part of associated farmers distorted economic policy-making in favor of private or short-sighted interests, causing mismanagement, corruption and inefficiency (Kolumvas, 1991: 102–3; Papageorgiou, 2010: 39–42).

By the end of the1980s the Agricultural Bank needed to clear outstanding debts and demanded their recovery from the government and the coops. In consequence, the latter soon became strapped for cash, they lost markets, were forced to sell fixed assets, and key regional and national associations were dissolved to the benefit of private business (Papageorgiou, 2010: 39–41). In the public opinion, farmers' coops had become synonymous with business failure, the widespread corruption of political parties and farmers, heavy dependence on state subsidies, the theft of public money and party-political interests.

Nowadays, a sizeable number of the remaining agricultural coops are economically viable and are even success stories in their markets. They develop local production on ecologically responsible terms, and they protect small local farmers against global competition and agri-business corporate models (Association of Agricultural Cooperatives of Thesprotia, 2012). On the other hand, the violent neoliberal turn in government policies has also sought to assail the remains of farmers' cooperativism. New legislation in 2011 forces primary local associations to set up anonymous corporations if they want to combine, abolishing the second-degree unions, while also reinforcing state control on coops (Association of Agricultural Cooperatives of Thesprotia, 2012; Law 4015, 2011). Moreover, in 2012 the Agricultural Bank was sold to a private bank, leaving them with few sources of funding.

In the face of this forceful assault of capital, the deep recession engendered by devastating austerity measures, the neoliberal restructuring, privatization and dismantlement of the welfare state, the institutionalized cooperative movement in Greece is seeking now to re-launch itself on new foundations. It is claiming its independence from the state political system and capitalist forces and it is reaffirming the international principles of cooperativism: democratic self-management on the basis of equality, tight collaboration and confederation of the various associations on local, national and international levels, care for the community and sustainable development (PASEGES, 2011).

Workers' control

Greek industrial relations have been characterized overall by the scanty involvement and participation of workers in industrial management. Most efforts in this direction have been sporadic, short-lived and ultimately unsuccessful (Koutroukis and Jecchinis 2008: 31). Among the few instances of workers' participation, the oldest dates back to the middle of the 19th century, when workers' councils were operating in the emery mines of the island of Naxos. Luminous later examples include the factory councils which were set up in the shoe and tobacco industries between 1920 and 1936.

In the aftermath of the military disaster in Asia Minor in 1922, social crisis was exacerbated in the mainland, triggering the mobilization of Greek labor. The trade union of tobacco workers was among the most populous, well-organized and class-conscious, maintaining close liaisons with the new Communist Party of Greece. Tobacco workers in northern Greece initiated the most exciting experiment in workers' participation to be made up till then. They put together informal shop-floor committees directly elected by workers themselves and engaged in the direct self-administration of labor. The committees liaised with trade unions, overseeing the compliance of business administration with collective agreements and industrial legislation. They defended workers' rights, promoted workers' education on the shop floor and represented the interests of labor in struggles with capital. Despite the repressive measures and the persecution of shop-floor committees that started with renewed vigor in 1929, they managed to survive and keep fighting until 1936, when Metaxas' dictatorial regime was forcefully imposed (Koutroukis, 1989: 44–7).

After World War II, participation in policy-making through labor representatives was introduced at the national level, as in the Economic and Social Policy Council. But effective workers' control was virtually absent in most private and public enterprises. It was only in 1983 that new legislation was enacted promoting workers' participation in line with the "socialist ideology" of the new Panhellenic Socialist Movement government (Raftis and Stavroulakis, 1991: 294). The results, however, were miserable, as there was little independent mobilization on the part of employees themselves and their actual input was overshadowed by the involvement of government agencies, political parties and trade union factions. The privatization processes which started in the early 1990s and continue at a faster pace to date issued the death certificate of such plans (Koutroukis and Jecchinis, 2008: 35).

Overall, the failure of legislative initiatives and state-driven policies championing workers' control in the 1980s and 1990s should be put down to a set of intertwined factors: the hostile attitudes and manipulative interference of business and trade unions; the culture of managerial authoritarianism in the workplace; government interventionism and the lack of a tradition of employee participation in the running of companies. Moreover, workers' demands were more general in their content and exceeded the context of particular workplaces; trade union activism and participation in the workplace had not been institutionally enshrined for a long time; here was insufficient understanding, motivation, commitment and training on the part of labor and Greek industrial relations were polarized along the party-political lines. The dismal record of workers' participation should be also traced back to the fact that in Greek industry "participatory arrangements have been introduced solely through legislation, while in the USA and most Western European countries legal provisions were mainly used to validate arrangements already established by custom and practice" (Raftis and Stavroulakis, 1991: 295).

It is worth noting, however, that in a dozen of cases during the same period workers took militant action and were actively engaged in the management of their industries. We pause to consider two such instances in which workers' control was pursued through spontaneous initiatives of the workers themselves (Raftis and Stavroulakis, 1991: 297). The I. Pantelemidis company, located in the district of Thessaloniki in northern Greece, produced wheel rims and held a near monopoly in this field. When its founder died in 1981, his heirs declined to take over the company due to its outstanding debts, and the rim factory faced immediate closure. Its 23 employees mobilized to avert this danger and in November 1981 they resolved to take over the industry, assisted by the local municipal authorities and the metalworkers' trade union. This was a genuine and militant workers' take-over. No legal framework was available for such an initiative, so the company hung in a legal vacuum and they had to operate informally (Koutroukis, 1989: 50–2; Raftis and Stavroulakis, 1991: 307). The workers entertained close ties with the company and each other, as most of them were in their fifties and sixties and had been employed at the factory from the start. Party and trade union politics played no role in their everyday activity and their decision-making.

The general assembly functioned as the main governing body but, gradually, a production coordination committee, made up of three informally elected and revocable members, took charge of the operations of the factory. Initially, the workers were excited at the prospects of their business and achieved impressive results, raising productivity by 100 percent in the first months, increasing their wages and reducing working hours. Later on, however, there was a drop in efficiency due to reduced enthusiasm and commitment, slackened work rhythms, and the lack of efficient business planning. Both objective and subjective obstacles, such as continuous bureaucratic impediments, the old age of most workers, who were soon to be retired, the absence of relevant background and class and political consciousness, contributed to this unfortunate outcome. Six and a half years after the original takeover, the remaining workers of the factory surrendered ownership to the municipality of Evosmos (Raftis and Stavroulakis, 1991).

A similar experience took place in the Koulistanidis Textile Company in the same period, again in the area of Thessaloniki. Heavy indebtedness forced the company to suspend all payments in February 1980. In October 1980 the remaining 117 employees asked the son of the former owner to assume the post of emergency administrator, while a court-appointed supervisor controlled all daily transactions. At the end of 1983 the burden of debt made closure inevitable, but in the meantime the workers ran the company effectively without any authoritative supervision on the shop floor, managing production and carrying out transactions with banks, social security funds and government agencies. Decisions were taken collectively and often unanimously by all workers.

There are many noticeable affinities with the Pantelemidis case which may help to shed light on its record. The workforce consisted mainly of laborers in their fifties and sixties who had worked together for a long time. They avoided party and trade union politics and they refused to form a union on these grounds. They preferred instead to operate autonomously without any formal structure, at a time when there was no legal framework or other established agency to uphold and legalize their self-activity (Raftis and Stavroulakis, 1991: 302).

Despite their final collapse, both instances of workers' independent action and collective control took place in an unfavorable environment where they had to walk a solitary road without precedent. Their capacity to manage their industries effectively against the odds and lacking any relevant experience, bears witness to the latent potential of labor for self-direction. The ties they had forged over the years by laboring together and the emphasis on their independence from formal party politics and bureaucratic trade unionism underpinned their limited but exceptional achievements. On the other hand, cultural traits fostering the construction of passive and consumerist subjectivities which were indifferent to workers' democracy, the absence of a broader labor and social movement nurturing their autonomy and solidarity, the lack of a supportive financial, legal and political infrastructure and the non-existence of any network of self-managed industries and communities explain their short life and eventual demise.

Fresh starts in an emerging economy of solidarity

Social dislocation as an effect of neoliberal crisis-governance

From the 1980s onwards, key shifts in Greek political culture involved the wide diffusion of utilitarian individualism and the eventual eclipse of collective concerns, projects and commitments. Social self-mobilization was gradually confined to voting for a party in the elections and to seeking private benefits through patronage relations and clientele networks (Sakelaropoulos and Sotiris, 2004: 203–6; Sevastakis, 2004: 11–22). In the 1990s and the early 2000s a consensual post-democracy crystallized in Greece in line with similar mutations in liberal democracies across the world. The confluence of the mainstream center-right and center-left parties on a liberal-modernizing agenda enjoyed the consensus of middle-class individuals. The consumerist, apolitical individualism of a critical mass of the citizenry was the flipside of the shared allegiance of ruling parties to the neoliberal doctrine as they finally found the key to an abundant hyper-capitalism (Crouch, 2004: 4, 59–60, 103; Kioupkiolis, 2006).

From 2010 onwards, however, the neoliberal hegemony brought about an authoritarian turning away from post-democratic consensus. In the state of exception instituted under the acute sovereign debt crisis, the commitment of ruling parties to the same basic coordinates (private market economics, the EU and the Eurozone) has enforced recession policies and an upward redistribution of wealth, in line with the hegemonic monetarist-neoliberal policies of EU elites and the International Monetary Fund (IMF) who dictated the terms of the "bailout". This shook the material ground under the feet of middle and lower classes, who had hitherto consented to an impoverished democracy in return for a debt-financed affluence.

Between 2010 and 2012, the cluster of structural reforms foisted on the Greek economy and society in return for the bailout package has inflicted harsh material pain on popular majorities, terrorizing and traumatizing them. Statistical indicators can convey a very rough idea about the wartime economic collapse and material devastation visited on Greek society. The real GDP shrank by -21.3 percent in this period, and it is expected to contract further by -4.2 percent in 2013. Private consumption decreased by -23.2 percent, while unemployment skyrocketed from 7.7 percent to 24.4 percent in 2012 (IMF 2013). More than 100,000 private enterprises closed in 2010–2012, leaving so far 500,000 unemployed and generating a humanitarian crisis due to the lack of an adequate social safety net (Hellenic Confederation of Professionals, Craftsmen and Merchants, 2012, 1013). Full-time employment fell from 67 percent in 2010 to 56.5 percent in early 2012, while there was a 337 percent rise in the forced change of full-time contracts into flexible forms of labor (Mouriki, 2012: 71–2).

This traumatic shock paved the way for repeated cutbacks in wages, welfare expenses and living standards, for privatizations, the abrogation of numerous social rights (such as social benefits, protection from unemployment and labor rights), an effective disregard for political liberties and the removal of legal barriers to the unfettered exploitation of labor. Such cataclysmic changes would have been unthinkable without the rhetoric and the politics of terror deployed in an undeclared state of exception (Balourdos, 2011: 165–92; Mouriki, 2012).

The new social economy, biopolitical labor and the commons

The emergence of a network of self-organized collectives, which are active in various fields of commerce, exchange, production and social services (health, education, care for the homeless, and so on), marked a turning point in the actually existing social economy in Greece in 2010–2011. This was a response to urgent social needs in light of the massive economic collapse. But it also constituted a qualitative shift in the historical function of cooperatives and social enterprises, which now operated within the context of a broader resistance movement and placed an enhanced emphasis on autonomous self-organization, social solidarity, networking and the opposition to neoliberal capitalism (Lieros, 2012; Solidarity4all, 2012; Varkarolis, 2012). Confronting head-on the hegemonic neoliberal strategy which sets out to reconfigure the body social and to fashion atomized and impoverished modes of subjectivity, they strive to construct bonds of solidarity and to effectively bolster the capacity of individuals for autonomy and collective cooperation. They intervene in the same terrain of social life, bodies and affects that is being targeted by neoliberal biopower and they struggle against this power with a view to advancing an emancipatory and solidaristic counter-project.

This is why the wedge driven between the wider not-for profit social economy, which fosters collective goods and social interests, and a solidarity economy, which is more politically oriented and antagonistic to market and state politics, has become particularly pertinent in crisis-ridden Greece.

Broadly construed, the social economy can be defined as "commercial and non-commercial activity largely in the hands of third sector or community organizations which give priority to meeting social (and environmental) needs before profit maximization" (Amin, 2009: 4). The first Greek law on social economy and social entrepreneurship (4019/2011) has instituted the social cooperative enterprise and pledges to support all economic entities whose statutory purpose is the provision of social services and are democratically self-managed (Nasioulas, 2012: 165–6). In 2012 a total of 7197 cooperatives (agricultural, banking, plumbing, pharmacists, women's agrotourism, and so on), 11 mutual societies (mutual help funds and so on) and 50,600 associations, foundations, non-profit and voluntary organizations fall under a general description of the contemporary social economy in Greece (Nasioulas, 2012: 152).

To gauge the socio-political function of those endeavors we should view them against the backdrop of the current transformations in the mode of capital accumulation. As De Angelis (2012) points out, the very existence of capitalism is dependent upon the social and cultural reproduction of labor. On the other hand, maintaining its current rate of growth presupposes now the demise of all redistributive arrangements, the dismantling of the welfare state and the privatization of the provision of public goods. By withdrawing from the social reproduction of labor power, capital is pulling the rug from under its own feet. This is why "capital needs the commons, or at least specific, domesticated versions of them" (De Angelis, 2012: 185). It needs to accept economic arrangements founded on the principle of social cooperation so as to cope with the devastation inflicted by the neoliberal advances, to fill the gaps left by the retreating welfare state and to contain generalized discontent.

However, a commons-based economic activity can also produce the exactly opposite effect: It can "create a social basis for alternative ways of articulating social production, independent from capital and its prerogatives" (De Angelis, 2012: 185). This subversive possibility is made effective when social economy activities are situated within a wider transformative project that strives to supplant the dominant capitalist institutions with bottom-up alternatives grounded in equity, justice and solidarity.

From this perspective we can single out the collective economic endeavors that were initiated by the resistance movements from 2008 onwards, unerstanding them in terms of a distinct solidarity economy that seeks to reconstruct social bonds. This economic field is oriented towards direct democracy and mutual aid. It sees itself not as charity or as a substitute for the shrinking welfare state, but as a socio-political attempt at collective self-empowerment. It has an anti-systemic edge, purporting to transform relations of production, exchange and consumption through cooperative, free associational and mutual help institutions. Rooted in neighborhoods and localities, it struggles against the privatization of the commons and resists cooptation by market and state forces (Lieros, 2012: 46–7; Nikolopoulos and Kapogiannis, 2012: 29–31, 35, 108). Such a solidarity economy is antagonistic to heteronomous state politics, capitalist hierarchies and the reign of profit, as distinct from a social economy which operates as a third sector that complements the public (state) and private (market) economy (Lieros, 2012: 37, 71, 82, 159; Varkarolis, 2012: 45).

According to existing rough estimates, this solidarity economy in Greece comprises nearly 150 collective initiatives which include social clinics and pharmacies for the uninsured and the unemployed; social kitchens and movements for the collection and distribution of food; social grocery stores and circuits for the distribution of consumer goods without middlemen; free share bazaars, time-sharing banks and local exchange trading systems; social evening classes; immigrant support centers; urban art collectives and alternative cultural spaces; legal support groups; work collectives such as coffee shops, courier delivery companies, bookshops, agricultural cooperatives of unemployed women and one occupied factory, the Vio.Me. industry (Solidarity4all, 2012).

These initiatives make plural and imperfect, grassroots endeavors to advance social self-organization and to intervene in everyday life, unsettling the established norms of state rule and profit-driven market economies (Varkarolis, 2012: 39, 45–9). They thus stage struggles for the defense and the expansion of the commons:

> [T]he commons of culture, the immediately socialized forms of "cognitive" capital, primarily language, our means of communication and education . . . but also the shared infrastructure of public transport, electricity, post, and so on: the commons of external nature threatened by pollution and exploitation . . . the commons of internal nature (the biogenetic inheritance of humanity). (Žižek, 2008: 429, emphasis in the original)

The means of the production and reproduction of common life that have been privately appropriated in the past or that are now targeted for new enclosures by global capital are arguably the locus of key social antagonisms in our era, which are articulated around collective resources and the shared substance of our social being.

The commons are used today in a more specific sense that captures mutations in the dominant mode of production and new relations of social self-governance in the management of collective goods. The new social economy of solidarity may be grasped today in connection with post-Fordist forms of immaterial labor or biopolitical production which give rise to expansive webs of communication, the spread of diffuse information and knowledge and extending social relations through new technologies across the globe (Hardt and Negri, 2004: 66, 109, 114–15, 208–11, 337–40). Biopolitical labor is not confined to the manufacture of material goods but it also transforms and generates knowledge, affect, images, communication, social relationships and forms of life. According to a much advertised but controversial argument advanced by Hardt and Negri, the collective subject of the multitude laboring in biopolitical production embodies a distinctive type of economic, social and political organization, where the commons does not arise from the subordination of differences to an overarching particularity; it is rooted in participation and collective decision-making without centralized leadership or representation.

What is more significant for us is that contemporary social mobilizations such as the Indignados and Occupy movements of 2011 can be seen as manifestations of a multitudinous subject along these lines. They have contested the rule of both private and public property, pointing to the possibility of a social self-administration of the commons. They have turned their backs on centralized direction, closed ideologies and representation by political parties, trying to win back effective self-government. Following in the footsteps of such innovations, social self-rule could be refashioned along federalist lines, which would weld together an extensive variety of interacting forces and assemblies without being subsumed under any overarching central authority (Hardt and Negri, 2012: 89–90).

The Greek Aganaktismenoi (Outraged) was likewise a leaderless and self-organized initiative of common citizens. Its organization was fluid and open, it lacked any pre-fixed program or ideology and it was committed to the collective deliberation of the multitude as the final authority. The Aganaktismenoi conjured up institutions of popular self-rule through regular open assemblies that were held in central squares across Greece. They set about debating new national policies and effective ways to spread the "squares' movement" in popular urban neighborhoods, workplaces and other key sites of everyday life, in an attempt to put in place an entire network of alternative power structures (Douzinas 2011; Giovanopoulos and Mitropoulos 2011).

From August 2011 the mobilization gradually petered out but, as Manuel Castells said with regard to the Spanish Indignados:

> [T]he movement did not disappear; rather it spread out into the social fabric, with neighborhood assemblies . . . spreading . . . alternative economic practices such as consumer cooperatives, ethical banking, exchange networks and many other such forms of living differently so as to live with meaning. (Castells, 2012)

The incipient economy of solidarity in Greece is indeed an off-shoot and a continuation of the movement described above. By dwelling on a few actual undertakings we now elaborate the logics, the potential and the prospects of these experimental forays into building new economies of autonomy, equity and solidarity.

Pagkaki: a workers' collective running a coffee shop

The idea to set up a coffee shop along the lines of collective ownership, autonomy and solidarity gained ground in late 2008 amid a group of individuals who had already participated in Sporos, a cooperative of fair and solidarity trade in Athens (Pagkaki, 2010). The coffee shop, designed as a traditional Greek kafeneio serving coffee, drinks and snacks, opened in June 2010 in a central district of Athens. It is run by a workers' collective of 10 members in 2012, and it is constituted in the legal form of an urban cooperative, the closest to work collective that is permitted by Greek law (Pagkaki, 2010; Varkarolis, 2012: 115). From the outset the intent was to craft and promote the commons in their twofold dimension as collective goods and as a particular type of social relations of community, equality, participation, both inwards and outwards.

First, *inwards*. The commons were established in the fields of ownership and the distribution of goods in the kafeneio. No member of the collective owns a personal share in the workplace, which belongs to the cooperative and not its current members (Pagkaki, 2011). There are no employers and employees, no surplus value extracted from the labor of workers. Everyone is equally remunerated at the same hourly rates for all kinds of labor, and all alternate at the different job posts. All workers are equal members of the collective and its decision-making body, the general assembly, which strives for the highest degree of consensus.

Second, *outwards*. The work collective is committed to building a space of social communication, debate and conviviality accessible to all. It supports like-minded ventures in the economy of solidarity, it takes part in wider social struggles and it contributes to the construction of socio-political networks with a view to realizing an equitable, autonomous society for all. Its constitution stipulates that any remaining monthly surplus after the payment of wages, running costs and an initial internal loan will be used to aid like-minded collective initiatives.

Enacting the commons as social relations anchored in equal freedom, the collective is interested, first, in advancing the social dimension of the coffee shop and its social space, through the creation of an especially accessible and affordable place for meeting and entertainment. In addition to being a place for socializing, leisure and communication, Pagkaki hosts also information-sharing events and discussions which bear on collective self-organization, its practices and its prospects (Pagkaki, 2011). Moreover, it is engaged in weaving a wider network of autonomous ventures in workers' self-management, solidarity and cooperation. It stands by grassroots labor unionism which is structured in horizontal and direct democratic forms. And it strives to function as a collective experiment in producers' radical self-organization that will furnish a viable example for others to reflect upon, emulate and expand (Pagkaki, 2011).

Vio.Me.: a self-managed occupied factory

A prominent place among current experiments in economic self-management should be accorded to the Vio.Me. building materials factory, situated at the outskirts of Thessaloniki. This is the first experiment to date that is the product of industrial conflict and involves the occupation of the means of production by the workers.

Vio.Me. was a subsidiary of Philkeram-Johnson that produced complementary items for the construction industry: adhesives, sealants, mortars, plasters, and so on In May 2011, at the height of the financial crisis, the factory was abandoned by its owners and the workers were left unpaid. In response, they occupied the factory and started legally withholding their labor (Katsoridas, 2013). After several months of unfruitful negotiations, the general assembly of the workers decided to operate the occupied factory under direct democratic workers' control. They started production on 12 February 2013 under the now emblematic motto "If you cannot do it, we can!" (Initiative of Solidarity with the Struggle of Vio.Me., 2013).

The Vio.Me. project lies at the intersection of traditional labor struggles and the budding movement of solidarity economy. At the heart of this effort lies the Vio.Me. workers' trade union, driven by sharp class consciousness and militancy. In the numerous deliberations leading up to the decision to embark on self-management, the workers of Vio.Me. resolved to get rid of the traditional positions of authority in the union and to install the workers' assembly as the ultimate instrument of decision-making, both over the political decisions required in the struggle and the factory's production process (Katsoridas, 2013). This arrangement seeks to eliminate inequalities in the workplace, to ensure equal participation, to unleash workers' creativity and to secure workers' control over the production process.

Their decision to turn away from the established ritual of protest and negotiation, which has been re-enacted in countless industrial conflicts during the Greek economic recession, triggered a visceral reaction from the Greek Communist Party (KKE) and its affiliated labor unions, which accused the Vio.Me. workers of aspiring to become petty capitalists and of pursuing partial and individual solutions (see, for example, Panergatiko Agonistiko Metopo, (All-Workers Militant Front) PAME Arkadias, 2013). Gradually, through a series of ranting criticisms, the KKE evolved into one of the foremost critics and opponents of the struggle of Vio.Me.

In response, the workers of Vio.Me. agreed on a series of measures that would prevent their cooperative endeavor from turning into a profit-driven capitalist company. In line with the principles of cooperativism, the workers decided to put a cap on their individual proceeds. They opted instead to direct any surpluses towards the purposes of the wider community and similar struggles and endeavors, thus consciously discarding the profit principle. All workers have a share that is, an enshrined right to voice and vote, in the new cooperative: "There will be no worker who is not a shareholder, and no shareholder who is not a worker", they affirm (Avramidis and Galanopoulos, 2013). Thus, the means of production they have occupied are seen as a collectively managed commons rather than as the property of individuals:

> The commons are what is considered essential for life, understood not merely in the biological sense . . . the structures which connect individuals to one another, tangible or intangible elements that we all have in common and which make us members of a society. (Fattori, 2011)

On this conception, labor itself is treated as a common good. According to the capitalist mythology, labor is the property of the worker who enters into a voluntary agreement with the owner of capital to exchange their labor for money. In contrast, on this new understanding, our capacity to create, its individual dimension notwithstanding, is seen as an inherently social activity that is socially realized and socially beneficial, based on collectively produced and learned skills and on collectively managed tools and means of production (Wainwright, 2012). Labor is not treated as a commodity to be exchanged in the labor market but as a plentiful resource that a self-instituted community can tap into so as to secure its subsistence.

The workers of Vio.Me. have thus mobilized a commons-based vocabulary that is radically different from both the private property vocabulary deployed by capitalist firms, and the state-run public property vocabulary rehearsed by parties of the left. One could indeed argue that the market and the state, with their corresponding forms of property, function as mechanisms that deprive communities of control over their own means of reproduction and hand it over to bureaucratic elites, in the case of the state, or to business elites, in the case of the market. Conversely:

> [T]he decentralized, self-governing systems of co-production . . . offer fairer, more direct access to resources . . . that expands the distribution of the means of production and decision-making far more widely than through the top-down systems of the modern market/state. (Quilligan, 2012: 76)

The second component of the struggle, the Open Initiative of Solidarity with the Struggle of Vio.Me., was established in Thessaloniki (as in many other Greek cities and abroad) immediately after the announcement of the workers' decision to undertake self-management. The Initiative is open to participation by any and all. It operates on the same principle of horizontality and consists of collectives and individuals who are motivated by the principle of social and economic self-management. While it always respects the political decisions taken by the workers' assembly, the Solidarity Initiative plays a key role in organizing mobilizations, protests and marches, as well as in coordinating national and international communication, fundraising and solidarity campaigns (Katsoridas, 2013). But, most importantly, it has a pivotal role in ensuring the participation of the wider community in the struggle, extending thus the scope of the project from material to biopolitical production.

We are witnessing thus the crystallization of structures that go beyond simple workers' control over production and aspire to a wider social control, which encompasses the production of new ideas and values (including common ownership, solidarity, cooperation and the protection of the environment), new relationships (through a network of decentralized collectives revolving around the issue of self-management) and, above all, new subjectivities. The workers are ceasing to be mere followers of orders, and they are taking responsibility for their actions, releasing their creativity and realizing the importance of collectivity and mutual dependence.

Micropolis: A social space of prefigurative experimentation

The idea behind Micropolis originated in the heat of the December 2008 uprisings which shook the country and brought new political actors to the forefront. In the second half of the 1990s a critical mass of young people and others underwent a growing radicalization. This erupted into violent clashes with the police, an exhilarating feeling of liberation from social norms and an unleashing of social creativity. Social imagination in action transfigured the public space in urban centers – for the duration of the uprising at least – initiating numerous occupations of public buildings, parks and squares as well as permanent neighborhood assemblies, festivals, street art, interventions in malls, theaters, museums and conferences (Nasioka, 2012).

In one of these temporary spatial re-appropriations, in the occupied premises of the Drama School of Thessaloniki, parts of the anti-authoritarian movement, along with many other collectives and individuals, felt the need for a space that would facilitate permanent contact of the social movements with society, where this atmosphere of radical self-institution could become an everyday, lived experience.

After a long period of search, they rented a 900 m² neoclassical three-storey building right in the center of the city. They put in place a commons run by a community that met weekly in a general assembly. This community grouped together an assortment of collectives and individuals under three basic principles: horizontal decision-making, radical independence from existing institutions (the state, the church, political parties, companies and so on) and the absence of personal economic profit. The vagueness of these criteria of inclusion allowed a multitude of collectives that were not political in the strictest sense of the term to incorporate themselves in the process. We mention only a few of the activities initially sheltered in the building: drama, furniture refurbishment, music rehearsals, wild animal rescue, concerts, a library, talks and movie projections, political meetings and many different free classes, from yoga and violin to pottery and sign language. The bar on the first floor was soon established as an alternative to Thessaloniki's hyper-glamorous nightlife. Members of Micropolis performed voluntary work behind the bar as part of their duties to keep the place alive and help pay the rent.

The selection of the name was intentional: this stretch of space was designed to be a miniature (micro) of the city (polis) that the participants envisioned, the locus of extensive prefigurative experimentation (Micropolis Social Space, 2009). Micropolis soon became for many people the point of entry to the activity of social movements. With conflicts and contradictions, charting its way through endless heated discussions and a perpetual quest for the elusive consensus, this project evolved into a successful experiment in social self-management.

However, the squares movement of 2011 brought forward new issues and actors, and provided an opportunity to enrich and deepen the insights gained by the 2008 uprising. Moreover, voluntary work started taking a toll on the participants, and the crisis started affecting their personal circumstances in ways that drove them away from the project. This brought up a whole new range of issues that had not been addressed by the project thus far, such as access to cheap and nutritious food, defense of the rapidly privatized commons, solidarity and mutual support. There was a prompt realization that the private circumstances of each member should not remain a private matter. The issues of what is produced, who produces it and how it is distributed and consumed should not remain outside the scope of the project.

At first, the question of remuneration sparked a process of intense but creative theoretical debate that seems to have been going on at the same time in a series of self-managed projects in Greece throughout 2011 (see, for example, Varkarolis, 2012: 86). Following a long period of reflection and debate, a new constitutive process was initiated to amend the existing framework in a manner that would enhance equal participation, common access to the labor commons and collective control over all decisions involved.

The first vexing issue was access to food. Entrenched agribusiness and trade interests in Greece, in tandem with the dwindling incomes of middle and lower classes and the skyrocketing prices, brought about a situation bordering on humanitarian disaster. The community set about devising a structure that would bring the producers of good food in direct contact with the consumers, cutting out the middlemen and ensuring a fair price for both. A new assembly coordinated the creation of a small food dispensary where members of the community, alternating at regular intervals, were remunerated for shop-keeping. A similar structure was launched to run the kitchen. Soon thereafter a furniture workshop, a kindergarten, a bookstore and a print shop started operating along the same lines. The constitutive process went on, seeking to craft institutions that would enable a collective control of the economic processes, preventing the asymmetrical influence of any actor but ensuring also workers' participation in decision-making. This last point is decisive. Labor as a common good belongs to the community, not to the individual worker. How can we, however, guarantee the social and communal control of production without reducing the worker to a waged laborer servicing the community?

The answer was twofold: firstly, all interested members alternated regularly in the remunerated posts, so as to diffuse all the necessary skills and to avoid the entrenchment of particular individuals in specific positions. Secondly, a series of assemblies with different competencies were instituted. Each new economic unit is administered by its own assembly, where everyday management decisions are taken jointly by remunerated and non-remunerated members alike. A joint assembly of all the economic units coordinates all economic activity and prepares proposals to be submitted to the weekly general assembly, where all members of the community are required (and encouraged) to attend. The general assembly has the final say over all activities within the bounds of Micropolis. At the same time, a rotating administrative assembly attends to the smooth functioning of the social center (over supplies, repairs, and so on). All assemblies are open to members and non-members alike.

The whole economic activity of Micropolis is non-profit, and any small surpluses are directed towards two funds: a mutual fund that covers the workers' medical expenses, and a solidarity fund destined to provide financial aid to political struggles, new social centers and related experiments in the solidarity economy.

Beyond the fulfillment of material needs, the thrust of experiments like Micropolis lies in their intervention in biopolitical production and the cultivation of a new culture rooted in the values of solidarity, equity, mutual recognition, participation and collectivity. Indeed, the constant reinvention of the community as a collective subject is a fundamental dimension of the project that embodies at the same time a critique of traditional figures of community:

> Community has to be intended not as a gated reality, a grouping of people joined by exclusive interests, . . . but rather as a quality of relations, a principle of cooperation and of responsibility to each other and to the earth, the forests, the seas, the animals. (Federici, 2012: 50)

This communal link helps thus to forge non-alienated subjectivities that can break loose from the work–consume–sleep pattern imposed by capitalist accumulation. Social control, extended over many areas of communal life, is complemented by workers' control over their own activity and their active participation in decision-making over production, distribution and consumption. Indeed, in Micropolis, as in many other similar structures throughout Greece, the various needs of the participants – food, child care, entertainment, learning – can be met collectively in their own terms. This has triggered a motion towards autonomy in the proper sense of the term: autonomy as setting the nomos (rule) that governs our existence.

Autonomy, however, does not imply isolation or the creation of islets of liberty. Micropolis was conceived as an antagonistic project, and today it is probably even more so ever since it overcame its introversion and sectarian attitudes and started nurturing meaningful relationships of mutual support and cooperation with a multitude of militant grassroots projects. Today Micropolis provides an important node in a wide network of collective endeavors that try to challenge both pillars of the capitalist system – the state and the market – and to gradually displace them through radical democratic alternatives from below.

(In)conclusive thoughts

All the contemporary experiments in the self-constitution of a new social economy of the commons described above embody a distinct take on political change and social self-emancipation which is worth contemplating and pursuing as a promising avenue of social transformation.

Firstly, they incarnate a practice of prefiguration whereby the envisaged aim of the process, that is, the institution of workers' autonomy, social solidarity and responsibility, is embodied in the very means through which it is pursued.

Secondly, they opt for a politics of immanent and horizontal change, that is, for a direct, grassroots, self-mobilization of social agents on a footing of equal participation. Direct collective self-rule in the spheres of production and circulation kick-starts the politicization of the commons in everyday life that breaks through the divisions between the economic, the social and the political and restores to societies their power of effective self-direction, abolishing the rule of separate, formal politics and "free" markets.

Thirdly, they stitch together partiality with pluralism. They do not project themselves as fully-fledged and exclusive pathways to social reconstruction, but as just one among the various roads that need to be travelled so as to reach a new social constellation of greater freedom and equality. Issues of broader political strategy, alliances, grassroots union militancy and engagement with the formal political system remain wide open and subject to debate.

Fourth, the ventures in question are intrinsically agonistic not only in the sense that they set themselves against the hegemony of the state and private economies or that they are riddled with contradictions and internal fights. They also pose an ongoing reflections, experimentation and self-questioning over the best practices that will advance collective emancipation under given conditions.

Lastly, they have crafted particular responses to the challenge to build an association of associations that will topple hierarchical models, bureaucratic domination and state centralism: the network structure and the open assembly. The establishment and spread of networks linking different collectives together is today one of the most common ways in which cooperative ventures in the solidarity economy seek to mutually sustain themselves, to expand and to start building autarkic economic spheres of production and distribution outside the markets and the state.

At the same time, the networks themselves tend to be decentralized, voluntary, loose and open to newcomers, thus making room not only for enhanced diversity but also for the expression, diffusion and negotiation of conflicts in a non-authoritarian manner that respects the equal autonomy of each. In this context, the open assembly provides a forum of collective deliberation that can enable access and influence to all those concerned without requiring the continuous presence of all, charting a path between bureaucratic, authoritarian representation and a direct democracy that would demand the unremitting commitment of all. Hence, the network structure and the open assembly foster openness, participation, direct involvement and social integration around the commons while eschewing the unlikely and dangerous dream of a society that takes charge of its own affairs by incarnating a unified subject, always fully present to itself and devoid of internal divisions.

In this perspective, workers' control of production and distribution encompasses, but it is not confined to, industrial democracy centered on individual factories. Situated within an inclusive, plural and networked democracy of the commons, the self-management of labor seeks to extend itself to the new forms of biopolitical production in the service sector, the administration of natural resources, the production of information, social relations and culture. This movement gestures towards a new type of social holism. An increasing plurality of sites of self-management which govern production units, vital social resources and key collective goods in a direct, autonomous, diverse, open and agonistic manner come together in extensive networks of broader coordination and self-regulation. Such networks of open assemblies strive to break down the divide between consumers and producers or workers in particular enterprises and wider communities of interest. They thus advance social integration in ways that cater to the common good and organize an effective economy of the commons, whereby production and consumption are handled in terms of a common ownership of assets and a general concern for sustainable and equitable consumption.

References

Amin, A. (ed.) (2009) *The Social Economy*. London and New York: Zed Books.

Angelidis, M. (2007) *Developmental Dynamics and Social Transformations in Athens* (In Greek). Available at http://courses.arch.ntua.gr/fsr/138722/ Angelidis-et-al_Athens.pdf (accessed 27 March 2013).

Association of Agricultural Cooperatives of Thesprotia (2012) Cooperatives under attack (In Greek). Available at http://www.paseges.gr/el/news/ Oi-synetairismoi-sto-stohastro (accessed 6 March 2013).

Avramidis, C. and Galanopoulos, A. (2013) Vio.Me.: Labour experiment with worldwide resonance (In Greek). UNFOLLOW Magazine, 15. Available in English at http://borderlinereports.net/2013/05/23/ viome-a-workers-experiment-with-global-appeal/ (accessed 5 December 2014).

Balourdos, D. (2011) Impact of the crisis on poverty and economic exclusion (In Greek). *The Greek Review of Social Research*, 134–65.

Castells, M. (2012) Where are the "indignados" going? Available at http://www.irishleftreview.org/2012/01/27/indignados/ (accessed 25 March 2013).

Crouch, C. (2004) *Post-democracy*. Cambridge: Polity.

De Angelis, M. (2012) Crises, capital and co-optation. Does capital need a commons fix? In Bollier, D. and Helfrich, S. (eds) *The Wealth of the Commons: A World Beyond Market & State*. Amherst: Levellers Press.

Douzinas, C. (2011) In Greece, we see democracy in action. Available at http://www.guardian.co.uk/commentisfree/2011/jun/15/greece-europe-outraged-protests (accessed 11 June 2012).

Fattori, T. (2011) Fluid democracy: The Italian water revolution. *Transform! Magazine*, 9. Available at http://transform-network.net/ en/journal/issue-092011/news/detail/Journal/fluid-democracy-the-italian-water-revolution.html (accessed 3 May 2013).

Federici, S. (2012) Feminism and the politics of the commons. In Bollier, D. and Helfrich, S. (eds) *The Wealth of the Commons: A World Beyond Market & State*. Amherst: Levellers Press.

Gibson-Graham, J.K. (2006) *A Postcapitalist Politics*. Minneapolis and London: University of Minnesota Press.

Giovanopoulos, C. and Mitropoulos D. (eds) (2011) *Dimokratia under Construction* (In Greek). Athens: A/Synecheia Editions.

Hardt, M. and Negri, A. (2004) *Multitude. War and Democracy in the Age of Empire*. London: Penguin.

Hardt, M. and Negri, A. (2012) *Declaration*. New York: Argo-Navis.

Hellenic Confederation of Professionals, Craftsmen and Merchants (2012) More than 100 000 private enterprises closed in two years (In Greek). Available at http://portal.kathimerini.gr/4dcgi/_w_articles_kathbreak_1_08/10/2012_465163 (accessed 15 March 2013).

Initiative of Solidarity with the Struggle of Vio.Me. (2013) The machines of self-management have been switched on (In Greek). Available at http://www.viome.org/2013/02/the-machines-of-self-management-have.html (accessed 3 May 2013).

International Monetary Fund (IMF) (2013) *Country Report on Greece*. Available at http://news.in.gr/files/1/2013/01/18/cr1320.pdf (accessed 15 March 2013).

Kamenidis, C. (1996) *Cooperativist Economics*. Thessaloniki: Aristotle University of Thessaloniki.

Katsoridas, D. (2013) *Vio.Me.: The first experiment in workers' self management of an industrial unit* (In Greek). Available at http://bit.ly/10ijBxL, (accessed 3 May 2013).

Kioupkiolis, A. (2006) Post-democracy and Greek politics (In Greek). Translator's introduction in Crouch, C. *Post-Democracy*, trans. A. Kioupkiolis, Athens: Ekkremes Editions.

Klimis, A.N. (1991) Some notes on the history of cooperatives in Greece (In Greek). In *Cooperatives and the Common European Market* Conference proceedings. Athens: Institute of Cooperativist Studies and Research.

Kolumvas, N. (1991) The condition of Greek agricultural cooperatives in view of the changes in Europe (In Greek). In *Cooperatives and the Common European Market* Conference proceedings. Athens: Institute of Cooperativist Studies and Research.

Koutroukis, T. (1989) *Workers' Participation in Greece: the Difficult 80-Year Trajectory*, Athens: Eidiki Ekdotiki Editions.

Koutroukis, T. and Jecchinis, C. (2008) Aspects of worker participation in Greece: A legal revolution and the evolution so far. Available at www.special-edition.gr/pdf_ees_59/koutroukis.pdf (accessed 16 May 2013).

Kroustallaki-Beveratou, S. 1990. *Agricultural Co-operatives: An Institution of Economic and Social Development* (In Greek). Athens: ATE Editions.

Law 4015 (2011) Available at http://www.dsanet.gr/Epikairothta/Nomothesia/n4015_2011.htm (accessed 6 March 2013).

Lieros, G. (2012) *An Actually Existing New World* (In Greek). Athens: Editions Ekdoseis ton Sunadelfon.

Linebaugh, P. (2012) Enclosures from the bottom up. In Bollier, D. and Helfrich, S. (eds) *The Wealth of the Commons: A World Beyond Market & State*. Amherst: Levellers Press.

Micropolis Social Space (2009) *Presentation Text of Micropolis* (In Greek). Available at http://micropolis-socialspace.blogspot.gr/2009/07/blogpost.html (accessed 3 May 2013).

Milios, Y. (2013) *The Greek economy in the 20th century* (In Greek). Available at http://users.ntua.gr/jmilios/Oikonomia_Eikostos1ab.pdf (accessed 27 March 2013).

Mouriki, A. (2012) On the altar of competitiveness. In Mouriki, A. and Balourdos, D. (eds), *The Social Portrait of Greece* – 2012. *Aspects of the Crisis*. Athens: EKKE editions.

Nasioka, K. (2012) The adventures of a desert flower. 21st century Athens: a city in a state of emergency (In Greek). Available at http://ratnetblog2.blogspot.mx/2012/04/21.html (accessed 5 December 2014).

Nasioulas, I. (2012) Social cooperatives in Greece. Introducing new forms of social economy and entrepreneurship. *International Review of Social Research*, 2 (2) 151–71.

Nikolopoulos, T. and Kapogiannis, D. (2012) *Introduction to the Social and Solidarity Economy*, Athens: Editions Ekdoseis ton Sunadelfon.

Ostrom, E. 1990. *Governing the Commons: The Evolution of Institutions for Collective Action*, Cambridge: Cambridge University Press.

Papageorgiou, C.L. (2010) Usage and mis-usage of co-operatives. The example of Greece. *International Journal of Co-operative Management*, 5 (1) xxx–xx.

Pagkaki (2010) *A few words about us*. Available at http://pagkaki.org/en (accessed 28 November 2014).

Pagkaki (2011) *Work collective Pagaki: one year on* (In Greek). Available at http://pagkaki.org/node/89 (accessed 28 March 2013) (URL no longer available).

Panergatiko Agonistiko Metopo (PAME) Arkadias (2013) Comment of PAME on the event of VIO.ME. (In Greek). Available at http://youtu.be/dh2l4dCCK0M (accessed 5 December 2014).

Panhellenic Confederation of Unions of Agriculture Cooperatives (PASEGES) (2011) Theses of the Pan-Hellenic Confederation of Unions of Agricultural Co-operatives on the Framework for the

Reconstruction of Agricultural Co-operatives. Available at http:// www.paseges.gr/el/news/Oi-theseis-ths-PASEGES-gia-to-plaisio-anasygkrothshs-twn-agrotikwn-synetairismwn (accessed 7 March 2013).

PASEGES (2013) Members, activities. Available at http://www.paseges. gr/el/member-activities (accessed 05 March 2013).

Quilligan, J.B. (2012) Why distinguish common goods from public goods? In Bollier, D. and Helfrich, S. (eds) *The Wealth of the Commons: A World Beyond Market & State*. Amherst: Levellers Press.

Raftis, A.C. and Stavroulakis, D.G. (1991) Attitudes towards workers'participation in Greek industry: a field study. *Spoudai*, 41 (3) 290–315. University of Piraeus.

Sakelaropoulos, S. and Sotiris, P. (eds) (2004) *Readjustment and Modernization* (In Greek). Athens: Papazisi Editions.

Sevastakis, N. (2004) *Ordinary Country. Aspects of the Public Space and Antinomies of Values in Contemporary Greece* (In Greek). Athens: Savalas Editions.

Solidarity4all (2012) *Solidarity for all*. Available at http://www.solidarity-4all.gr/sites/www.solidarity4all.gr/files/aggliko.pdf (accessed 10 May 2013).

Varkarolis, O. (2012) *Creative Resistances and Counterpower* (In Greek). Athens: Editions Kafeneion to Pagkaki.

Wainwright, H. (2012) From labour as commodity to labour as a common. Available at https://snuproject.wordpress.com/2012/10/29/ from-labour-as-commodity-to-labour-as-a-common-via-michel-bauwens/ (accessed 3 May 2013).

Young, M. (1984) European Co-operatives. Perspectives from Greece. In Mutual Aid Center (ed.) *Prospects for Workers' Co-operatives in Europe*. London and Luxembourg: Office for Official Publications of the European Communities.

Žižek, S. (2008) *In Defense of Lost Causes*. London and New York: Verso.

Index

www.ingramcontent.com/pod-product-compliance
Ingram Content Group UK Ltd.
Pitfield, Milton Keynes, MK11 3LW, UK
UKHW040741020325
455689UK00002B/7